**Proposition 13
and Land Use**

Proposition 13 and Land Use

A Case Study of Fiscal Limits in California

Jeffrey I. Chapman
University of Southern California

Lexington Books
D.C. Heath and Company
Lexington, Massachusetts
Toronto

Library of Congress Cataloging in Publication Data

Chapman, Jeffrey I
  Proposition 13 and land use.

  Bibliography: p.
  Includes index.
  1. Land use—California. 2. Real property
and taxation—California. 3. Local finance—
California. I. Title.
HD226.C2C46   333.73'15'09794   79-3749
ISBN 0-669-03471-1

Published simultaneously in Canada

Printed in the United States of America

International Standard Book Number: 0-669-03471-1

Library of Congress Catalog Card Number: 79-3749

To Elaine
and
Michael and Allison

Contents

List of Figures

List of Tables

Preface and
Acknowledgments

When Proposition 13 passed on June 6, 1978, it not only slashed property taxes but also set in motion a string of events that changed the entire public financial system of the state of California. As local jurisdictions attempted to recoup revenue losses, they often intervened in the land-use market. In the long run these interventions may prove every bit as cataclysmic as Proposition 13 itself. It is the purpose of this book to investigate the interrelationships between the private land-development market and the public sector during a time of change.

Although this book utilizes some simple economic methodology, it is designed for use in public administration and urban planning classes as well as in public finance economics classes. Students of administration must be aware of how government interventions affect the use of land, and planning students must also be aware of how land-use interventions affect the financial stability of the public sector. It is only through analyzing the interrelationships between private suppliers and consumers of development and the public sector that the full impact of Proposition 13 on land use can be interpreted.

The evolution of the ideas and concepts in this book owes a great deal to my colleagues who have been willing to read, criticize, and argue about the subject. Although I have not agreed with everything they have suggested, this book would have been far more difficult to write without their aid. In particular, several persons should be singled out for their insightful comments: John J. Kirlin, Donald Winkler, David Dale Johnson, Philip Emmi, Peter Gordon, and William Baer of the University of Southern California; John Schunhoff from the City Economic Development Office of Los Angeles; and John Fitzgerald of the Merrill Lynch White Weld Capital Markets Group. All these individuals were free with their time, analysis, and penetrating critiques. It is my hope that they were able to prevent any errors; those that remain are, of course, my responsibility.

Particular thanks must also go to research assistants Michelle St. Germaine, who assisted at the initiation of the project, and Joanne Short, who provided an immense amount of time and effort in the empirical sections of the various chapters. Special thanks must also go to Artimese Porter and Linda Perry, who typed and retyped drafts of the manuscript, and to Lenora Villeral, who carefully helped to edit the book.

The Lincoln Institute of Land Policy financed the data collection. Arlo Woolery of that institute graciously encouraged my initial work in this area. The School of Public Administration financed the computer time for the analysis.

Finally, and most importantly, this book is dedicated to my family, who were always encouraging and willing to help and to bear with an author who was immersed in his subject.

Proposition 13
and Land Use

1 Introduction

Proposition 13, a California property-tax-limitation initiative, overwhelmingly passed on June 6, 1978. In so doing, it nearly crushed the property tax as a financial pillar of local government in California. This book's subject is the reactions of local and state government to this perceived catastrophe, particularly with respect to private land-use implications. This California case study will examine three principal topics.

First, the analysis will consider the impact on land use of the various types of development-controlling mechanisms. Some rules, regulations, and prices are more efficient than others in determining future patterns of development; and these must be recognized. The second area under consideration is the impact of Proposition 13 on land-use decision making, and thus on the ultimate patterns of land development. The final area of analysis will be the integration of the tax system and the land-use implications of that system into a model based on the interdependence of the public and private sectors. This model revolves around private developers and consumers as well as public-sector decision makers.

Land Use

The history of population growth in the United States over the past seventy-five years has been that of movement first from the rural areas to the central cities and then back from the central cities to the outlying suburbs, so that today the population of the suburban ring exceeds that of the central city. At the same time, there has been a movement of industry and commerce to the suburbs, where there was more space for expansion and a greater proximity to a semi-skilled and skilled labor force. The majority of metropolitan jobs are now found outside the central city. Both these trends have been encouraged by public policies as varied as federally subsidized mortgages for new single-family dwellings or local tax abatement for businesses.

The results of these movements have been mixed. Many families are now able to live in larger homes, on larger lots, in more comfortable economic and environmental circumstances than before. But the central cities have been left with a large service-dependent population and a poor tax base. The isolation of the poor and minorities away from the suburbs has led to increased societal friction. At times, public services have not been adequately provided to rapidly

1

growing development, and property-tax rates have been forced to rise to provide for new public infrastructure.

In response to these problems and in an attempt to retain the benefits of particular life styles, growth controls began to be enacted in the late 1920s. They were designed to prevent the misuse of land and to alleviate inequities that might arise from the use of the private market to dictate land policy. They override both private incentives and market signals to change land-use patterns.

There are several different ways of controlling land use. Growth and type of development can be controlled by direct laws and restrictions or by the selective provision of facilities and infrastructure. Fees, charges, and taxes on both the developer and the consumer can also affect the way land is utilized. These latter methods, although more indirect, can lead to more efficient resource allocation, since individuals can arrange their activities to take account of the new prices. The former methods do not allow this opportunity.

Some growth controls are nearly ubiquitous. For example, zoning now exists in every major city with the exception of Houston, Texas. But other types of little-noticed controls are also becoming important. For example, 50 percent of the builders in the West have experienced sewer moratoriums, and 35.5 percent have experienced deliberate public-facility constraints—two very effective control devices (Burrows 1978, p. 8). Complex growth controls are now often enacted to prevent the fiscal problems that accompany development —in particular the demands on the local government (which enacts the controls) to provide services to the new areas. When taxes are cut, causing available resources to fall, it should not be surprising to see more controls enacted.

Proposition 13

California has always been characterized by growth. Less severely affected than many other sections of the country by the 1973–1975 recession, it made a rapid recovery. During this recovery, population in-migration caused many areas of the state to grow rapidly. These events had two financial implications: They forced local jurisdictions to provide services to new developments, and they increased the price of property. Both effects were translated into higher property taxes for both new and old residents. Combined with legislative inaction and a large state surplus, this set the stage for Howard Jarvis and Paul Gann to launch their property-tax-cutting initiative. Proposition 13 qualified for the June 1978 ballot with over 1 million signatures—more than twice as many as needed.

The proposition had six sections. Section 1 limited the maximum property-tax rate to 1 percent of the full cash value of the property. The 1 percent was to be collected by the counties and apportioned to the units of government within the county. There was no longer to be a separate county, city, school-district, or special-district rate. The 1 percent of the cash value would be used to form a pool, which would then be allocated. Also included in this section was the provision that the limitation did not apply to the rates necessary to pay off debt approved prior to July 1, 1978.

Section 2 of the initiative affected the tax base. Full cash value was defined to be equal to the appraised value of the property in the 1975-1976 tax year, adjusted upward by no more than 2 percent per year. However, if property was constructed or purchased, or changed ownership, after 1975, the appraised value at that time would form a new base for the tax. This new base would be subject to the 2 percent limit.

Section 3 of the proposition limited changes in state taxes. After approval of the initiative, any increases in state taxes would have to be approved by two-thirds, rather than the previously required one-half, of both the California State Assembly and the California State Senate. Excluded from this constraint were all property taxes, which were flatly forbidden.

Section 4 imposed a constraint on the taxing ability of the substate units of government. Cities, counties, and special districts could increase nonproperty taxes if they could obtain a two-thirds vote of the "qualified electors." Although this last phrase is not defined in either the state constitution or in statutes, it has been interpreted as meaning two-thirds of those voting in the election. Increases in property taxes were prohibited.

The last two sections of the initiative gave starting dates for its implementation—July 1, 1978 for all but Section 3, which would take effect immediately. It also dealt with potential unconstitutional clauses and phrases. The entire initiative is reproduced as appendix 1A.

The campaign against Proposition 13 was intense but unsuccessful. The proposition passed by a 65-35-percent margin, cutting about $7 billion from local-government revenues. The state immediately wrote a one-year bailout measure that utilized the state surplus to replace over $4 billion of the shortfall. The next year the state passed a longer-term bailout bill which is still in effect. Both private and public sectors have learned to live within the law's confines; in fact, some jurisdictions have been able to convince more than two-thirds of the voters to increase some types of taxes to allow for increased city expenditures. Until recently, however, some of the long-run land-use consequences of the initiative have not been studied. In order to do this, some of the economics that underlie both land-use interventions and the ways in which local jurisdictions raise money must be examined.

Some Economics of Land Use and Taxation

Constrained by some relatively strong assumptions, consumers and producers, each in his own perceived best interest, interact to establish a market. In this market suppliers offer goods and services for specific prices and consumers purchase these commodities subject to income constraints and the relative prices of the commodities. The net result of these transactions is a situation of optimum welfare for both seller and buyer.

Unfortunately, perfect markets seldom exist in practice. There are two land-use problems in particular that might arise to cause a departure from this optimum. The first problem arises from the potential existence of externalities. An externality exists when the activities of a buyer or seller interfere with the welfare of another buyer or seller, and when this interference is not compensated. If output prices do not reflect externalities, the market equilibrium will not be optimal. The second problem arises from the existence of public goods—goods that might be desired by the populace but that offer no economic incentives for their private production; that is, there is no way to induce the consumer to reveal a preference for the good by paying for it. This happens because one of the good's characteristics is that any one individual's consumption does not diminish the availability of the good for other individuals. Government intervention is often designed to offset the inefficient equilibrium reached when these problems exist.

Reducing externalities has been the justification for the most prevalent form of land control—zoning. Zoning attempts to prevent development that might cause negative externalities. For example, zoning laws would forbid the construction of a steel mill in the middle of a residential neighborhood, because of the negative impacts that the steel mill would have on the property values of the homes. Although zoning may appear to add certainty to land-use decisions, it is also a political process that will always contain some degree of uncertainty.

In some cases, land-use controls can also provide public goods. For example, controls can secure the preservation of open space or prime agricultural land. Generally, however, it is the responsibility of the local government to provide most of the public goods and services desired by the residents. And in order to provide these services, governments need money.

The types of goods and services that governments provide are varied. Many of these services directly affect the way that a community develops. For example, if government is willing to extend service-delivery boundaries and provide adequate infrastructure to new developments, there is likely to be more development than would occur if the reverse were true. Both developers and government officials are very much aware of their interrelationships and often take actions to accommodate one another.

In order to raise money for provision of both capital and operating services, governments resort to a variety of instruments. To provide capital, they issue debt. But because of Jarvis-Gann (as Proposition 13 is sometimes known), they cannot issue any debt that is dependent on a property-tax base. This severe restriction will cause local governments to shift as much of the financing of the urban infrastructure as possible to the local developer. In California the property tax played a varied role in funding city operating expenses, ranging from a negligible role in some cities that had no property tax to that of raising over 50 percent of city revenue in others. With this source gone, cities must cut back in real terms on some services and hope that increased efficiency will occur.

To the extent that capital and services are cut back, development will be affected. To the extent that development slows, there will be less need for the dilution of services to finance that development. The interrelationships between land-use controls, land use, and the public budget are varied, numerous, and generally complex. This book will attempt to illuminate some of these relationships.

The Scope of the Book

There are three reasons that caution must be exercised in discussing the various subjects of this book. The first is that the role of the federal government is often relegated to the background. It is impossible to discuss any specific type of land use or local budget fully without examining the role of the federal government. Federal subsidies encourage housing development, federal money-market policies affect interest rates which in turn have an impact on development, and federal grants encourage communities to take specific actions. Although this book does note some specific examples of federal-government impacts, in general this factor will remain implicit in the discussion. A second reason for caution is that most of the analysis in this book deals with cities. Counties, school districts, and enterprise districts also enact land controls and are affected by land use and by Proposition 13. However, far fewer data have been developed for the special districts, and school districts have few land-use controls available. Counties are a significant unit of government in California; however, the primary focus of the book is on the more disaggregated city responses, although significant county impacts will be noted whenever appropriate. Finally, the data base of this analysis is a short-run base. These data were collected within eighteen months after the passage of Proposition 13. The long-run impacts of Proposition 13 may not be manifested until more time has passed.

The basic outline of the book is straightforward. Following this introductory chapter will be a series of chapters that discuss the various aspects of land-use controls, local budgets, and fiscal-limitation movements, including Proposition 13. More specifically, these can be identified as follows.

Chapter 2 examines the political economy of land use. In this chapter a typology of land-use regulations is developed and examined for the determination of land-use effects on economic efficiency, political usefulness, and administrative feasibility. The chapter will conclude with a brief analysis of the impacts of these rules on the public and private sectors.

Chapter 3 has two principal parts. The first section will analyze the role of the property tax in municipal finance and present some of the results of the economic debate concerning tax capitalization. The second part of the chapter will develop a simple model of the interactions of the three sets of activities that take place in the urban land market: development supply by developers, development demand by consumers, and jurisdictional intervention by government. The model will then be used to examine changes that might occur when fiscal limits are imposed.

Chapter 4 examines the California public-budgeting and land-use environment that existed prior to the passage of Proposition 13. This analysis will be primarily institutional as it discusses principal public revenues and expenditures in California and the major land-use controls that are available to local jurisdictions. Some constraints that local governments face and the debt-financing tools that were available will also be examined from a specific land-use perspective.

In order to understand the impacts of the fiscal-limits movement on budgeting and land use, it is necessary to analyze it in partial isolation. Chapter 5 presents a brief overview of this movement and then examines the particular political, economic, and institutional reasons for the proposition's passage. The initial state bailout provisions and the longer-term bailout plan will also be discussed.

Chapter 6 will also be divided into two sections. The first section will present data concerning what actually happened after the proposition passed. Revenue, expenditure, and land-use-activity changes of local jurisdictions will be examined. The second half of the chapter will present some empirical estimates of the impact of charges and rules on the amount of construction that occurred in the year following the passage of the initiative.

Chapter 7 will take a closer look at three specific land-use topics that are linked to Proposition 13: rent controls, development changes, and debt financing. Each of these specific subjects will be examined in terms of present and future problems resulting from the initiative.

The final chapter will draw together the relationships between jurisdictional budgets and land use, and will take a long-run look at the land-use implications of the initiative. Finally, tentative conclusions and policy recommendations will be developed.

Appendix 1A:
Proposition 13

That Article XIIIA is added to the Constitution to read:

Section 1.

(a) The maximum amount of any ad valorem tax on real property shall not exceed one percent (1%) of the full cash value of such property. The one percent (1%) tax to be collected by the counties and apportioned according to law to the districts within the counties.

(b) The limitation provided for in subdivision (a) shall not apply to ad valorem taxes or special assessments to pay the interest and redemption charges on any indebtedness approved by the voters prior to the time this section becomes effective.

Section 2.

(a) The full cash value means the County Assessors valuation of real property as shown on the 1975-76 tax bill under "full cash value," or thereafter, the appraised value of real property when purchased, newly constructed, or a change in ownership has occurred after the 1975 assessment. All real property not already assessed up to the 1975-76 tax levels may be reassessed to reflect that valuation.

(b) The fair market value base may reflect from year to year the inflationary rate not to exceed two percent (2%) for any given year or reduction as shown in the consumer price index or comparable data for the area under taxing jurisdiction.

Section 3.

From and after the effective date of this article, any change in State taxes enacted for the purpose of increasing revenues collected pursuant thereto whether by increased rates or changes in methods of computation must be imposed by an Act passed by not less than two-thirds of all members elected to each of the two houses of the Legislature, except that no new ad valorem taxes on real property, or sales or transaction taxes on the sales of real property may be imposed.

Section 4.

Cities, counties and special districts, by a two-thirds vote of the qualified electors of such districts, may impose special taxes on such district, except ad valorem taxes on real property or a transaction tax or sales tax on the sale of real property within such city, county or special district.

Section 5.

This article shall take effect for the tax year beginning on July 1 following the passage of this Amendment, except 3 which shall become effective upon the passage of this article.

Section 6.

If any section, part, clause, or phrase hereof is for any reason held to be invalid or unconstitutional, the reamining sections shall not be affected but will remain in full force and effect.

2

The Political Economy of Land Use

A myriad of rules, regulations, and charges affect land use. This chapter will examine the political economy of these interventions into the private land market by categorizing and analyzing their impacts.

Almost all land-use interventions can be examined for economic, political, and administrative effects. At times these impacts may be extremely important and obvious; at other times, although still crucial, they may not be as clearly seen. The principal economic criteria are concerned with allocative efficiency and public-expenditure decisions; the principal political dimensions are those of equity and acceptability, while the principal administrative implications are those of management and control. Unfortunately, often only segments of this typology are used to evaluate land policies.

These three generic areas are not always distinct and independent. Policies that are efficient for some allocative dimensions may lead to quite inefficient results in other dimensions. For example, tax reductions for farmers to encourage the maintenance of farmland at the urban fringe to prevent sprawl (perhaps an efficient short-run allocation) may actually lead in the long run to an inefficiently small amount of land being converted to urban use. In this same example, large land owners may receive the major share of the benefits (an equity consideration), and the law may be written so that compliance is relatively easy (the administrative dimension) so that benefits are likely to accrue. Identifying some of the evaluation dimensions so that the interventions can be analyzed will be the first task of this chapter.

Nearly all land-use interventions that occur because of market failure can be categorized as one of two types, direct or indirect. Direct regulations, characterized by such examples as zoning and growth-management rules, are deliberately designed to override market preferences in favor of the tastes and preferences of public decision makers for the course of the city's future growth. The result of this type of intervention is the supplantation of decentralized economic decisions by centralized decision making.

Indirect incentives also interfere with the market. However, this type of interference uses the private, profit-making incentives of consumers and developers within the market structure. Typical tools of this type are fees, charges, and economic-development incentives. The indirect tools work by changing the relative costs of development. Land developers and consumers can then freely react to these new price signals. Land use is regulated indirectly using economic incentives within the context of the market.

Although the enactment of either type of regulation affects private land-use rights (Erwin et al., 1977, p. xiv), indirect interventions tend to be oriented more toward private-property rights than are direct interventions. To the extent that individuals, for a price, can utilize their land in any way they wish, there is less infringement on private rights than if they are forbidden land-use activities by government fiat.

In some cases direct and indirect techniques are not independent. Most jurisdictions use combinations of tools to direct growth and development, and the use of any one measure—whether direct or indirect—must be examined in the context of an entire set of rules. It is not unusual to find one type of intervention used in conjunction with another; for example, tax abatement for economic development (an indirect tool) might be coordinated with zoning changes to allow different land uses. Furthermore, the boundaries between indirect and direct can be indistinct. Certain activities have effects that might be analyzed as both. For example, environmental regulations may be both direct (a developer cannot build homes that generate waste products in excess of the capacity of a particular sewage-treatment plant) and indirect (but he can build—for a price—an increment to the plant so that the development can occur). However, as generic categories, direct and indirect are useful in analyzing the types of rules, regulations, and fees that are enacted.

The final section of this chapter will briefly analyze the effects of interventions on the private and public sectors. By influencing the quantity and type of development that occur, interventions affect both the private developer and the consumer. Some of them also raise revenues for the local government or reduce local-government costs, thereby affecting the local-government budget. This interrelationship, which will be developed in more detail later, argues that the local private sector is partially dependent on public land-use regulations, which in turn, by influencing the types of land use, affect the financial position of the government.

Economic Criteria

Two basic economic criteria can be employed in evaluating local-government land-use interventions. The most important is the impact of the regulations on allocative efficiency of the market. The second is the impact on the local governments' budgets. In many jurisdictions, lip service only is given to the former, whereas the latter is examined very closely.

Economic Efficiency

If perfect competition exists, it is possible to make positive statements about economic welfare.[1] In particular, prices will exist that induce individuals to move to a position where it is no longer possible to increase the welfare of any one individual (in that individual's judgment) without directly reducing the welfare of another individual (in that individual's judgment). This state, called a *pareto optimum,* reflects, for a given income and wealth, property-right distribution, the optimum allocation of resources within the economy. This optimum reflects consumer preferences as well as producer decisions. Sometimes referred to as economic efficiency, it is much more than maximization of output. Under perfect market conditions with all assumptions met, the prices necessary to ensure optimality will exist, and the state will automatically occur. A pareto optimum can exist for each income and wealth distribution in society.

Pareto optimality is more than a positive description of individual welfare maximization for all sectors of the economy. It is also a normative goal. Land-use regulations can be evaluated based on whether they contribute to economic efficiency. It is sometimes contended that these regulations interfere with efficiency and ought not to be adopted. However, if the land-use market is not at an optimum, then these rules can force the equilibrium to be more efficient. This justification is somewhat suspect, however, because it implies that the efficient solution is known and that rules are applied rationally.

A necessary (but not sufficient) condition for a pareto optimum is that the existing price accurately reflect the benefits that occur and the costs that must be paid in any transaction. If an individual or firm engages in an activity that has an impact on the welfare of any other individual or firm, and if there is no compensation for that impact, an externality is present and prices are no longer accurate.

Externalities can be either positive or negative. Positive externalities are uncompensated welfare additions; negative externalities are uncompensated welfare losses. The existence of either type distorts the market processes because the full evaluation of the activity is not calculated. Externalities primarily exist because it is too expensive to design a system that will force the necessary compensating payments to be made. The transaction costs of convincing all parties to agree to a voluntary settlement are too high. To the extent that a compensating payment does occur, perhaps because of a change in the definition of property rights or a more specific enumeration of those rights, the externality is said to be internalized.

An example of a positive externality occurs when an individual home owner's improvements increase a neighbor's property values. If there is no compensation for this activity, the home owner may decide that the activity should not be undertaken. There are thus economic forces that prevent any individual landowner from improving his property. The subsidy of land improvements in poor areas through tax abatements or subsidized low-cost improvement loans is one approach that government uses to deal with such externalities.

Another common externality in urban areas is a negative one. If a glue factory locates next to a private home, the factory's fumes and noises will probably annoy the resident of the house; and it is likely that if the family attempts to move, it will find that the property value of the house has fallen. The reduction of these types of negative externalities has been one of the primary rationales for zoning—the technique designed to separate noncomplementary users of land.

Budgetary Impacts

The impact that land-use interventions have on the budget of the local jurisdiction is a second economic-evaluation criterion. These regulations should help the locality provide an efficient level of public services and raise revenues to pay for them. This is yet another way of examining efficiency problems, since citizens prefer to have optimal quantities of goods and services provided and financed by the public sector.

The class of goods called *public goods* has two characteristics: Any individual's consumption of the good does not detract from the potential consumption of the good by another individual; and it is not feasible, using the market, to force people to pay for the consumption of the good (Musgrave and Musgrave 1976). Many goods exhibit varying degrees of these characteristics. To the extent that they do so, the market will not work to provide for their efficient allocation, since there is an incentive for consumers to understate their preferences in an attempt to avoid paying for a good that they can consume anyway if it is provided at all. In these cases, it has been traditional for government to provide the good.

Land-use regulations have an impact on some types of public goods. These regulations have been invoked to protect such public goods as open space, historical monuments, or prime agricultural lands. Since typically the regulations restrict the conversion of this land to more intensive development, which would generate increased taxes, there is also an impact on city revenues. The city government must determine how much of this type of activity should occur. The tradeoff is between the higher tax revenues that would accrue if the land were utilized at its highest and best use, and the benefits the public receives from the controlled land use.

Land-use interventions are also frequently justified for their impacts on growth. Some land-use instruments can act to encourage growth (for example, tax abatements), while others act to discourage growth (for example, strict residential zoning to discourage commercial development). Patterns of growth are also controlled by land-use regulations. Developments in particular areas can be guided through the use of infrastructure-provision or construction limits. Since growth affects city revenues, land-use instruments also have an impact on these revenues.

Some types of city revenues can also be traced directly to land use. The clearest example is the property tax, which is a direct function of both land value and improvements. However, how the land is used is also important. Commercial use provides property- and sales-tax revenues to the jurisdiction, whereas construction provides building fees and charges.

But development also imposes service costs on the jurisdiction. Proper land-use planning can direct the development of the jurisdiction to reduce the costs of providing some public services. For example, a strict growth-management plan in Brooklyn Park, Minnesota, has resulted in a savings of about 40 percent in capital sanitary-sewer, water, and storm-sewer facilities without affecting service (Gleeson 1979).

Political Criteria

The political dimensions of land-use planning may ultimately be as important as the economic. The political process may not adopt economically efficient land-use policies because of constraints faced by locally elected decision makers. These constraints become the evaluation criteria that the political decision maker utilizes.

The politician employs three types of criteria in examining potential land-use regulations: equity, property rights, and acceptability. It is the behavior of the local decision maker in response to these criteria that gives rise to major discrepancies between pareto-optimum interventions and the interventions that actually occur.

Equity

A specific pareto optimum, depending on a specific initial distribution of resource efficiency, can exist for any initial distribution; and efficient solutions will vary as the resource distribution varies.

The initial and succeeding distributions are societal problems. Although redistribution may entail some loss of efficiency, so that there may be an inverse relationship between the two concepts (Okun 1975), the choice of the final distribution of goods and services among the individuals in a society is ultimately a political choice.

Equity considerations in land-use interventions concern the identification of the principal beneficiaries and losers in any land-use decision. Initially, demands for equity may reflect only the concerns of those actively involved in the particular intervention. In these cases participants in the land-use dispute may gain at the expense of nonparticipants. If land-use-intervention externalities exist because individuals who incur costs are not compensated by those who benefit from the intervention, redistribution occurs. In practice, however, it is difficult to tax fully the benefits and compensate the losses that arise from land-use decisions. It is often a formidable task to identify all the affected parties, and real welfare changes are hard to measure since the necessary market prices may not be available. But if there is no provision for dealing with these gains and losses, the decision becomes solely a political power struggle between the potential gainers and losers. The ultimate distributional outcome often depends upon the bargaining skills, access to information, and legal rights of each group.

Property Rights

Changing land-use policies involves changing the distribution of property rights. These rights tend to be strongly held in the United States, and changing them involves serious political decisions. Both the land owner and the non-land owner have property rights. The land owner has rights concerning the development of the land; the non-land owner has rights that protect him from having his welfare affected without compensation. The decision maker is often concerned with the distribution of these rights without regard for related economic-efficiency problems.

Property rights are in part products of social norms reflecting current concepts of equity and justice. Changing them involves the careful use of the political process to ensure that decisions are treated as legitimate. Typically, land-use legislation requires that a particular sequence of steps be followed before the distribution of the rights is altered. Public notice, community hearings, and citizens' committees are often used to ensure this legitimacy. For example, before the city of Los Angeles instituted rent control, there were public hearings, and a citizens' committee to enforce the provisions of the legislation was instituted. Further, this legislation was limited to one year, and mandatory hearings were required for reenactment. The prevailing concepts of property-right equity are in part dependent on the distribution of the rights. A different distribution will lead to different norms. In the rent-control example, once some of the landlords' rights have been shifted to tenants through the limitation of rent increases, it may be difficult to shift the rights back to the landlord and remove the controls.

The constraints of equity and historic property rights determine the existence of the particular distribution of income, wealth, and rights at any particular time. They are therefore closely interconnected. If a jurisdiction changes land-use laws, it also changes the distribution of property rights. In turn, this directly changes the existing distribution of wealth in the community. For example, changing the zoning of a parcel has a direct impact on the wealth of the landowner, since his right to develop the property has been affected. If the zoning has been changed to allow apartment construction, the wealth of the landlord has increased. Furthermore, the wealth of other landlords has decreased (since there is more competition in the apartment market), and the income of apartment dwellers has risen compared to that of home owners. However, any equity impacts that the jursidiction initiates, such as changes in the tax structure, only indirectly change property rights, since only over the long term will the income or wealth distribution change enough to cause property-rights changes. Because changing property rights will always have equity implications, whereas changing income or wealth distributions will not always cause a change in property rights, these two criteria can be separated for analysis.

The constraints of equity and property rights also have long-run impacts, although often the political decision maker may have only the option of taking the short run into account. For example, rent control may help tenants and hurt landlords in the short run. But if, as its opponents claim, it leads to less apartment construction, then future tenants are being significantly discriminated against in favor of present tenants. Any analysis of these constraints must examine their ultimate impacts.

Acceptability

Acceptability, the third political constraint facing the local decision maker, depends on three interrelated factors: certainty, legitimacy, and responsiveness.

Certainty is the ability to determine what societal changes will occur when land-use policy is modified. A change in the status quo entails costs and benefits to the politician; and unless he is confident that these can be identified, he is not likely to alter the prevailing rules. As citizens' values change (for example, as the environment becomes less important and affordable housing becomes more important), the successful political decision maker will modify his actions to take account of these changes. The criterion of certainty leads to incremental changes, since large deviations from the status quo are likely to be linked to uncertainty.

The second aspect of political acceptability of land-use controls is legitimacy; the preferences of the relevant participants must be determined and responded to. The determination could involve guaranteeing access to the decision-making process to individuals who may either benefit or lose because of the changes, or it could make use of some other technique such as survey measurements.

Legitimacy also means that the change process must be clearly understood. Specific rules for substantive decision making must be clearly articulated, with the procedures for developing, accepting, and changing land-use regulations understood by the participants, in order for legitimacy to be maintained.

Traditional economic theory argues that local communities are usually better able to respond to local citizen preferences than are higher levels of government. If externalities exist, this implies that land-use interventions are best made at the level just high enough to take them into account. Although California does have state laws regulating land use, the bulk of the decision making is done at the local level. If local jurisdictions respond better than higher levels of government, then this is where the reaction to preferences should occur.[2]

Political criteria range from equity considerations to political acceptability. The best plans of the economist and planner will collapse if these criteria are not met. Yet even if both economic and political criteria are satisfied, if administrative concerns are not adequately addressed, land-use planning will not succeed.

Administrative Criteria

Administrative criteria revolve around two concerns: ease of administration and determination of the institutional relationships that must be considered when the regulations are enacted.

One crucial question is that of the feasibility of enforcement. There is a continuum of ease of enforcement, with some of the tools that are utilized being self-enforcing, permitting market incentives to drive the system. For example, in order to reduce the rate of construction of single-family dwellings, a steep tax could be imposed that would induce developers voluntarily not to develop in response to the price signal. At the opposite extreme a rigid bureaucratic system, perhaps a zoning code, could require developers to go to the government in order to be allowed to do any new development. Furthermore, some fees and charges are realtively easily collected, since the developer is known, as is the quantity of development (the usual fee base). At the other extremes, imperfectly drawn rent-control ordinances (for example, those that allow subletting) evade the purpose of the law. One goal in intervening, from the administrative perspective, should be to have a set of rules, exactions, and regulations that are easily enforced, since this will help to minimize administrative costs.

A second administrative goal should be to minimize uncertainty, delay, and duplication of effort. If met, this goal is important for at least two reasons: It saves money for the jurisdiction, and it can be used to encourage the type of development the community wants.

A major problem of the land-use regulatory system from the point of view of the developer is a lack of certainty and predictability. Administrators may have some power to mitigate at least two causes of this uncertainty. The first cause is vague standards that allow for enough government discretion to make decisions unpredictable; the second is an unsatisfactory vested-rights doctrine that fails to protect the developer adequately from vagaries in the regulatory process (Kolis 1979). These uncertainties can be reduced by consistent administration; and as they are reduced, fewer administrative hearings will be necessary, since the rules and enforcement patterns will be known to all the participants. Fewer decisions will be appealed, also, since obvious rejections will be anticipated.

Institutional Concerns

Formal institutions must also be considered in the administrative criteria. Land rules must be evaluated for their impacts on both public and private institutions. Rules that ignore these impacts also lead to administrative difficulties.

The private institutions concerned with development are the development corporations and the banking system, which finances both the supply and purchase of development. Rules that are easily understood, clearly enforced, straightforward, and quantifiable are preferred by all parties since they minimize profitability risks.[3]

Another important institutional consideration in the public sector is the relationship of the local planning department to the local finance department. In some cases, this relationship is nonexistent. Plans that severely affect the city budget may be implemented; conversely, revenue sources that have major impacts on its planned growth can be tapped. It is important for administrators to recognize that they are not independent and that the actions of one often directly affect the functions of the other.

These three generic criteria—economic, political, and administrative—constitute a framework that can be applied in evaluating the types of rules, regulations, exactions, and fees that can exist in local jurisdictions. The next section will identify some types of land-use interventions.

Types of Government Land-Use Interventions

As seen in the preceding sections, market mechanisms do not always work efficiently; government intervention is sometimes necessary to ensure that an optimum allocation of land-use resources occurs. It is impossible to enumerate all the land-use rules and regulations used by local jurisdiction. Rather, this section will provide a sampling of some of the types of interventions possible. This analysis will be based on a categorization of interventions into direct and indirect ways of affecting land use. The categorization will be based on the primary impact intended by the intervention.

Direct Interventions

Direct intervention into the land-use market means that the jurisdiction has opted to overrule the market directly through the use of rules and regulations that affect the participants. In this case builders must meet certain development criteria, consumers are restricted in their choice, and the city may take control over some types of land use. The efficiency outcomes that would exist in a perfect market are supposedly legislated through these direct interventions.

Direct rules and regulations have four basic characteristics: sureness of results, quickness of impact, palatability to voters, and legalistic style.

When a direct regulation is implemented, the desired response is generally clear and the outcome will be relatively certain. Since certainty is the object of planning, this is an important outcome. But at least two factors offset this apparent certainty. The first is that almost any law has loopholes that were not anticipated by its writer. The second is that there may be secondary effects that are perversely divergent from the intended impacts. Both these factors add to the uncertainty of the law. The public sector should be more surprised by the ultimate impact of the law than the private sector, since it is in the private sector's interest to seek out the loopholes. Compared to indirect interventions, however, direct techniques are more certain.

A second characteristic is that direct regulations have an impact quickly. When a law is enacted, it takes effect immediately. Primary impacts can be quickly perceived and evaluated by the jurisdictional decision makers.

The third characteristic of direct controls is that their financial implications are often hidden. They are, therefore, not as likely to provoke the post–Proposition 13 California voter as much as some of the indirect interventions (Chapman and Kirlin 1979a). Direct controls, since they typically do not utilize market processes, do not tend to be perceived as new taxes and thus are more politically acceptable.

Finally, indirect controls are more legalistic. This means that the regulations easily lead to litigation, that both government and developers have incentives to add legal counsel to their staffs, and that ultimately many of the regulations end up having their precise impacts determined by the court.

Direct controls can be loosely divided into those that control the rate of development and those that control the type of development. Examples of the first type, which tend to slow growth by creating impediments, are excessive subdivision controls, moratoriums or planning pauses on water or sewer connections, and cap rates. Examples of the second type are public land acquisition and zoning ordinances.

Subdivision controls may require the developer to provide certain site-specific improvements for the subdivision. These improvements can include such things as street and sidewalk construction, storm and sanitary sewers, open space, schools, and maintenance contributions. Subdivision controls can also be used to guarantee that future development will minimize negative externalities. In addition to attempting to mandate the growth rate of the infrastructure, subdivision controls can prohibit a proposed development if it is not consistent with the overall general plan of the community. A second type of subdivision control—fee and land-dedication exactions from the developer—are indirect controls and will be discussed later.

Another direct way of affecting the development process is through interim development controls: planning pauses, suspension of sewer or water hookups, or infrastructure provision and building moratoriums. All slow down the process. During these pauses, existing property owners (assuming that demand is increasing) will get windfall gains, since supply has been fixed. This helps to explain why existing inhabitants vote for moratoriums. In California, infrastructure moratoriums have been used by several jurisdictions to regulate the development process and to bring the development into compliance with environmental standards. Wastewater treatment and air-pollution standards, mandated by state and federal agencies, are often the ostensible constraints that cause the community to institute these pauses.

Cap rates (absolute ceilings on population) and annual permit limitations are two additional examples of direct regulations. Cap rates have the political appeal of appearing not to exclude any particular income group, but to only control population size. They are theoretically similar to minimum-lot-size requirements (Hirsch 1977), with the inhabitants of the jurisdiction again receiving the benefits of economic rent. They also tend to be artificially precise, with an ad hoc determination of the optimum population. There is also no guarantee that growth up to the population ceiling will be uniform or occur in the areas in which it is desired.

Annual permit limitations authorize the issuance of a specific number of building permits annually. They differ from cap rates in that development permission is given to the best plans after the plans have either competed directly or have met significant development criteria.

Jurisdictional acquisition of land is one technique utilized to control the type of development that occurs. It is based on the assumption that government can direct growth when it owns the land on which growth occurs. This method can be used to protect open space, to remove land from development, and even to improve the marketability of surrounding (but unencumbered) parcels (Burrows 1978). The simplest technique of government acquisition of land is to have the government buy it outright. However, this does not imply that the land will remain undeveloped, since the government itself may end up using the land. A main deficiency of government acquisitions is that they tend to be very expensive. This occurs for a variety of reasons: The owner may not wish to sell; a legally justifiable public purpose must be invoked if condemnation proceedings are to occur; and government expenditures do not end when the acquisition is complete, since maintenance and tax-opportunity costs remain. The major efficiency justification for public land purchase is that in some cases public goods are supplied. But this rationale must be used carefully.

The Petaluma Plan

The Petaluma Plan is an important example of direct growth controls. Petaluma is a small city located about forty miles north of San Francisco that was once an agricultural center (known to local inhabitants as the "egg basket of the world"). Because of its reasonably priced housing, its population increased by 77 percent from 1960 to 1970 and by another 29 percent from 1970 to 1975 (Schwartz et al., 1979, p. 3). In 1972 the city adopted a strict comprehensive growth-management plan. This plan was upheld by the U.S. Supreme Court in 1976 and therefore gave legal assistance to any jurisdiction that wanted to restrict growth. From 1973 to 1977 growth was to be limited to an average of 500 dwelling units per year by means of an annual allocation of subdivision units. There were some exceptions to the plan (notably very small new subdivisions and buildings on existing lots), but it did include multifamily units as well as single-family dwellings.

The key feature of the system is a housing-allocation program designed to control the location, type, quality, price, and number of new units. The allocation program is administered by a seventeen-member citizen board, which acts in an advisory capacity to the city council. The evaluation board reviews each subdivision proposal and awards points to each subdivision based on two major sets of criteria. The first set is concerned with the public infrastructure and has six items, scored from 0 to 2 points each. These items are: water system, sewage, drainage, fire protection, schools, and streets. The second set deals with the quality of the house or the subdivision. Items in this set include architectural-design quality, site-design quality, character of landscaping and screening, usable open space, provision of foot or bicycle paths and equestrian trails, contiguousness to existing development, and provision of low- and moderate-cost housing. The first set of items serves as a screening device, with 9 of the 12 possible points needed in order to pass on to further review. The subdivisions then are arrayed by type and location, and final allocation of permits up to the maximum number of units allowed are developed. The city council holds hearings after the citizens' committee makes recommendations and makes the development awards (Schwartz et al., 1979, p. 8).

The results of this direct intervention into land use are not unexpected. Compared to housing costs in nearby cities that did not have this program, the prices of standard homes in Petaluma increased significantly, by between $400 and $7,000, depending on house size. Single-family homes built in Petaluma after enactment of the program were fewer, larger, and more expensive (in constant dollars) than those built before the advent of growth management (Schwartz et al., 1979, p. 59).

However, by 1976 home construction in Petaluma was growing at little more than half of the 500-dwelling-unit maximum rate. Developers had found that the regulations were cumbersome and that it took too much time to complete the permit process. Furthermore, once the process was completed, some developers held their permits for speculative value. The plan was then modified by excluding more development from the permit system and by allowing developers to apply for and reserve permits further into the future. Perhaps as a result of these changes, residential construction increased by more than 60 percent in 1979 (Hager 1980).

It is sometimes argued that the juxtaposition of noncompatible land uses causes negative externalities. In particular, this would occur in two situations (Davis 1963). The first occurs when one individual is neutral with respect to location but when, if the location is next to a different land usage, the value of the adjacent land is depressed. The previously mentioned example of the glue factory illustrates this externality. The second case occurs when one individual is attracted by positive externalities to locate next to another, but once he is there, his presence causes negative externalities for the other. An example of this might be cheap apartment construction near expensive homes. The apartment owner benefits from the expensive neighborhood, since he can charge higher rents; but the property value of the single-family dwellings may deteriorate. It is crucial to realize that it is the location that is important. Some cities need glue factories and apartments in order to have a secure economic base. It can be argued (Lafferty and Frech 1978) that each land use generates externalities at two levels: the small-neighborhood level (where they are usually negative) and the citywide level (where they are usually positive).

Zoning is the primary legal tool used by local government to control land use. Zoning codes typically regulate the type of use (such as commercial, industrial, or residential); the density of use (single-family dwellings, duplex, triplex, or multiple); height; and setbacks. Zoning is used primarily to prevent negative externalities and to provide an incentive for specific types of economic development. To the extent that it prevents negative externalities, it encourages economic efficiency. Zoning may also help to ensure an adequate supply of land-use-oriented public goods, and proper zoning can cause development to occur in a pattern that helps minimize the costs of providing some public services.

In practice, zoning seldom meets these goals, for several reasons. The first is that zoning primarily controls land use and only indirectly deals with the impact of negative externalities. For example, pollution impacts might be better controlled by fees or subsidies than by zoning practices. A second reason is that if zoning and economic incentives conflict, the incentives will eventually dominate (Siegan 1972) and zoning will no longer regulate. A third problem is that often the land-use pattern caused by zoning increases private costs; for example, the segregation of industry and housing has increased travel costs. Finally, transaction costs necessary to change zoning patterns to a more efficient use are often high, and land-use rigidities often exist.[4]

Zoning has some significant equity effects. For example, if localities use zoning to ensure minimum lot sizes, the effect is to screen out poor people. If the distributions of the costs and benefits from zoning are examined, the potential beneficiaries will be the higher-income groups while a large share of the costs will fall on the low-income groups (Erwin et al. 1977). Finally, if zoning also increases the probability of capitalization occurring, it makes benefit taxation, which tends to be regressive, more likely (see chapter 3).

Indirect Controls

Individuals respond strongly to price changes that affect their welfare. If the prices of goods or services change, behavior patterns will also change. Indirect land-use incentives are based on these assumptions.

Under the indirect-intervention concept, the local jurisdiction affects land-use alternatives by affecting relative prices. It is assumed that entrepreneurs respond to varying prices as they decide on development patterns, and that consumers will respond as they choose preferred locations. There are shifting possibilities in any land-use price change that is imposed; and, depending on the varying supply-and-demand elasticities, these price impacts might be shared among developers and consumers.

Compared to direct regulations, indirect controls have less-certain effects, are slower to have an impact, could antagonize voters, and are less legalistic.

Since indirect controls influence behavior through changing prices, their short-run impacts tend to be less predictable than direct-control impacts. This is because individual responses to prices may vary with individual tastes and preferences. However, the aggregate effect should be predictable under most conditions.

Indirect controls tend to have their impact more slowly than direct controls. This is because producers and consumers take time to recalculate welfare or profitability equilibria after price changes. In the long run, however, this equilibrium should be more stable than that reached under direct controls.

Since indirect controls change relative land prices, at times they appear to be indistinguishable from ordinary taxes. In California this tends to make the use of these controls less politically acceptable; this factor may be one of the most serious weaknesses of indirect controls.

Indirect controls are straightforward. They are generally stated in dollar terms, and all parties can see the intentions of the jurisdiction, although the ultimate effects might be more difficult to discern. Loopholes are much less likely to exist, and litigation is seldom necessary to determine the role of the fee.

It should be emphasized that indirect controls may lead to land uses identical to those determined by direct controls. However, the process utilized to reach this end state is quite different. Direct controls override market activities; indirect controls utilize market processes. Indirect techniques range from additional fees, charges, and tax abatement techniques to indirect profit controls, environmental regulations, and biased assessment practices.

There are two types of exactions from developers: The developer can be forced to provide infrastructure such as streets, lights, sewers, or waste-treatment facilities; or he can be made to pay various fees and charges. Both techniques have long been utilized in California; although since the passage of Proposition 13, exactions have increased in importance. In both cases the marginal costs to the developer increased. These fees often are determined in an ad hoc manner, with the city charging an estimated average cost of service.[5] It is theoretically possible to determine a proper fee for a particular land use. This should be the present value of the difference between the estimated costs of service for the additional development unit and the anticipated revenues that would arise from the unit. This approach would eliminate all distortions in land use (Hirsch 1977).

Financing techniques and tax incentives can also affect development. Two examples of financing techniques utilized to encourage development in California are federal grant funds and tax-increment financing. One example of a federal grant is the Urban Development Action Grant (UDAG) from the Department of Housing and Urban Development. These grants enable a local jurisdiction to assemble property and provide infrastructure to encourage private commercial development. Their ultimate aim is to improve the city's economic base and to provide jobs. Private-sector cooperation is crucial for the receipt of the funds; and in most cases the federal government is jointly approached by the city and the private developer.[6] Tax-increment districts are formed when the local jurisdiction "freezes" the value of part of the jurisdiction. Any taxes derived from an increase in this value are used to finance the redevelopment of that district. With proper planning, the redevelopment can generate enough revenues to pay for itself. Of course, the existing tax rate is potentially higher than it would have been if the increases in value of the frozen parcel had been included in the base. After the passage of Proposition 13, this form of financing became far more difficult since the district's property values seldom grow fast enough to generate enough revenues to cover the redevelopment costs.

Tax changes can also be used to affect development. At least two techniques can be used to encourage development. It is possible to allow tax concessions in areas where development is to be encouraged; or land can be taxed more than structure, thereby encouraging more land development in order to generate enough income to pay the land taxes. To discourage development, land taxes might be lowered so that the land owners feel less pressure to utilize their land intensively to generate income. In practice, however, this technique may not always work smoothly, since it subsidizes the holding of land while waiting for the best offer.

The California Land Conservation Act, sometimes called the Williamson Act, was enacted in 1965 and is an example of the use of this tool. This act enables farmers to voluntarily enroll their land (supposedly on the urban fringe) in a ten-year, annually extended program. Once enrolled, the land would not be taxed at its highest and best use, but rather be taxed at agricultural use, based on capitalizing the agricultural income. If the farmer wished to develop the land in other ways, a penalty would have to be paid. This act was popular with rural land owners, since it lowered their taxes, and with counties, since it ensured that the farmland, which demanded few services, would remain as farmland and still generate taxes in excess of service costs.

The ostensible purposes of this act were to preserve prime agricultural land, to prevent premature and unnecessary conversion from agricultural to urban use, and to provide a "fair" level of property tax. The actual results of the act, however, were somewhat different (Goodenough 1978).

Most of the benefits of the act, in terms of property taxes saved, went to the large land owners. However, because these are taxes saved rather than direct sums paid out, there has been little publicity concerning these benefits. Most of the enrollment has been for nonprime farmland (70 percent of the contracted land). This land produces little commercial product and is far from incorporated and growing areas. There has been little enrollment of land around the true urban fringe. The lower estimate of the decrease in tax revenue that occurred because of the act in fiscal-year 1972–1973 was over $22 million. State general-fund subventions to replace these losses in 1972–1973 were about $13 million. It is generally considered to be unsuccessful as a land-control measure, because it has not really controlled land changes. In part this is because it is a voluntary program with an emphasis on strong local independence; but it is also in part because the tax incentives are not strong enough to outweigh the private-sector incentives for the changing land use.

Another type of indirect control is more subtle—a control on potential profits. An example is the rent-control ordinance, which constrains landlords from raising rents to market levels. Rent controls affect profit margins and, therefore, apartment construction by limiting the price of apartments. Further, financial institutions are hesitant to make development loans for apartment construction if rent control exists or is considered imminent, since additional risk is attached to the realization of apartment builder's profits. Rent control is an example of land-control ordinance enacted for equity considerations. Other equity-based regulations that have an impact on profitability and indirectly on land use are inclusionary housing programs (where developers must provide low-cost housing in order to get development permits) and condominium-conversion ordinances, which prohibit the converting of apartments into condominiums.

An additional indirect regulation method is the use of environmental controls. Typically, these either force a developer to provide certain services, such as sewage treatment, or insist on an upper limit of polluting materials that can be released into the airshed.[7] These become part of development costs and are indirect impacts on land use; that is, the government is *not* telling the private-sector developer what can be built. Rather, it is telling the developer what additional costs must be incurred in the construction of different types of projects. For example, strict air-pollution requirements will tend to forestall industrial use.

A final example of an indirect tool is misappraisal of a particular property. This typically is not a formal tool of the jurisdiction, since it often happens by accident; but it could clearly have an impact on the use of the property. If it is known that expensive development is consistently underassessed (for example, the ratio of assessed values to market values for expansive homes is consistently less than the ratio for inexpensive ones), this might well encourage development of more expensive property.[8] It should be noted that both direct and indirect regulations affect both supply and demand for land, and thus have an impact on the property value, which the assessor ascertains. As these activities change, the assessed value and market value should also change to reflect the regulations' impact. The more regulations, the greater the likelihood that there will be a decline in market value that the assessor should observe (Baxter 1979). In California, Proposition 13 now determines assessment procedures and has eliminated much of the artistry of assessment practices.

This listing of direct and indirect ways of affecting land use is only partial and is primarily useful as a set of relatively simple examples of government intervention. There are two important concepts to remember when examining these interventions. First, interventions by themselves may not guarantee economic efficiency or political palatability. Even if there are market failures, formal intervention will not guarantee either efficient resource allocation or equity. Second, it is very difficult to intervene in a purely direct or purely indirect sense. Most rules, regulations, and fees have both direct and indirect consequences. In many cases the secondary effects, which may be of opposite character, can be nearly as important.

Evaluation of the Types of Interventions

This section will examine direct and indirect rules in the light of the economic, political, and administrative criteria. Table 2-1 summarizes these results.

Table 2-1
Relationships between Types of Interventions and Evaluative Criteria

Type of Intervention	Direct	Indirect
Criteria		
Economic		
Efficiency	–	+
Revenues	0	+
Expenditures	+	0
Political		
Financial equity	0	–
Property rights	–	0
Acceptability	+	0/–
Administrative		
Ease	–	0/+
Institutional relationships	–	+

– negative effect of intervention
0 neutral effect of intervention
+ positive effect of intervention

Economic Criteria

Economic efficiency may be the most important of all the criteria. Without the intent of increasing individual welfare, most land-use interventions would be hard to justify.

With perfect knowledge of consumer tastes and preferences, producer technologies, and the economic impacts of all the externalities, it is conceptually possible to design a set of direct controls that would leave the economy in precisely the same position as a set of perfectly designed taxes and fees (Buchanan and Tullock 1975). However, the extent of knowledge needed to tailor these rules and to regulate accurately each individual's and firm's behavior is far greater than that needed to develop indirect interventions. Because of this, direct and indirect rules have different results when evaluated by economic-efficiency criteria.

Direct rules change conditions of ownership. They deliberately ignore market preferences, and instead reflect the best judgments of decision makers as to what an efficient land-use pattern should be. There needs to be a considerable knowledge concerning the prerule behaviors of the participants in the land-use market in order for the rules to be precisely specified. This information is expensive to gather, and there is a much greater chance of an inefficient equilibrium being reached. Only if there are so many other distortions that market incentives cannot be used will direct intervention possibly be efficient. Indirect interventions, through a tax or subsidy mechanism, are usually more efficient means of changing land-use patterns. These augment the incentives facing the individual consumer and developer and, if utilized correctly to compensate for externalities, are more likely to lead to an optimum result. If the present pattern of land use is efficient, both direct and indirect interventions will lead to inefficiency. However, given other systemic problems, indirect methods, since they allow individuals options of response, are likely to be more economically efficient than direct methods.

Direct activities seldom directly generate additional budget revenues. Any revenue impact that they may have would be secondary and arise from land-use patterns that they create. For example, zoning is justified for its externality-mitigating impacts. Yet, it may force a different type of land use than what the market would imply and, in so doing, cause different revenue patterns to exist. Zoning for a housing development because of political pressure for more housing rather than for the commercial or industrial use that might be indicated by the market leads to less total revenue to the jursidiction, since the sales-tax revenues are eliminated. Indirect tools are partially designed to generate revenue. In imposing fees and charges, jurisdictions argue that development imposes additional costs and that the fees are designed to defray these costs. In these cases, this type of intervention produces the direct result of more money for the jurisdiction. However, the land-use changes that occur because of the use of fees and charges might be unanticipated if the jurisdiction only examines their revenue potential.

Direct regulations can be used to ensure concentrated development that leads to cost minimization. Although this has been successful in some instances, there is no guarantee that all direct controls will lead to this result. In California some jurisdictions attempt to use growth controls to ensure that the development that does occur utilizes a minimum amount of city services. The minimization of city costs is seldom the primary focus of indirect interventions. They are not necessarily designed to ensure concentrated development patterns, although, as secondary effects, they may well induce them. They are probably neutral with respect to costs.

Political Criteria

Income wealth or consumption equity is as much a political as an economic problem. Most direct interventions are not concerned with this impact, although they do have significant effects. However, because most of their impacts are either secondary or long run, the citizenry is not particularly aware of them. One of the selling points of direct effects is their legal neutrality, although the economic effects derived from the law may not be equitable.

Indirect interventions in the land market have clear equity impacts. These are so visible that they cannot be categorized as secondary. Fees and charges must be paid by someone—the consumer, the developer, the construction worker, or the land owner. Since they typically tend to be flat fees, the apparent result is a regressive fee structure. However, because of the various shifting possibilities, the incidence of the fee is always uncertain; and if the fee replaces a property tax, the ultimate burden becomes even more difficult to ascertain. Finally, if these fees are accurate benefit charges, they are as inequitable as any other price charged in the market, since all individuals face the same price for a given commodity, regardless of income.

Property rights are directly affected by direct interventions. The economic value of the limiting of these rights is shown by a fall in the land value that occurred as the regulations were imposed. New land owners, who buy at the lower price, have purchased a constrained piece of land, whose use has been appropriately discounted.

Indirect controls are designed to work within the existing framework of property rights. Since direct interventions leave property rights unchanged in the short run, but change instead the relative costs of alternative activities, these incentives are neutral with respect to these rights.

Political acceptability involves the ease of acceptance of the political decision and depends on perceived legitimacy, responsiveness, and certainty. Direct interventions all rank high with respect to these criteria and under most circumstances are politically acceptable. However, individuals may be differentially affected by rule changes, so that it is difficult to predict the degree of acceptability of all changes. For example, downzoning helps home owners, hurts future apartment dwellers, and hurts developers. Yet the law will be obeyed because it did meet acceptability criteria.

For the very same reasons, indirect land-use controls are less likely to be acceptable. They are less certain in impact, and they run counter to the tax-revolt ethic that is quite pronounced in California. They rank low in both perceived legitimacy and responsiveness dimensions. However, they may be easier to justify in a cost-recovery argument. At best the indirect-intervention impacts are negative to neutral in acceptability.

Administrative Criteria

Direct controls are difficult to administer. They usually entail the existence of a large bureaucratic framework, since formal approval is usually necessary to get something done. Direct controls tend to be rigid, and the administrator has little formal discretion as to their implementation. Any flexibility is found in the appealing of adverse decisions on technical grounds.

Most indirect controls are easier to administer, since the fees, charges, or other interventions, once enacted, do not require further government approval.

They are more flexible in dealing with unanticipated situations since the primary locus of decision making is at the individual level, and the various developers and consumers can arrange their behavior and still be within the law. Furthermore, since they are simpler to administer, a secondary effect is that they are also less expensive for the government to administer.[9]

Direct rules tend to increase the difference between public- and private-sector institutions, since they ignore private-sector incentives. Further, since the direct interventions have fiscal effects as secondary impacts, they do not tend to increase communications between the planning and finance departments of a local jurisdiction. For these reasons, direct rules would rank relatively low on this criterion.

Indirect interventions do somewhat better. Since they are oriented toward the same incentives that guide the private sector, they are more easily understood by private-sector institutions. Furthermore, since they entail a revenue flow, they force the relevant departments within the jurisdiction to communicate.

There is no obvious "winner" in terms of what should be the type of intervention utilized. Land-use decision making is complex, and public interventions increase its complexity. Any intervention depends on the type of problem to be solved and how the relevant criteria are weighed. In most cases the indirect interventions appear to be more economically and administratively worthwhile, while the direct rules tend to be more politically palatable. Since political considerations explicitly involve basic value judgments to a greater extent than the other dimensions (which are also not value free), direct rules tend to dominate.[10] But with the overlay of Proposition 13 on the system, fiscal considerations will become more important; and a movement toward more market-like interventions is likely to occur.

Some Simple Impacts of Land-Use Controls

The purpose of land-use controls is to have an impact on the pattern of land development. In so doing, the interventions affect developers, consumers, and city finances. Some of these simple interventions will be discussed in this section.

Private-Sector Impacts

Land-use controls have an impact on developers and consumers in the private sector. Rules almost always increase development costs. At a given market price, then, the developer will supply less housing, the greater the number of rules, regulations, or fees relating to development. Consumers are indirectly affected. Unless there are perfect substitutes for the desired land use, at least some of the cost increases will be shifted to the consumer. In equilibrium, the quantity of development bought and sold on the market will be less than it was before the interventions.

In addition to developers and consumers, other individuals are also affected and change their activity as the rules change. Retail merchants, for example, are affected when residential development is curtailed through the interventions. Financial institutions who loan money to both sides of the market—that is, to both developers and consumers—also change lending policies in accordance with land-use changes.

It should be emphasized that these price and quantity effects may, indeed, lead to a more efficient allocation of resources in the economy. To the extent that the regulations accurately force an internalization of the externalities that exist in developing areas, or to the extent that the fees and charges truly reflect the benefits of services and should be paid by the consumers of those services, the economy could be closer to an optimal state. However, if these interventions are not carefully thought out, the economy could move in the reverse direction— away from optimality.

Public-Sector Impacts

Land-use controls have an impact on the type of economic development that takes place in the jurisdiction. This development affects the public budget in several ways.

The more development amenable to the imposition of fees and charges, the greater the revenue flow from this source. However, if some of these are earmarked for specific purposes—for example, in lieu of park fees—then the city must take this money and use it to provide additional service increments to the residents of the new development. In this case the city's net financial position does not change the types of development allowed but has an impact on the revenue structure. If the city, through zoning, encourages commercial and industrial growth as opposed to residential growth, the revenue flow may be larger.

If regulations cause a more efficient clustering of similar-service demanders, the city can anticipate falling per-unit costs of service provision.

In California, after the passage of Proposition 13, the variety and application of ways of intervening in the land-use arena are crucial concerns of city policy; but their effects may well have been broader than initially intended. Chapter 3 will present a model that will capture some additional relationships between land-use interventions and the local public economy.

Notes

1. See Leftwich (1963) or any other intermediate text for a delineation of the extremely strong assumptions necessary for perfect competition to exist.

2. Changing the location of a decision could be important in some land-use decision making because two of the major groups that have constrained the usefulness of zoning at the local level may be less effective at the state level: the local developer and the neighborhood organization. The exact opposite is true for the large developer.

3. This is true at least in theory. In practice, complicated local practices may given unfair advantages to local developers over potential competitors who may not understand some of the arcane ramifications of the laws.

4. Hirsch argues also that large-lot residential zoning, compared to a property tax, gives rise to three inefficiencies: More communities are required for an efficient level of public goods to be provided, there are inappropriate lot sizes for some communities, and it could lead to inefficient scale for some local-government operations.

5. This crudeness will disappear. Proposition 4, which passed on the November 1979 ballot, allowed, as an exception to expenditure limits, fees not to exceed the full costs of services. This is a strong incentive for accurate fee determination.

6. A tool used in other states—industrial-revenue bonds—is currently not allowed in California. These tax-exempt bonds are usually issued by a jurisdiction, which then loans the proceeds to qualifying firms for plant and equipment financing. These plants pay lower-than-market interest rates for these loans.

7. Environmental restrictions that forbid development, as in some Coastal-Zone areas, are more similar to zoning restrictions than to indirect techniques.

8. There is evidence of this in some areas. For example, Pollakowski (1976) found that in Seattle lower-valued dwellings were overassessed, whereas higher-valued dwellings were underassessed. Black (1977) has discovered the same situation in Boston.

9. Rent control is an obvious exemption to this argument, since it requires a large bureaucracy to administer it. See chapter 7.

10. See Buchanan and Tullock (1975) for another explanation.

3 Public Budgeting and Land Use

The Importance of the Property Tax

For most cities in California the property tax, prior to Jarvis-Gann, was the major revenue source, although its relative importance had been declining over the past ten years. Immediately prior to the election, about one-fifth of total city tax revenue and one-third of total local revenue was provided by this tax to the average California municipality. In the year preceding the enactment of Proposition 13, California property taxes were more than 50 percent above the national average. It is estimated that in the year following Jarvis-Gann they will fall to about one-half of their former level and be about 35 percent below the national norm (see chapter 4 for more details).

The academic view of a property tax has long differed from the view of the practitioner. However, with the formalization of this view by Rolph and Break in the 1960s and Mieszkowski and McClure in the early 1970s, this view became somewhat more widely disseminated and accepted. These new analyses indicated that if the property tax is considered a national tax on the owners of capital, then the average tax on all property will be borne by all owners of capital through a fall in the average rate of return. In this case, if capital income is a higher percentage of the income of wealthy individuals than of poor individuals, the tax is progressive. If the property tax is considered only a national tax on housing, then the income elasticity of the property tax would be identical to the income elasticity of the demand for housing. This elasticity appears to be slightly less than 1 (although its estimates vary from study to study), which would make the tax slightly regressive (Carliner 1973). These results are distinctly different from the old view that the tax was shifted forward to consumers and was likely to be heavily regressive (McClure 1977).

However, the property tax is a local tax that varies between localities. This differential in the tax affects the relative value of capital in different regions in different manners and, with all else equal, tends to drive mobile capital from the high-tax localities to low-tax localities. The tax is borne in the long run by the immobile factor, land. Those residents living in a low-tax jurisdiction benefit, since the inflow of mobile capital will increase competition in that market and drive consumer prices down. It can also be shown that a local property tax used to finance public goods whose benefits vary by location will result in a more compact city than would occur if the public goods were financed by benefit charges (Wright 1977). The tax can also cause locational inefficiencies, instability of aging communities, and a decline in the variety of available jurisdictions (Hirsch 1977). Finally, variants of the property tax, such as site-value taxes or development-value taxes, can have an impact on the speed of development and the amount of land available for urban growth (Smith 1978; Rose 1973). It does appear as if property-tax price effects are important at the local level, although they may vary by local idiosyncrasies. This implies that the tax can be an important local-policy instrument.[1]

There is also an important relationship between assessment and the incidence of the tax. If assessment is not accurate—that is, if more expensive properties are assessed at lower fractions of their market value than less expensive properties—then there is likely to be an additional forward shifting of the tax to the consumer. If true, this implies that the tax is more regressive than previously thought; and better administration in terms of accurate assessment will make the tax more progressive.

The concept of capitalization may be one of the most important in local public finance. Capitalization occurs when the present value of a durable asset changes because of a change in either the benefits or costs associated with that asset. If the price of the asset reflects the present value of the asset (under conditions of certainty they are equal), capitalization is measured by the change in the asset price. For example, if taxes on an asset are lowered, then its price should increase to reflect the tax change.

In the short run, capitalization is a demand phenomenon, because it is assumed that the supply of durable assets is fixed. If a tax on a particular type of asset is imposed, then the holders of that asset, recognizing a decreased return, will attempt to sell it and invest in other nontaxed assets. The price of the taxed asset falls until its new buyer receives an identical return based on the after-tax income stream and the lower price. The original owner has borne the entire tax. Theoretically, in the short run both taxes and expenditures can be capitalized into property values.[2]

There are several preconditions necessary for capitalization to occur. Tax or expenditure changes must extend into the future, must be on durable assets, and cannot be shifted. Furthermore, any change must not affect all assets equally (Wendling 1979). Capitalization thus refers to differences in property values that arise between jurisdictions because of differences between fiscal packages offered to their inhabitants.

An example might be useful. Assume that there are two communities, X and Y. Assume further that they receive all their revenues through the use of property taxes and that, although they provide the same service level, their residents have different tax liabilities (say, because of geography). Because of these geographical differences, the owner of a piece of property worth $40,000 in X pays $500 per year in property taxes, while the owner of an identical piece of property in Y must pay $1,000 per year to receive identical services.

Assuming all the conditions for capitalization are present and that the discount rate is 10 percent,[3] the property in Y will be valued at $35,000. The $5,000 difference in prices is the present value of the $500 property-tax differential. A mover can thus buy in X for $40,000 and face a $500 tax liability or can buy in Y for $35,000 and face a $1,000 tax liability. It is possible to have capitalization with no changes in observed property values. If the present value of the benefits exactly offsets the present value of the increased taxes, and both are capitalized, property values will not change. If benefit and cost capitalizations are not exactly offsetting, then property value will vary.

There are at least two important local implications of capitalization. Tax capitalization involves tax rates. If the rate is reduced and thus the tax base increases, then it may well be that the tax revenues collected will not fall by the full amount anticipated by the tax decrease. Conversely, if rates increase the base may fall, and the tax revenues collected will not increase as much as anticipated. Only under specific conditions, to be discussed later in this chapter, when both service changes and tax changes are entirely capitalized into property values, will there be no change in the base and, therefore, will projections be accurate.

In the short run, the owner of the asset bears the full burden of the tax. However, for the new mover into the community, the lowered price is offset by the increased taxes. If capitalization exists in a long-run equilibrium, then it would convert the property tax to a benefit charge for the new residents of the community and would be regressive, since it is imposed regardless of income.[4] Resource-allocation efficiency, however, is greater under a benefit tax.

Local Finance and Capitalization

A crucial public-finance question concerns the circumstances that must be present in order for variations in tax rates and expenditures to be capitalized. The first attempt to address this question, a 1956 article by Charles Tiebout, never discussed capitalization, but implicitly used it in his analysis. His purpose was to show that a conceptual solution to the problem of determining the efficient level of local public goods and taxes exists. In Tiebout's model, jurisdictions offer specific bundles of public services and taxes to potential residents.[5] Each household then chooses a specific community that offers a set of taxes and expenditures and moves to that community.

In order to get this result, Tiebout makes a series of assumptions:

1. Households are fully mobile.
2. They have full information about the bundles of taxes and expenditures that are offered.
3. They can choose where to live from among a large number of communities.

4. There are no employment restrictions on their residential choice.
5. There are no public-service externalities between communities.
6. There is an optimum size for every pattern of community services.
7. Communities attempt to achieve their optimum size.

At any given time there may be families in any one community who are unhappy in their location. These families will attempt to move to a community that better matches their preferences. To do this, they must bid away a place from the home owners in the community in which they wish to relocate if the community is already at optimum size. The price of property increases in the desired community. If this increase in property value is the present value of the variation of taxes or public services in the desired community compared to the other, then capitalization has occurred. Tiebout, however, never explicitly described this bidding process.

There are several problems with the realism of this model. Although normal moves may be sufficient for the model, they are not costless; and the local market might not easily clear (Mills and Oates 1975). Many jurisdictions that are close to employment are needed. Local budgets are fixed, although in the real world voter preferences can be reflected. Because of the federal income-tax laws, which allow deductibility of some local taxes, if the community utilizes property taxes (but not benefit taxes), then there is too low a price being paid for location; and a possibility exists for an excess demand for living in specific jurisdictions.

But most importantly, there needs to be a shortage of space in any community that offers a specific combination of desired goods and taxes. This shortage is what causes households to pay premium prices for location. If there were no shortage, households would not be willing to pay a premium for the location and there would be no capitalization. If land is in short supply in the long run, there will be capitalization in the long-run equilibrium.

Tiebout's model leads to the demonstration that local government can provide an efficient level of public services. Households reveal preferences for the public-service tax set by voting with their feet. A second implication of Tiebout is that if demand for public services is a function of income, then communities will be homogeneous. Finally, if these variations are capitalized into land rents, there are likely to be land-price discontinuities at the borders between cities that offer vastly different bundles (assuming homogeneous service delivery within each of the adjoining jurisdictions) (Ellson 1980, p. 198). This could explain, for example, why there exist such large discontinuities between jurisdictions in parts of California that are located close to each other (for example, Beverly Hills prices are far above those of adjacent West Hollywood, an unincorporated part of the county).

Several extensions of the Tiebout model were developed in the 1970s. In particular, three weaknesses of the Tiebout model were examined: the lack of a pricing mechanism, the demographic instability of the homogeneous communities, and the inefficient supply of low-income housing (for example, see Hamilton 1975a, 1975b, 1976b, 1977).

In his article, Tiebout never identified a system of prices that would operate for local public services. Because of this, the consumption of these goods will be rationed by some inefficient method, for example, queuing or zoning. However, if a proportional property tax is used to finance these services, it would be in the interest of any individual household to locate in a community of high property value in order to consume public services at a low tax rate. The poor would attempt to invade wealthy communities, and the Tiebout conclusion of homogeneous jurisdictions would not occur (Mills and Oates 1975; Hamilton 1977). If existing residents could restrict low-income households to ensure that the tax base per household remains high, they would not face increasing tax rates. Thus there is an incentive to support restrictions to prevent small lots—perhaps through zoning. Support for restrictions comes from all the property owners in the jurisdiction, regardless of their income level, since an increase in the supply of low-income housing on small lots will cause a decrease in assessed value per household and an increase in the tax price for public services. But the value of the existing low-income housing is increased because of the zoning. Furthermore, since there is less land available for the low-income housing, there will be an increase in supply of the high-income housing and the price of high-income housing will fall.[6] Zoning is a roundabout method of transferring wealth from the poor to the rich.

Under some types of zoning ordinances, specifically those that force the household to consume a minimum level of housing, the local property tax is converted into a benefit tax. This is because a household must pay a fixed sum to live in the community and receive the public benefits. If this occurs, then the local public service could be distributed efficiently; and the tax rates and levels of public-service provision would not be capitalized, since the tax price would be considered identical to a benefit charge and would not distort the price of housing (Hamilton 1975b).[7]

Whether capitalization occurs at all has also been under discussion. Some authors maintain that in the long run there are no fixed factors, and that capitalization does not occur (Edel and Sklar 1975, Hamilton, 1976b). However, Hamilton further argues that it is in the interjurisdictional differences in tax rates relative to expenditures that are capitalized, not only the rates (Hamilton, 1976a). Under this assumption, it is the differences between the per-household benefits and taxes that have an impact on property values even in the long run. In any one community, however, the capitalization effects net to zero, since any fiscal gain enjoyed by the low-income households (who pay less in taxes than they receive in benefits) is exactly offset with a loss by the high-income households (who pay more in taxes than they receive in benefits) (Hamilton 1976a). Once again, current residents might attempt to zone out new low-income residents, since the old residents' housing values would decline if low-income housing caused them to absorb a fiscal deficit.

The principal implication of the capitalization of a differential fiscal surplus is that full capitalization leads to horizontal equity.[8] A given housing and public-service bundle receives the same price everywhere. In effect, this is a movement toward benefit taxation. A numerical example makes this easier to follow.

Assume that initially there is a homogeneous community of 100 homes, each worth $75,000. The community has determined to spend $1,500 per house for public services and to raise this money by a 2-percent property tax. This also raises $1,500 per household; and, since the tax liability equals the benefits, no change in property value is observed.

If this community is compared to a community that is not homogeneous, say, one having three-fourths of the homes being worth $75,000 and one-fourth being worth $50,000, the Hamilton situation occurs.[9] If the heterogeneous community wishes to spend the identical amount per household, it must use a tax rate of 2.18 percent. This would raise $1,635 from the higher-priced houses (they would run a fiscal deficit of $135) and $1,090 from the lower-priced houses (they would run a fiscal surplus of $410). Again assuming a 10-percent discount rate, the price of the higher-priced houses would fall by $1,350 to $73,650, whereas the price of the less-expensive houses would rise by $4,100 to $54,100. Horizontal equity exists since the price paid for the benefit is the same no matter where in the heterogeneous town one lives. A mover can purchase a $75,000 home for $73,650, a savings of $1,350, which exactly equals the present value of the fiscal deficit associated with that house. Or a mover can purchase a $50,000 home for $54,100, a price increase of $4,100, which exactly equals the fiscal surplus associated with that house.[10]

If capitalization occurs, then the tax advantage of low-income housing is offset by the increase in the price of housing. The tax structure is perfectly inelastic with respect to income. This makes the property tax regressive, although efficient. Further, Hamilton (1977) has calculated that this regressivity is substantial. If local governments could ignore this regressivity and argue that income distribution is the purview of the federal government, the problem would be moot.[11] However, it is unlikely that local politicians will ignore this concern. If this political constraint is important, property-tax reforms, as with Proposition 13, will act to make the tax system more progressive, although less efficient.

Ultimately, the question of capitalization is empirical. Most of the work examining the theory, starting with Oates (1969), has shown that at least some capitalization has occurred, especially with respect to taxes. The more complex models (for example, Meadows 1976; Hamilton 1979; Lea 1979; Brueckner 1979) do not always indicate as large a degree of capitalization as some of the simpler models (for example, Noto 1976; McDougall 1976), yet most of the results indicate that in the short run some capitalization occurs (Edel and Sklar 1974). Furthermore, although not all of the empirical work discovers the same set of results—see, for example, Pollakowski's (1973) critique of Oates, and the Oates response (1973)—all appear to be based on the same framework. There have also been studies that examine the impacts of the fiscal variables by income class. One found that, in the aggregate, middle-class location decisions are quite sensitive to fiscal influences. But when declining central cities are separated from growing central cities, fiscal inducements are only important in the growing cities (Ellson 1980). In the declining central cities, the fiscal differences were more of an effect of decentralization than a determinant. Another study found that taxes and expenditures have different impacts on moving decisions by income group and tenure of ownership (Reschovsky 1979). It found that tax rates were negatively related to moves for all income strata and tenure categories and were significant for low-income owners and renters and for middle-income renters. Furthermore, the expenditure variables were positively correlated with moves for the same six classes and significant for the same three.[12]

Proposition 13 transformed California from a high-property-tax state to one with lower-than-average property taxes. From both theory and empirical work, it is tentatively possible to predict some effects. In the short run there should be windfall capitalized gains for most areas of the state, since the effective tax rate is lowered. California economic activity should increase relative to other states. Within the state there will be less differentiation between regions in the property-tax rate (all rates in excess of $4 per $1,000 assessed value demonstrate different debt requirements). This reduction in tax differentials should minimize this tax as an incentive for within-state development locations. However, with the lowering of this differential there may be some slight shifting in activity from the suburbs to the central cities, since central cities may have less outstanding debt than suburbs. For example, one study has found some tentative evidence that the deterioration of the Los Angeles economy relative to the suburbs has either slowed down or reversed (Shulman 1979). It is also likely that a Tiebout equilibrium will not occur in California since the high-tax–high-service jurisdiction cannot easily exist after the proposition (Shulman 1979). Hamilton's fiscal zoning impacts are also likely to occur as jurisdictions attempt to keep out projects that lower the average local tax base.

A Model of Budgeting and Land Use

When the local government attempts to have an impact on land use, it will also affect the public-revenue and -expenditure flow. At the same time, if the local government changes the tax structure and service-provision pattern, it will also affect land development. The construction of a model of public intervention in the land market and the description of the simultaneous impact of development on the local budget will be undertaken in this section.[13] There will be three sets of actors in the model: developers, consumers, and jurisdictional decision makers. Each set of actors has an impact on the other two sets. The model is a specification of the interrelationships among the three groups.

Increased development provides additional revenues to the jurisdiction by augmenting the local property-tax base and by providing residences for additional taxpayers who may cause increases in such revenues as sales taxes, fees, or population-based intergovernmental grants. The development may also cause increased expenditures since the jurisdiction must now provide additional services.

The local budget also has an impact on development. If the jurisdiction imposes specific taxes or requirements on the developer, he may decide that it is too expensive to build. If this occurs, the city will not get the anticipated revenues. At the same time the jurisdiction can encourage development by providing high-quality services.

After describing a model that amplifies these points, this chapter will examine the impact of Proposition 13. Later, in chapter 6, the limited empirical data that has been collected after the passage of the initiative will be analyzed in this context. The model itself is limited. Its primary emphasis is on the residential sector because a full data set necessary to estimate the model after Proposition 13 does not yet exist in usable form; and there is scant evidence that property taxes have a major impact on industrial or commercial location (Van Ness and Shoup 1979).[14] Furthermore, the analysis will generally not be concerned with the existing housing stock, but rather only with new development. In the context of the model, it is the marginal development that is being examined in relation to the marginal revenue and expenditure concerns of the jurisdiction.

The Supply of Development

Several factors influence the decision of the potential developers. This section will analyze some of these factors and derive the supply curve of development for a typical jurisdiction. It is assumed that construction is a competitive industry, and the supply curve is the marginal-cost curve of the developer.

A developer must first obtain construction financing. If the developer is a large company, retained earnings may be the source of funds. However, most developers must obtain construction financing and commitments from a lending institution. Only if the lender's analysis indicates that the loan will be adequately secured will it be granted. The political climate of the jurisdiction can affect the financing of the project by increasing uncertainty about its profitability. For example, the existence of rent-control ordinances increases the uncertainty of the lender and makes apartment loans difficult to get. The riskier the project, the more likely it is that the developer will have to borrow at high interest rates, which in turn increase the costs of development.

The rules that the jurisdiction imposes on developers set the constraints. Many of these rules revolve around the necessary permits and approvals that a builder must obtain in order to develop. The more rules and approvals that a developer must abide by, the greater are his costs. These costs involve not only the additional labor necessary to fill out the forms and present the case for development, but also the opportunity costs that the developer incurs as he waits for approval, holding the vacant land.

However, the rules and planning processes that exist in a jurisdiction may also help the developer in some situations. In particular, the local developer probably knows the quickest way to get approvals. The nonlocal developer does not immediately have this information and incurs the costs of obtaining it. This gives the local builder a decided advantage over the outsider.

If the regulations have not changed over a long period of time, their impacts on risk and uncertainty may be minimized. In fact, if it is anticipated that the regulatory process will remain consistent, the rules may even act to lower uncertainty. For example, if the rules restrict the issuing of building permits and are expected to remain the same, a developer with permission to build has an advantage because the tighter supply will increase the odds of a profitable development. Of course, if rules or requirements are often changed, then there will be an increase in uncertainty, which is likely to be reflected in increased borrowing costs.

It should be noted that rules may also constrain the supply of buildable land. By affecting this supply, the jurisdiction affects the housing market. Since much of the argument over the occurrence of capitalization revolves around the long-run existence of a perfectly elastic supply of land for each jurisdiction, if this supply is limited, then much of the capitalization debate has been settled. In terms of the earlier Tiebout discussion, it is likely that he assumed a perfectly elastic supply of land for all communities, but a fixed supply for any one community.

There is another set of laws, exogenous to the jurisdiction, that affect the developer. These are regulations imposed by the state and federal governments. For this model, these additional development interferences will be held constant.

It is within this political and institutional climate that the developer must operate. Once approval and financing have been obtained (and this may take years in some jurisdictions for some projects), the developer can begin to build. There are three primary costs that the developer incurs. He must buy land, he must either rent or buy equipment, and he must hire workers. The appropriate technology will determine the most efficient use of these resources, based on the relative prices. It can be assumed that the small developer is a price taker for all three of the inputs; that is, he can hire as much labor as he wants at a given wage, rent as much equipment as he wants at a given rate, and purchase as much land as he wants at a given price. For a given community, however, there is a fixed supply of land; at the aggregate level, therefore, the marginal cost of land is probably increasing.

In addition to these primary costs, the developer also faces the taxes, fees, and charges that the jurisdiction is imposing. As will be seen in chapter 6, some of these can be very large. The developer has two choices: to pay the fees and hope to be able to pass them on to the consumer, or to leave the area. The more elastic the demand for development, the less likely it is that the increases in costs will be shifted forward.

It might be noted that the developer will also pay attention to the service-delivery policies of the jurisdiction. If the development is in a city with high-quality schools, police services, parks, and museums, then it is likely that interjurisdictional quality differences may be capitalized into the price of the land; the developer, who has paid for them when the land was purchased, now passes them on in the price of the house. Additional changes in either expenditures or taxes can thus be reflected in changing raw-land prices, which affect developers' costs. Additionally, if a developer is responsible for providing the capital infrastructure of the development and if there is some likelihood that the benefits of all of his expenditures will not be captured in the price of his homes, the profitability picture worsens.

Given the structure of the financing, political, and input costs, the developer must then decide whether to proceed. The basis for this decision is the expected profitability of the venture. The key to this profitability is the price at which the dwelling units can be sold. In a competitive market, higher output prices will, in the short run, increase the rate of return to existing firms as well as encourage these firms to increase output. To ensure the greatest profitability, the developer takes the output price (that is, the additional revenue received from selling one more unit) and compares it to the marginal costs of producing that unit. The developer produces when the two are equal. If prices increase, he produces more; if prices fall, he produces less. The marginal cost and supply curves are the same (at least above average costs in the long run). Since there is a short-run fixed supply of one of the inputs—land—the marginal-cost curve will slope upward.

In the long run, however, the supply of land can increase. The supply of land and its uses are at least in part a political phenomenon. It is possible to increase the aggregate supply of buildable land by changing the rules and constraints that face the building industry. While this supply can be increased only marginally for boundary locked in jurisdictions that can no longer annex, suburbs on the urban fringe face a large potential land source. If land is not fixed, the supply curve of new development will be more elastic.

This discussion is important for tax-shifting arguments. For a given demand, the greater the elasticity of supply of development, the greater the likelihood of much of the fees, charges, and taxes placed on the developer or landowner being passed on to the consumer. Since this model is basically a short-run model (although in equilibrium), it is assumed that the aggregate supply curve is upward-sloping and that it looks like *MC* in figure 3-1. As selling prices increase, there will be an increase in development supplied and vice versa. If marginal costs were to change, the curve would shift to reflect that change. For example, if fees and regulations increased, the marginal-cost curve would shift up, and the quantity of development supplied at a given price would decline.

The Demand for Development

Consumers make purchasing decisions in light of the income restrictions on their consumption. They must be aware of the relative prices of the goods and services they would like to purchase. If housing services are considered as part of a potential consumption bundle, then the price of housing services relative to that of other goods is an important variable. The higher this price becomes, the fewer housing services are demanded. If the housing units offered for sale are comprised of the housing services, then the price of the housing unit is examined by the consumer in the consumption decision.

However, factors other than the price of the unit are also important. Perhaps just as important as the price is the cost and availability of financing. The lending institution must ascertain not only that the purchaser can afford the house, but also that the house is worth what the buyer is willing to pay. If the lending institution does not find favorably in both of these questions,

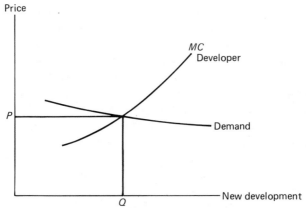

Figure 3-1. The Market for New Development

the consumer will not get the loan. Furthermore, the loan is financed at a particular interest rate, which largely determines the monthly payment in the early stages of the loan. For many, it is this monthly payment and not the total price of the house that is the crucial variable. Since interest rates are largely a national phenomenon, a major component of the monthly payment has little to do with the local housing market. Finally, the down-payment requirement may be the largest handicap, since a large lump-sum payment is difficult to accumulate. Overall, the intricacies of financing may be the most important short-term consideration in determining the demand for new construction.

In addition to the prices of the residence, the prices of the substitutes and complements to the particular housing unit must be noted. For example, if the price of apartments is less than the annualized price of the single-family dwelling, the consumer might opt for the apartment. Or, if the additional complementary costs of owning a home (for example, utility costs, insurance, or gardening) are quite high, there may be strong incentives for renting an apartment. In this analysis, these relative prices will be assumed to remain constant.

The demographic characteristics of the household reflect the tastes and preferences of consumers. In the past, single individuals rarely owned homes, but were more likely to rent, whereas families usually bought residences. Family income is also important, since wealthier families are better able to afford the large down payment and higher monthly costs connected with home ownership.

It is also anticipated that government activities affect the decisions of the consumer. In particular, the expenditure and taxation patterns of the local jurisdiction may affect the decision of the consumer to move into the area.

Expenditures reflect service-delivery patterns of the local agency. It can be assumed that high-expenditure cities provide more services to their residents than low-expenditure cities provide to theirs. Although residents may not always be aware of the exact expenditure levels, at least some of the results of the expenditures are known, so that the mover has an idea of the city's service levels. Holding all else constant, the higher the service levels, the greater the desire to live in the particular area. However, if service levels are constant among jurisdictions, then this variable will be unimportant. As the state begins to take more interest in the financing of city services as a result of the Proposition 13 bailout, there is some likelihood that this will occur.

The importance of taxes as a determinant of a specific interjurisdictional move may lessen after the passage of Proposition 13, since there will be less variation in property taxes among jurisdictions. In theory, if local taxes vary among areas, households will consider this as they make their residential choice, tending to avoid high-tax cities.

Besides the property tax, other taxes are also important in the consumer's decision to buy. If the consumer also has to pay a large amount of sales and income taxes, he will have less disposable income with which to purchase a house. These tax payments may affect the amount of development demanded in the jurisdiction.

The consumer-demand curve (D) in figure 3-1 reflects the marginal evaluation of the consumer for the particular type of development. It assumes that an increase in price is associated with a decrease in the quantity of new development demanded. If other elements should change (for example, if taxes should decrease as they did under Proposition 13), the curve would shift to the right. More development would be desired at the same price.

There is some question as to the elasticity of demand. It has been argued that in California demand is highly inelastic; that is, the quantity demanded is not very responsive to price. There has been little empirical work on this precise parameter, although Hamilton (1975a) has estimated the price elasticity for all housing to be around -1.

It is sometimes argued that newly constructed houses are homogeneous with the existing housing stock. If this were true, the market price of housing would be determined by the intersection of the demand for total housing and a vertical supply curve representing the housing stock. The market price would be the same for old and new housing, and the demand curve for new development would be perfectly elastic at that price, since the two types of housing units would be perfect substitutes (Dale Johnson 1980a).

In California, however, the prices of old and new housing are different. This difference could reflect differences in quality or in materials used, or it could indicate that the new development market does differ from the market for existing housing stock. Because of this possibility, the model will assume that the demand curve for new development will have some slope, although because of the possibility of substitution, it will be highly elastic. Small price changes will heavily affect the quantity demanded.

A caveat might be added to this section. It has been assumed that the purchase of a residence is a consumption decision. If it is an investment decision, the previous analysis does not hold. What becomes important is the competing returns on other types of investments that the household could make. It may be that in times of significant inflation, housing takes on investment aspects that have an impact on the elasticity of demand. If future returns are anticipated to be high, demand might be more inelastic.

Private-Sector Equilibrium

The intersection of the supply and demand curves, as illustrated in figure 3-1, defines the development-market equilibrium. At price *P*, *Q* units of development will be sold, and the market will clear. At higher prices, there will be a greater quantity supplied than demanded, and housing inventories will increase. At lower prices, there will be excess demand, and queues will form for the right to buy a house. In the California housing market, both have occurred, indicating that at times the market has been in disequilibrium.

Although California development lotteries have received national attention, there have also been cases in which the number of unsold homes has reached historic highs. For example, in the fourth quarter of 1978, the inventory of unsold single-family homes in Orange County reached its highest level since 1970. It was primarily the expensive homes that remained unsold—there was a 12.9-percent difference between the price of a sold home and the price of an unsold home (Doti 1979). The reason that the developer gave for the overbuilding of expensive homes was inflation in land and development costs, owing in part to pressures from present landowners for increased land-use amenities and lot-size restrictions (Doti 1979).

The concept of a supply-demand equilibrium is important for the model for several reasons. It illustrates that there are two separate groups of individuals who must be satisfied in order for the development market to clear. It also shows that under most circumstances, the claim that all fees and charges on the developer are passed on to the consumer is not accurate. These additional costs will cause the marginal-cost curve of the developer to shift upward and the market price to increase. But given the elasticities of the curves, the new market price is not at all likely to be above the old equilibrium price by the full amount of the additional costs. Only if demand were perfectly inelastic or supply perfectly elastic would the full amount be passed on. Neither of these events is likely to be true in California. Also, since the new equilibrium quantity is lower than before, the construction sector is also likely to bear some of the burden through reductions in work time and therefore in income. Finally, if the homogeneous-housing argument is true, the developer bears all the short-run costs through reduced profits, although in the long run the landowner will end up bearing the burden (Dale Johnson 1980a). In this case any price shift to the consumer would indirectly occur in the long run through a slower-than-usual growth in the housing stock.

The Public Sector

The principal actors in the public sector are the city decision makers. These decision makers reflect the tastes and preferences of present home owners, who may have very different interests than do the households moving into the community, especially regarding the proper scope of government activity.

Cities receive revenues from a variety of sources. The principal local revenue source for most cities before Jarvis-Gann was the property tax, with charges and fees as well as sales-tax revenues also important (see chapter 4). For this last source the rate is fixed, and the locality influences the revenues by encouraging commercial activity. Since Jarvis-Gann, the property-tax rate is also fixed so that property tax revenues also can be increased only by increasing the property-tax base. An example of this activity occurs if the locality controls the mix of land between residential and commercial-industrial, thereby affecting the property-tax and sales-tax bases. Further, by zoning for residential versus apartments, the locality can affect the type of residents who inhabit the jurisdiction, and indirectly affect the sales-tax base (as well as service demand).

Local jurisdictions receive about one-third of their revenues from nonlocal sources—either state or federal subventions. If these grants have no relationship with the economic activity of the city, they are exogenous to the model. However, the level of many grants depends on such variables as local tax effort or population, both of which are related to development. Many of these nonlocal revenues also have strings attached: Cities must spend the money in specific ways. This reduced flexibility makes the nonlocally raised money less useful than the locally raised money.

To recapitulate, there is a direct relationship between development and the tax base. Additional property development increases the property-tax base, and the process of development also increases the revenues from various fees and charges. An increase in the population of the jurisdiction may increase sales-tax revenues (if shopping is available in the jurisdiction). Furthermore, new residents also pay fees and user charges, so this source of revenue increases. New development also affects at least some of the revenues received from state and federal governments. Any grant that has population as one of its determining factors will be augmented when new development occurs, although perhaps with a lag. As new development increases, the tax base increases. Figure 3-2

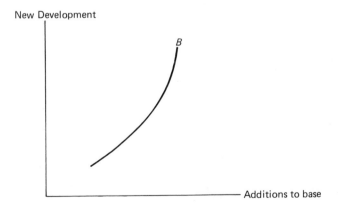

Figure 3-2. Postulated New Development—Additions to Tax-Base Relationship

Source: Adapted from Jeffrey I. Chapman and John J. Kirlin, "Land Use Consequences of Proposition 13," *University of Southern California Law Review* 53 (1979): 95-124. Used with permission.

illustrates this relationship. The curve is assumed to be monotonic, positively relating additions to the tax base and development, but not necessarily linear. It is also assumed that the rate of increase in the aggregate base is not as large as the rate of increase in development. This relationship is also assumed to be stable. The only reasons for a shift would be changes in assessment practices, changes in the sales-tax-subvention formula, or changes in grant formulas.

Once developed, the additions to the tax base can be translated into a set of additional revenues for the jurisdiction. For each element of the tax base there is a specific factor against which it is multiplied, which determines the revenues gathered from that element. For most elements this factor is the applicable tax rate. For example, the property-tax-base increment is multiplied by the property-tax rate; the increment in the sales in the jurisdiction is multiplied by 1 percent, and so on. For some of the components of the base, the appropriate variable is an implicit rate—for example, the factor in the grant formula that determines the allocation. Figure 3-3 illustrates this tax vector. This curve is positively sloped, since with constant tax rates a base increase will always result in a revenue increase. Since most of the revenue components are determined by this relationship, the tax vector is primarily linear. However, since there are some revenues that do not increase linearly with an increase in new development—for example, grants—a slight curvature will be assumed. The curve shifts whenever the relevant rate changes. Increases in the rate will cause the curve to shift to the right (the same base will generate more revenue); decreases will cause the curve to shift to the left (the same base will generate less revenue).

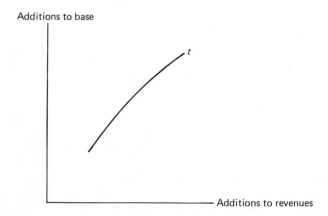

Figure 3-3. Postulated Additions to Tax Base—New Tax-Revenue Relationship

Source: Adapted from Jeffrey I. Chapman and John J. Kirlin, "Land Use Consequences of Proposition 13," *University of Southern California Law Review* 53 (1979): 95–124. Used with permission.

Jurisdictions provide a wide variety of services. The mix of these services, including differential emphasis on delivery patterns and on production techniques, varies between jurisdictions. While this increases the choice for a consumer, it also makes it exceedingly difficult to compare service outputs among cities. When quality dimensions are also included, the comparison problem worses.

Since most jurisdictions use line-item budgets, public-service decisions are typically made in terms of expenditures for inputs. This model will thus be concerned with the expenditures necessary to provide specific levels of services. It makes the implicit assumption that there is a positive correlation between expenditures on services and service outputs.

The jurisdictional decision maker faces the same types of production possibilities and cost constraints that face any private entrepreneur. The goal is to combine the quantities of land, labor, and capital to minimize the costs of service provision based on the production technology and the relative input prices. However, whereas the motivation in the private sector is to maximize profits, there is no such incentive for the public sector, since profits do not exist. It may be that decision makers do not attempt to minimize costs, but rather react to some other incentives, perhaps maximizing an agency budget or maximizing the accoutrements of office; see Orzechowski (1977) for a summary of a series of essays on bureaucratic incentives.

If cost minimization does not occur, what may happen is a movement toward an overutilization of labor. Certainly the primary component of city expenditure is labor. Many of the services that cities provide are by their nature labor intensive; even if cost minimizing was the goal, labor expenditures would still predominate. Since most of the city services are labor intensive, with few fixed inputs, and since there is not necessarily cost minimization, it is not surprising to discover that for most services, over most ranges of output, marginal costs for the jurisdiction are constant (Segal 1977, p. 286). This implies a linear relationship between service outputs and total service costs for the new development. Figure 3–4(4A) illustrates this relationship, assuming that some service delivery already exists in the jurisdiction.

There are some services that must be provided, regardless of what the city decision makers may think, because they are mandated by the state or federal government. These mandates provide a floor for the total service provision of the city, as shown in figure 3–4(4B). As development increases, additional services are necessary. At some point, however, because the land area of the development is fixed, satiation begins to occur. At this point, fewer and fewer additional services are demanded. This is illustrated by figure 3–4(4B). The combination of 4A and 4B in figure 3–4 generates 4D, the relationship between new development and additional service expenditures.[15] It postulates that as development occurs, with constant average costs of services and with quality held constant, the rate of increase of new service expenditures will begin to

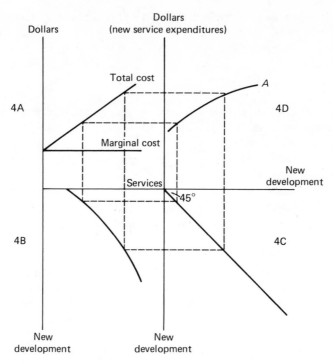

Figure 3-4. Derivation of New Development—New Local Public-Service-Expenditures Relationship

diminish (although it will probably always be positive). It might be noted that there will be positive expenditures even with an almost-zero level of development, because of the floor set by the state and federal mandates. Finally, the curve shifts as the quality of service or service mix changes.

Decisions being made in this sector also have an impact on the private sector. The private consumer may be concerned about services as he looks for a house. Since service levels are difficult to ascertain, the proxy that might be used is service expenditures. Thus the position of curve *A* in figure 3-4(4D) affects the position of the demand curve, *D*, in figure 3-1. If curve *A* shifts, the demand for the development shifts. As the jurisdiction makes service-level decisions, it also affects curve *A* and the private market. In addition, these decisions might have an impact on the marginal-cost curve of the developer if the jurisdiction either forces the developer to provide more services (moving marginal costs to the right) or if the services act to increase the supply of buildable land (moving marginal costs to the left).

By law, the operating budgets of California jurisdictions must be balanced.[16] However, there is no reason for the additional revenues and expenditures associated with any specific new development to be equal. But the jurisdiction can always force the equality by lowering the quantity or amount of service provision to the particular development and/or raising fees and charges so that the revenues that the development generates will increase.

Figure 3-5 indicates this situation. The perfectly elastic revenue function comes from the additional tax base and vector associated with the development as developed in figure 3-3. Expenditures are represented by a 45-degree line: Movements along the horizontal axis correspond to equal movements along the vertical axis. The intersection of the two is the situation in which the new revenues received from a particular project are exactly equal to the new expenditures on the project. If equilibrium occurs in this sector, it arises because of policy decisions, not because of natural economic forces, and reflects the jurisdiction's desires to have the additional revenue exceed or equal the additional expenditures.

Figure 3-6 shows the entire model, with the solid line indicating an equilibrium. It is drawn to illustrate the policy decisions that the mix and quality of services provided to the new development will precisely use up the revenues that the development is anticipated to produce. The private market is at equilibrium at price P and output Q. Given the service mix and quality level, represented by curve A, this quantity of development generates a new service-expenditure level E. Precisely at the same time, the development also generates a tax-base increment of level I, which, given the tax vector t, generates an additional-revenue stream equal to R. In equilibrium, this additional-revenue stream equals the additional-expenditure stream. Finally, the location of the private-sector demand and supply curves represents the E and R streams, respectively.

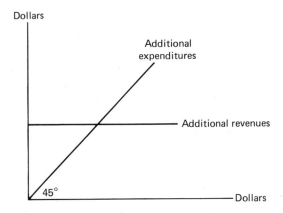

Figure 3-5. Additional Revenues and Expenditures Associated with New Development

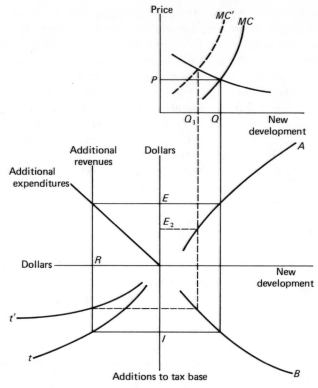

Figure 3-6. Assembled Private and Public-Sector Model of New Development

Source: Adapted from Jeffrey I. Chapman and John J. Kirlin, "Land Use Consequences of Proposition 13," *University of Southern California Law Review* 53 (1979): 95-124. Used with permission.

There are two crucial relationships in this model. The first is the tax vector, represented by curve *t*. Large elements of this vector are amenable to the political process. If the jurisdiction decides that more revenues are necessary from the development, it can impose additional fees and charges on the developer. This will affect the marginal-cost curve of the developer, moving it to *MC'* and the equilibrium to Q_1. Although this results in a lower additional base, the tax vector has also shifted, perhaps to *t'*. If this is so, the revenues generated would be the same. Compared to the old equilibrium, the new development would be yielding an excess of revenues over service expenditures of $R - E_2$—perhaps to be used to subsidize other areas of the jurisdiction. Perhaps more importantly, the development-expenditure relationship, illustrated by curve *A*, can also be changed. For example, the jurisdiction can change either the mix or quality of services provided to accommodate a shortfall of revenue caused by a shift in *t* that might be caused by Proposition 13.

Finally, if new development is identical to old, then, as previously noted, the demand curve for the new development is perfectly elastic. If the developer's marginal-cost curve shifts, there will be no price increases in the private sector but only a fall in the equilibrium quantity of new development. Even with the movement to t', which occurred as MC moved to MC', the additional revenues from the jurisdiction would be less than they were under the nonhomogeneity assumption. In this case, curve A would have to shift if the jurisdiction wanted to maintain the equality.

Reactions to the Property-Tax Reductions

Jurisdictions can engage in at least two activities in response to Proposition 13. They can ensure that their budgets balance through increasing user charges, decreasing expenditures, and accepting state aid. Or they can impose more regulations and service-provision demands on developers and thus ensure that only "profitable" development will occur.

It is clear that fees will become more important in the system of local finance. These fees can be imposed on the developer (which would shift the marginal-cost curve to the left) or they can be on the consumer (which would force a shift to the left in the position of the demand curve). In either case, if demand for new development has some elasticity, prices would increase and development decrease. Fees would also change the position of the tax vector. Fees, however, are subject to market constraints (see Break 1980), so that increases in the fee schedules might not raise as much money as anticipated if consumers react by not engaging as much in the higher-priced activity. Fees cannot be deducted from the individual income tax (although builders can deduct them from revenues to lower their tax liability), nor do fees help the city get more credit under the "local-tax-effort" portion of general revenue sharing.

Jurisdiction can also cut expenditures. In this case, the quality of service per unit of development falls which implies a shift in the A vector to the right. Furthermore, if services are complements to the new development, a decline would lead to a downward shift in demand and to less development occurring. This maybe exactly what the jurisdiction wants.

Finally, if the jurisdiction takes the state bailout money and does not change the mix of services or impose new fees, nothing in the model will change. Unfortunately for the jurisdictions, the state bailout (see chapter 5) was not sufficient to maintain budget levels in real terms; thus both the tax and expenditure effects also occurred. After the bailout there was far more interdependence between the revenue systems of the state and local governments, and any analysis in the future concerning local revenues must take account of this interrelationship (Shapiro and Morgan 1978; Vasché 1978).

There are at least two ways that jurisdictions can respond to the reduction in property taxes that also affect land use. They can change the regulations regarding land use to ensure that only "profitable" development will occur, and they can force the developer to provide more of the resources necessary for services (particularly infrastructure).

One regulation that has already been discussed is zoning. If jurisdictions wanted to ensure that any additional development generated enough revenues to pay for the additional jurisdictional expenditures, they would use their zoning powers to allow only specific types of development. The types of development most desired would be those that not only generated increments to the property-tax base but also increments to the sales-tax base, since these are most likely to provide fiscal surpluses. This means that commercial and industrial development will be preferred to residential development. There are other rules that jurisdiction can implement. Assuming that residential development is necessary, the jurisdiction can influence the type of construction that occurs. By requiring the developer to obtain a large number of approvals and spend a great deal of time obtaining them, the jurisdiction almost automatically encourages expensive development. Even if this development leads to large houses and thus to an increase in the number of families with children, the jurisdiction is still better off, since the state is now assuming the vast majority of educational expenses. As will be seen in chapter 6, there is a wide variety of rules and regulations imposed on local developers, many of which are in direct response to the passage of Proposition 13.

Since Proposition 13 has made it exceptionally difficult to issue debt, the lack of an existing urban infrastructure is crucial. By forcing the developer to provide more of the local infrastructure, the jurisdiction holds down its capital expenses and thus cuts back on service delivery to that jurisdiction. Some jurisdictions are also forcing the developer to put in higher-quality infrastructure in the hope of reducing future public expenditures for replacement or maintenance. This type of resource provision becomes quite similar to a charge that the developer must pay to the city, except that it is in terms of service provision rather than in dollars.

Equity and Efficiency Aspects of Tax and
Expenditure Changes

Substituting fees and charges for property taxes gives rise to serious equity questions. Examining the charges in isolation gives the impression that they lead to increased regressivity. Implicit in this argument, however, is that services financed by user-charge mechanisms would be better financed through general tax revenues. The equity problem can be decomposed into two parts: the role of the distribution of benefits of the services, and the substitution of one type of financing mechanism for another. If the individual recipient of the benefit of a service can be identified, then the recipient should pay for the benefit. This is especially true if the service is purchased voluntarily. Since the recipients of some of the benefits of government activities can be identified, candidates for user charges exist. The fact that the individual must then pay, regardless of income, does not necessarily make the situation any more inequitable than does forcing the individual to pay a price for any private good, regardless of income. However, if the purchase is required, the regressivity argument has more currency. Perhaps using charges to augment service levels above a base level might be a way out of the dilemma.

If it is possible to finance a good either through user fees or charges or through a particular tax, then an additional question is whether replacing a user charge by a tax is a movement toward or away from greater equity. Some types of taxes, since they are more general, might actually worsen the income distribution more than user charges. For example, financing a swimming pool out of general-fund revenues may be more inequitable than utilizing user-charge financing, if it is used only by wealthy children.

There are also some services that generate significant externalities. In these cases there is a strong likelihood that the level of consumption of the service will not be efficient, even if a user charge is applied. For example, even though it is relatively easy to identify the primary beneficiaries of garbage collection and to apply a garbage tax, for any given price the consumer will then demand an inefficiently low level of collection. This is because there are positive externalities to garbage collections (the prevention of disease, the cleanliness of a neighborhood, and so on). To take account of these externalities, the city may seduce the household with a subsidized user charge, with the subsidy coming from general revenues.

Expenditure cutbacks generate similar concerns. If expenditures are for public services that go primarily to the wealthy, then cutting back will make the entire distribution more progressive.[17] Since state aid generally financed most of the services that were going to the poor, it is likely that the expenditure cuts that actually did occur did come more from services received by the wealthy.

Since much of the financial assistance of the local jurisdiction came from the state, it is important to recognize the interdependencies between the state and local revenue systems in order to make equity judgments. There are three sources of these interrelationships: legal effects (for example, the property tax can be deducted from the federal income tax); income effects (for example, with a fall in the property tax, disposable income increases, consumption increases, and sales-tax revenue increases); and substitution effects (for example, if sales taxes increase, then the price of private goods relative to that of public goods increases, and there may be more public consumption) (Shapiro and Morgan 1978). Because of these interactions, it is quite difficult to ascertain precisely any specific equity impacts; however, since the primary source of revenue for the state is the progressive income tax, and since the other important source, the sales tax, does allow for food and shelter exemptions, it does appear as if the entire tax system is being made more progressive because of the shift, at least for movers. It is difficult to determine the equity impacts for existing home owners and renters.

Efficiency concerns are also important. If there were truly restrictive zoning designed to transform the property tax into a benefit charge, then a movement away from the property tax would not be efficient.[18] It is not likely that the zoning laws were set up to do this, and therefore a movement toward user charges is probably a movement toward greater efficiency.

If there were slack in government, then an expenditure cutback would not necessarily lead to a fall in services. This could mean an increase in efficiency. Furthermore, if the cutbacks result in a movement of services to the private sector, efficiency may also increase. Finally, if local decision makers do behave in a staff-maximizing (as opposed to a cost-minimizing) manner, then forcing staff cutbacks through reducing revenues might force a more efficient use of resources. However, if none of these examples apply, then there is no reason to expect efficiency to increase.

Local political leaders are probably more aware of the tastes and preferences of the local inhabitants than are either state or federal decision makers. If local leaders actually respond to these preferences, then when the state took over several functions of the local government, efficiency should fall, although equity might increase. If local leaders do not respond to local pressures, then state or federal assumption might improve the use of resources.

The Model and Fiscal Limits

This model can be used to illustrate some of the interactions that occur between new development and the local-budget revenue and expenditure responses to Proposition 13. Figure 3-7 illustrates a hypothetical sequence of events, beginning with the passage of Proposition 13.

Holding constant the tax-base-development relationship, B, and the development-service-expenditure relationship, A, assume that Proposition 13 passes. The relationship between the base and the revenues derived from that base does change. Curve t shifts to t', since the property-rate component of vector t has fallen.[19] Furthermore, consumers take taxes into account, so the demand curve should also shift, perhaps to D'. The equilibrium amount of development increases to Q' at the same time that revenues fall to R'. With no other changes, expenditures will increase to E' because of the increase in development. The new development project thus runs a potential deficit of $E' - R'$.

A potential solution to the deficit is to increase development fees. Assume that this occurs while the relationships illustrated by functions *A* and *B* again remain constant. If these fees are, initially, solely on the developer, then the developer's marginal-cost curve will increase, perhaps to MC''. For analytic interest, assume that this shift is not as great as the previous shift in consumer demand and that no charges are imposed directly on the consumer. The equilibrium amount of development will thus fall from Q' to Q'', but because of these assumptions will still be larger than the original Q. At the same time, the tax vector also shifts back toward *t*, perhaps to t'', since the fee component of the vector has increased. This partial makeup of the lost property taxes assumes

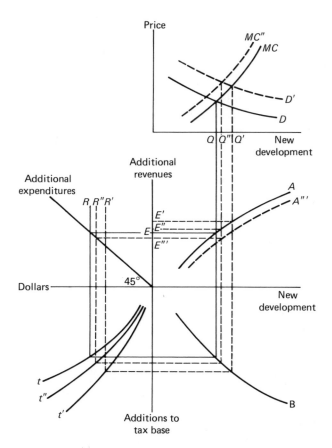

Figure 3–7. Illustration of Tax Cuts, Fee Increases, and Service Declines in the Model

Source: Adapted from Jeffrey I. Chapman and John J. Kirlin, "Land Use Consequences of Proposition 13," *University of Southern California Law Review* 53 (1979): 94–124. Used with permission.

that, politically, user charges cannot be implemented at a level necessary to cover the full property-tax loss. Since development is still higher than its original, pre-Jarvis-Gann equilibrium (although lower than before the implementation of the user charges), service expenditures, now at E'' are still greater than E (although less than E'). With the new tax vector, revenues have increased to R'', and the fiscal gap between expenditures and revenues has fallen to $E'' - R''$.[20]

Now assume that the jurisdiction still wants to get rid of this gap. In order to do so, it either changes the service mix or provides a lower quality of service. The development-service relationship changes, and A shifts to A''', indicating a decrease in quality per unit of new development. This decrease now generates a level of expenditure equal to E'''. Revenue stream R'' is still generated; and the fiscal gap disappears, since $E''' = R''$.[21]

As long as there are no additional changes in the environment, the jurisdiction is secure. But because of inflation, voter demands, or some other shock to the system, there is always the possibility that the model is unstable. One role of state assistance then becomes to stabilize the system. For example, if the bailout is less than inflation, and the user charges are at their politically feasible maximum, A might continually shift to the right to make up the difference. Because of the bailout, the rightward movement will be slower than what it would have been; but there is still deterioration. If the bailout is greater than inflation, A can shift back and service levels increase.

Some Extensions of the Model

The model can be used to examine the implications of various scenarios, ranging from improvement in local-government efficiency to alternative ways of reaching a stable solution. However, there are several dimensions for extension. The model is relatively naive; it does not include a significant public-choice dimension in explicit form; it is weak in its examination of how relationships change over time; and, most importantly, it only includes residential development.

The model can be made more sophisticated in many different dimensions. For example, the institutional role of various financing mechanisms for both the developer and the consumer can be more formally introduced. Or the interrelationships between the various sectors could be specified in more detail. Although mention has been made of the current residents determining the fiscal patterns of the jurisdiction, whereas the new residents have to accept what is offered, there is room for more public-choice analysis. For example, an explicit consideration of how public choice affects rules would be a useful addition to the analysis. Finally, an extension of the model applying the club concept of Buchanan to new development projects would add depth to the study.

The model is basically a short-run model. Tax, development, and service changes are all assumed to occur quickly. However, the assumption that land is relatively inelastic in the short run may not be true in the long run. If the supply of land is elastic, then the developer's supply curve will also be far more elastic. In this case, the fiscal equilibrium might be quite different, since long-run construction equilibrium will be greater than the short-run equilibrium. Furthermore, the long-run effects of service declines have not been examined for the public sector.

Most importantly, the model is for new residential construction. Models for commercial and industrial development might be similarly constructed. Further, a stock dimension might be a significant addition. A general model for all types of land use needs to be put together, since there are obvious interactions between the three sectors of the economy. These interactions might well prove to be of crucial importance.

Notes

1. After Proposition 13, the tax rate is no longer a viable tool for California jurisdictions, although outside of California the analysis still holds.

2. See Polinsky and Rubinfeld (1978) and Rose-Ackerman (1979) for formal models that imply some of these results in the long run.

3. Discounting is a procedure that translates future returns into a present valuation. A discount rate of 10 percent means that $1.10 received next year is worth only $1.00 today.

4. Capitalization exists in the long run only if there is a scarcity of an input factor. Yinger (1979) has demonstrated that this condition is often met in local jurisdictions.

5. Tiebout's (1956) public services are not pure public goods. For a given population the cost function for a public good may be U-shaped, but no additional inputs are required to extend the good to additional people. Tiebout assumed that the costs of providing additional services to additional citizens increased. Tiebout also never identified the property tax as the mechanism for raising local revenues.

6. This implicitly assumes a fixed supply of land.

7. Zoning can also restrict the entrance of potential high users of public services in order to ensure low levels of public-service expenditures.

8. See Dyer and Maher (1979) for a critique of this analysis.

9. Hamilton's analysis is framed in terms of differentials from homogeneous communities.

10. Or a mover can buy a home in the homogeneous community for $75,000 and realize neither a fiscal deficit nor a surplus.

11. It is inefficient for local government to redistribute income, since most programs will be self-defeating, and many of the effects of the program are inequitable (Sonstelie 1979, pp. 137–139).

12. For further summaries of the literature, see Dale Johnson (1980b).

13. A shorter, simplified version of this model will appear in Chapman and Kirlin (1979b).

14. Although there is evidence that sales-tax differentials do affect location (Fisher 1980), these differentials barely exist in California.

15. In figure 3-4, 4C is a 45-degree line used to translate 4A and 4B into 4D.

16. However, cities are allowed to issue debt for capital expenditures, which do not appear in their operating budgets.

17. See Thomas (1978) for evidence that some city expenditures are distributed regressively; see Gillespie (1965) for some counterevidence.

18. If restrictive zoning is practiced as strongly after the removal of the local tax, then the price differentials among housing classes are not burdens of the property tax (Hamilton 1977).

19. All of the illustrated merely indicate direction. The magnitude of each shift is an empirical question.

20. It is possible to impose enough development charges and requirements on the developer that the marginal-cost curve shifts upward enough to cause a decline in development. Expenditures would be much less, and the project could end up balancing revenues and expenditures at a lower rate of development.

21. The potential shift of D to the left has been suppressed in the anlaysis for graphical clarity. If D' falls, the private-market equilibrium amount of new development will also fall; and with the shift in A to A''', additional revenues will exceed the new expenditures.

4

California Dimensions of Public Budgeting and Land Use Prior to Proposition 13

It is important to understand the complex and sophisticated California fiscal and land-use environment preceding the passage of the proposition. This chapter will describe this environment. It will contain a brief description of California revenue and expenditure patterns and constraints and then examine land-use financing and planning within the state.

California Revenue and Expenditure Patterns

California State Revenues

The three major sources of revenue for the state are the personal-income tax, the state sales-and-use tax, and taxes on banks and corporations. Together, these three taxes account for nearly 80 percent of total state tax revenues (Jamison 1979). Taxes associated with motor vehicles account for about another 12 percent, with the remaining 8 percent derived from several smaller tax sources.

The contribution of the sales-and-use tax to state government has remained approximately stable over time; the major changes have occurred in the importance of the personal-income tax and the taxes on banks and corporations. In 1967–1968 the personal-income tax accounted for a little over 20 percent of state revenues; in 1977–1978 it accounted for almost 31.5 percent of the revenues—an increase of nearly 55 percent. Similarly, bank and corporate taxes increased in importance by about 14 percent. Most other taxes remained stable or showed marginal declines in importance over this ten-year period (Jamison 1979).

Table 4–1 indicates the escalation of the revenues from various sources of taxes from fiscal-year 1973–1974 to fiscal 1977–1978. The personal-income tax grew the most both in percentage and in absolute dollar changes. Total taxes over the five years increased by 88.6 percent for an average (uncompounded) yearly increase of over 17 percent.

There are several reasons for this growth in income-tax revenue. As workers received wage and salary increases, some became subject to the income tax for the first time. Further, the California income tax is steeply progressive, so that workers were subject to higher tax rates as their incomes increased. The reason for much of the increase in wages was inflation, and thus California received an inflation tax bonus.

Table 4-1
State Tax Collections, 1973-1974 to 1977-1978

Tax	Dollar Increase	Percentage Increase
Personal income	$+2,835,923,000	+154.8
Sales and use	+2,354,700,000	+97.0
Bank and corporation	+1,025,017,000	+92.1
Motor-vehicle fees	+279,963,000	+88.0
Insurance	+185,863,000	+57.4
Inheritance and gift	+133,158,000	+43.4
Motor-vehicle fuel	+107,479,000	+42.5
Horse racing	+33,302,000	+22.5
Cigarette	+14,737,000	+14.5
Distilled spirits	+8,534,000	+13.1
Beer and wine	+4,214,000	+12.9
Liquor-license fees	+2,769,000	+8.5
Private car	+944,000	+5.7
Transportation	-6,387,000	-100.0
Total taxes	$+6,980,217,000	88.6

Source: Conrad C. Jamison, *California Tax Study,* Security Pacific National Bank (1979). Reprinted with permission.

Table 4-2 illustrates that in the year preceding the passage of Proposition 13, all three major taxes and total state taxes went up faster than the income of California residents. The personal-income tax and taxes on banks and corporations went up especially fast, at a pace that would double them in about three years. The average citizen in California was paying almost 8.5 percent of income just for state taxes.

Table 4-2 also illustrates that the California tax system is a quite powerful generator of revenue. Between 1973-1974 and 1977-1978, on the average, for every 10-percent increase in personal income, California state taxes went up by 16 percent.[1] These are all nominal measures; that is, inflation has not been taken into account. With a total urban consumer-price increase during this period of 46.6 percent (U.S. Department of Labor 1980) the California resident could easily perceive himself to be caught between inflation and taxes, with perhaps little hope of escape.

California residents pay more per-capita taxes than residents of most other states (Jamison 1979). In 1977-1978, state tax revenues amounted to $673.69 per capita in California compared to $520.47 per capita for all fifty states combined (including California). The California rate is more than 29 percent above the national average. If expressed in dollars collected per thousand dollars personal income received, California paid $86.71, or almost 16 percent more than the fifty-state average of $74.82. California ranks eleventh in the United States in terms of revenue collection from the personal-income tax per $1,000

Table 4-2
Increases in California Taxes and Income Prior to Proposition 13
(in thousands of dollars)

Fiscal Year	Personal-Income Tax	Sales Tax	Taxes on Banks and Corporations	Other Taxes	Total of All State Taxes	Total Personal Income of California Residents[a]	State Taxes as a Percentage of Personal Income
1973–1974	$1,831,964	$2,675,738	$1,057,191	$2,312,171	$7,877,064	$112,641,000	6.99
1974–1975	2,581,584	3,376,153	1,253,673	2,363,087	9,574,497	125,579,000	7.62
1975–1976	3,086,611	3,742,524	1,286,515	2,591,075	10,706,725	139,472,000	7.68
1976–1977	3,761,356	4,314,201	1,641,500	2,838,696	12,555,653	155,626,000	8.07
1977–1978	4,667,887	5,030,438	2,082,208	3,076,748	14,857,281	175,155,000	8.48
Percentage change							
1973–1974 to 1977–1978	+154.8	88.0	97.0	33.1	88.6	55.5	
1976–1977 to 1977–1978	24.1	16.6%	26.8%	8.4%	18.3	12.5	
Percentage change in Tax Revenue ÷ Percentage change in income							
1973–1974 to 1977–1978	2.79	1.59	1.75	0.60	1.60		
1976–1977 to 1977–1978	1.93	1.33	2.14	0.70	1.46		

Source: Conrad C. Jamison, *California Tax Study*, Security Pacific Bank (1979). Reprinted with permission. State of California, *Annual Report of Financial Transactions Concerning Cities of California*, fiscal years 1973–1974 to 1977–1978, table 4.

[a]The personal-income figures shown are for the calendar years ending in the middle of the fiscal years. They are the latest estimates compiled by the U.S. Department of Commerce.

of personal income (139 percent of the national average); second in revenue collected from taxes on corporate net income per $1,000 of personal income (169.1 percent of the national average); and fourteenth in revenue collected from general sales or gross-receipts taxes per $1,000 of personal income (123.6 percent of the national average).

Local Revenues in California

In the aggregate, the major revenue source for cities before Jarvis-Gann was the property tax. However, the importance of this tax has fallen from the 1967–1968 share (31 percent of city revenue) to a 21-percent share for 1977–1978, a decline of nearly one-third. Close behind the property tax in 1977–1978 were federal grants, including revenue sharing. These grants were only about 1 percent less than the property tax in terms of importance to the city. About one-third of the local budget immediately preceding Jarvis-Gann came from federal, state, and county grants. The total of licenses, permits, and service charges provided about 10 percent more, while other local taxes also provided about 10 percent. These last two categories have been quite stable over the last decade, with almost no change in their importance since 1971-1972. It might also be noted that state grants have been falling over time, reaching a low in the year preceding Proposition 13.

The only major tax base that is utilized by the state, counties, and cities is the sales-and-use base. This tax accounts for a relatively stable 15-percent share of city revenues. In California the sales tax is collected by the state, and then a portion is subvened (returned) back to local jurisdictions utilizing a point-of-sale allocation formula. The basic ad valorem sales-tax rate in California is 6 percent. This is divided into three parts: The state gets 4.75 percent, the regional mass-transit district receives 0.25 percent, and the jurisdiction in which the sale takes place receives 1 percent (if the sale takes place in an unincorporated area, the county receives the money; otherwise the city receives the subvention).[2] This sales-tax formula has the effect of biasing city development decisions toward land uses that generate sales, since in addition to the property appreciation that occurs, there is also the increase in revenue owing to sales increases.

This subvention formula also leads to skewed distributions of the sales-tax receipts; for example, in 1977-1978 Bradbury, a dormitory suburb of Los Angeles that has virtually zoned out all commercial and industrial use, received $0.41 per capita from sales taxes, whereas Vernon, a city with boundaries drawn so as to maximize sales, received $15,186 per capita. This sales-tax-subvention formula is unlikely to be changed, since many cities have undertaken development plans to meet the formula's condition.

The property tax, as table 4–3 shows, grew faster than only a few types of

Table 4-3
Local Revenue Sources, 1973-1974 to 1977-1978
(in thousands of dollars)

	Dollar Rise	Percentage Increase
Property tax (total)	440,478	51.0
Sales and use	366,678	66.9
Other local taxes	263,279	76.2
Licenses and permits	56,578	97.2
Fines and penalties	19,518	24.0
State and county grants	163,963	26.3
Federal grants	837,209	235.9
Service charges	173,323	54.8
Other revenues	96,357	27.8
Total revenues	2,417,483	68.4

Source: State of California, *Annual Report of Financial Transactions Concerning Cities of California,* fiscal years 1973-1974 to 1977-1978, table 4.

revenues—state and county grants, other revenues, and fines and penalties—in the five years before the Jarvis-Gann initiative. It grew more slowly than the overall increase in revenues. The sources that grew the most during this period were revenues from the federal government (which grew by about 236 percent) and revenues from licenses and permits (which nearly doubled). In general, total revenues for cities went up more slowly than total revenues from the state during the same period. The "other local tax" category grew quite rapidly during these five years, exceeding the growth rate of property taxes, service charges, and other revenues. This category includes transient-occupancy taxes, franchises, business-license taxes, property-transfer taxes, and other nonproperty taxes. The citizens of California found themselves continually facing higher local taxes as well as higher state taxes.

During the year before the passage of Proposition 13, sales-tax revenues increased almost twice as fast as revenues from the property tax and more rapidly than those from any other tax (see table 4-4). In large part this increase in revenues was tied to two national phenomena: a large increase in inflation, and a tendency for the consumer to lower personal-savings rates. Both tendencies would lead to more consumption and more sales-tax revenues. There has also been only a very slight increase in the percentage of personal income that was taken up by local taxes (and, for the two years before Proposition 13, this percentage was constant). It was especially small compared to the state's average collections.

There are data available that allow comparison of some state and local taxes to the national norm. In fiscal-year 1977-1978, property taxes in California were about 52 percent above the national norm (after Proposition 13, in 1978-

Table 4-4
Increases in California Local Taxes Prior to Proposition 13
(in thousands of dollars)

Fiscal Year	Total Property Tax	Sales and Use Tax	Other Local Taxes	Licenses Permits Service Charges	Total Taxes[a]	Local Taxes as Percentage of Personal Income[b]
1973-1974	862,993	548,312	345,416	374,537	2,131,258	1.89
1974-1975	945,349	607,265	389,745	411,213	2,353,572	1.87
1975-1976	1,071,280	674,904	454,781	459,178	2,660,143	1.91
1976-1977	1,196,590	778,120	534,132	535,686	3,044,528	1.96
1977-1978	1,303,571	914,990	608,695	604,438	3,431,694	1.96
Percentage Change						
1973-1974 to						
1977-1978	51.0	66.9	76.2	61.4	61.0	
1976-1977 to						
1977-1978	8.9	17.6	12.2	12.8	12.7	
Percentage Change in Revenues ÷ Percentage Change in Income						
1973-1974 to						
1977-1978	0.92	1.21	1.37	1.11	1.10	
1976-1977 to						
1977-1978	0.71	1.41	0.98	1.02	1.02	

Source: Conrad C. Jamison, *California Tax Study,* Security Pacific Bank (1979); State of California, *Annual Report of Transactions Concerning Cities of California,* fiscal years 1975-1979, table 4. Reprinted with permission.
[a]Total taxes + (sum of other revenues, fines, penalties, grants) = total revenues
[b]Using personal income data from table 4-2.

1979, they will be about 35 percent below this norm). In 1976-1977, only three states (Alaska, Massachusetts, and New Hampshire) had a heavier property-tax burden per $1,000 of personal income. In fact, California ranked higher than New Jersey and New York states, which have extremely high taxes. But with the tax cuts that arise from the passage of Proposition 13, it is expected that only thirteen or fourteen states will have a property-tax burden (with respect to personal income) lower than that of California. (Jamison 1979, pp. 9-10). State and local sales-tax revenues in California exceeded the national norm by about 32 percent in 1976-1977, and it is expected that this margin probably grew in 1977-1978. In terms of sales-tax collections per $1,000 of personal income in 1976-1977, California ranked eleventh among the states.

State and Local Expenditures in California

Although most of the publicity preceding the passage of Proposition 13 was centered on the average Californian's tax burden, it is also important to recognize the expenditure patterns that existed in the state at that time. The principal expenditure in the state was for schools—over 37 percent of all state and local expenditures were in this category. Public welfare was the next most significant item with almost 15 percent of total expenditures. Health and hospitals were next largest, with about 6 percent of the total. Capital expenditures were about 10 percent of total expenditures, with about one-third of the capital outlay on education and another one-third spent on highways and sewers combined. Total direct general expenditures were about 6 percent above the national average, although this aggregate does disguise the over-30-percent underspending on capital (versus the national average) and the 12.5-percent above-the-national-average spending on other direct functions. The expenditure categories that exceeded the national norm by the largest dollar amounts were welfare (which was 38 percent above the norm), all other general expenditures (24 percent above the norm), education (6 percent), fire protection (41 percent), and financial administration (29 percent). The expenditure categories that were below the national norm by the largest dollar amounts were highways (45 percent below), interest on general debt (50 percent below), health and hospitals (9 percent below), sewerage (16 percent below), and sanitation other than sewerage (30 percent below) (Jamison 1979, p. 12).

If California revenues and expenditures are compared to the national norms over the five fiscal years preceding the passage of Proposition 13, it appears that expenditures were under tighter controls than revenues. Table 4–5 illustrates this trend. In 1973-1974 tax revenues in California were 15.0 percent above the national norm while expenditures were 10.5 percent above. By 1977-1978 revenues were 26.7 percent above, while expenditures were 9.8 percent above the nation. This widening gap leads to the accumulation of a large state surplus, on the order of $6 billion, which was later used to bail out local governments after Proposition 13 passed.

Table 4–5
Percentages by Which State- and Local-Government Expenditures and Taxes in California Exceed the National Norms

	Tax Revenues	General Expenditures
1973–1974	+15.0	+10.5
1974–1975	+21.7	+7.1
1975–1976	+21.3	+8.7
1976–1977	+22.8	+5.9
1977–1978	+26.7	+9.8
1978–1979	+0.7[a]	NA

Source: Conrad C. Jamison, *California Tax Study,* Security Pacific Bank (1980).
Reprinted with permission.
[a]Estimated.

There are two expenditure phenomena that are of particular importance for land-use considerations: the low amounts of expenditure on debt and the very low amounts of expenditure on capital improvements. Both may imply resistance at the state and local levels to public improvement of the development infrastructure through public-debt funding.

Using almost any measure of comparison, California ranks low in comparison with the capital-expenditure levels of other states: California ranks forty-third if per-capita expenditure is the variable, forty-eighth if personal income is the variable, and forty-ninth if percentage of total general expenditures is the variable. Furthermore, this is the continuation of a trend, not a one-year aberration. In 1966–1967 California was at 108.2 percent of the national average with respect to personal income for capital expenditures; it has consistently and steadily fallen until it reached the 1976–1977 figure of 69.7 percent of the average (Jamison 1979, section IVD). It appears that unless the developers themselves provide the necessary facilities, the development does not occur. However, some capital expenditures may be hidden in the operating budgets of the jurisdictions that utilize nontraditional debt instruments.

Constraints Facing Local-Government Finance Decisions

Even before Proposition 13, local budget decisions were not made in a vacuum. Rather, they were buffeted by a series of environmental actions that directly affected them. These impacts had financial consequences; yet because they were not linked to specific taxes, or because their expenditure implications were difficult to determine, often only the people immediately involved in the budget process were aware of their importance. This section will illustrate two examples of the many existing forces that have an impact on the budget—mandates and grants.

Mandates

A mandate is a constraint imposed by government action either as a direct order or as a requirement for government assistance. (Lovell 1979, pp. 32–34). They may be either programmatic or procedural. The local-government budget reflects the direct impact of mandates on its expenditure side and the indirect impact on its revenue side.

A recent study funded by the National Science Foundation identified approximately 1,260 federal mandates, of which 223 were direct orders and 1,036 were conditions of aid (Lovell 1979). In addition, it discovered that there were 1,481 potential California state mandates on local jurisdictions. Federal and state mandates differ significantly in their sources. Ninety-six percent of federal mandates are administrative regulations, whereas 80 percent of state mandates are directly derived from laws (Lovell 1979, p. 66).

Mandates appear to make a difference. In over 40 percent of the mandates that were studied, the mandated activity was not performed at all before the mandate was issued; and in about another 15 percent of the cases, the activity was only partially carried out before the mandate was imposed (Lovell 1979, p. 169). Nearly 50 percent of the studied mandates introduced entirely new programs or activities to the jurisdictions, with most of the new functions being in areas in which local governments have seldom supplied services, such as environmental protection and equal-rights participation. The traditional local-government services (police, fire, health, general government) have been relatively unaffected by mandates (Lovell 1979, pp. 176–177). Federal mandates have caused cities to begin new activities more often than counties, whereas for state mandates, the opposite is true. Many of the mandates have now been institutionalized, and thus the activities they introduced would be likely to continue even if the mandate were withdrawn. Cities are more willing than counties to drop activities if they can (Lovell 1979, p. 186).

Mandates have severe financial implications. Over one-half of all mandate costs and nearly two-thirds of direct-order-mandate costs are paid for by local government, predominantly from general funds. Direct-order state mandates are paid for either completely or partially in nearly 75 percent of the cases out of general funds, and nearly 40 percent of the combined state and federal conditions of aid and federal direct orders are paid fully or partially by the local government (Lovell 1979, pp. 168, 256).

Mandates significantly affect the revenue and expenditure patterns of the local budget. By making sure certain activities are undertaken, the mandates have an impact on the expenditures of the city; but by tying conditions to the receipt of revenues, the mandates are also affecting the likelihood of the city's receiving funds. No city budget can be examined without a specific inspection of the mandates that constrain the jurisdiction.

Grants

A second environmental phenomenon that affects the local-government budget is the intergovernmental grant. These grants augment the revenues of the local jurisdiction, but they may do this at the price of forcing the jursidiction to undertake activities that it might otherwise not have undertaken. To the extent that the budget reflects these grantsmanship decisions, it is affected by them.

There are two principal types of grants currently in existence in the United States: the categorical (or conditional) and the noncategorical (or noncondi-tional).[3] Categorical grants have strings attached to them: At the minimum, the local jurisdiction can get the money only if it spends it in a certain fashion. For example, grants for road construction must be used for road construction. An additional string that is often attached to categorical grants is the match. In order to get these grants, the jurisdiction must contribute a set percentage of its own funds. For example, to get highway-construction money, the state of California must put up 10 percent to match the 90-percent share contributed by the federal government. Noncategorical grants are basically unrestricted and can be used for almost any activity desired, including tax stabilization or reduction.[4] General revenue sharing is an example of this type of grant—it can be used for virtually any type of government program, and it has remarkably few requirements for its receipt.

The underlying theory of the categorical grant is that costs should be reduced for specific services so that jurisdictions will be able to afford to purchase more of those services. It is assumed that jurisdictions have demands for services, and a grant that lowers prices will cause an increase in the quantity of the service purchased. Some services have positive externalities, and thus they are underprovided. The grant is justified as a mechanism to ensure a more efficient provision of the services. The underlying economic theory of the non-conditional grant is somewhat less clear, since its justifications have usually been political. These grants do put unrestricted money into the jurisdictions that are closest to the people and should therefore be most knowledgeable as to how the money should be spent.

In practice, grants distort budgetary decisions. Expenditures tend to occur in the areas in which grants are available and, further, to be in the areas that require the least match. Many local and state jurisdictions appear to be willing to endure strings and constraints in order to get grant money. Once the money enters the local treasury, it can easily be substituted for other projects. Local governments may search out alternative grants that can be used for financing the same types of projects, and then utilize the grant that in the aggregate has fewest strings, and use the alternative grants for other similar projects (Benton 1980). Finally, there is a close connection between grants and the condition-of-acceptance type of mandate. By accepting conditional grants, jurisdictions are also accepting constraining mandates. These two environmental impacts are tied together, magnifying the resulting impact on the local budget.

Constraints, through their budgetary impacts, influence land-use decision making in at least two ways. Since they lead to expenditure and revenue patterns that would not have otherwise existed, most of the budgetary allocations in the jurisdictions are distorted, including those that affect land. These impacts can either enhance or restrict development but are not likely to be neutral. For example, if a jurisdiction can get grant money for additional sewage-treatment facilities, more are likely to be built and more development can occur. A second impact is that many of the mandates and grants directly require implementation of land-use planning. This perhaps forces jurisdictions to confront land-use decisions sooner than anticipated.

These environmental constraints have an impact on the city budget and make the city decision makers considerably more sensitive to undertaking new projects or responsibility for new development. This sensitivity, which was growing even before the passage of Proposition 13, dramatically increased after its passage. But any study of the impact of the proposition must be aware of the impact of the environment on the local public economy.

Land-Use Financing Prior to Proposition 13

In order for development to occur in an orderly and planned fashion, the urban infrastructure must be carefully provided in a logical manner. Prior to the passage of Proposition 13, these capital improvements and facilities were usually provided by the relevant jurisdiction, although the developer was already beginning to pay more of the capital expense. After the passage of the proposition, more and more of the necessary public improvements will become the burden of the developer.

Public improvements cover a wide variety of capital investments. A partial list of capital facilities necessary for substantial development to occur would include the following: streets, curbs, gutters, street lighting, drainage and flood-control facilities, sewers and wastewater treatment, water lines and water treatment, libraries, fire stations, police stations, public-works facilities, court houses, jails, office buildings, schools, parks and recreation facilities, and bridges (McTighe 1979, p. II-11).

The principal techniques used to finance capital improvements prior to the passage of Proposition 13 involved various types of debt financing, grants, special assessments or other requirements, and pay-as-you-go methods. Each of these methods imposed different costs on the citizens and had an impact on the type of development undertaken.[5]

General-Obligation Bonds

In the past, general-obligation bonds were the principal source of debt financing for capital improvements in local jurisdictions. These bonds, sometimes called GO bonds, were issued by local agencies after two-thirds of the voting electorate approved their authorization. The bonds were backed by the full faith and credit of the issuing government, and repayment of them was secured by the unlimited power of the issuing agency to levy special property taxes. Although these types of bonds were increasingly difficult to pass in the years immediately preceding Jarvis-Gann, most jurisdictions within the state that had debt, had GO debt. This was the primary debt instrument of school districts. GO bonds, since they were most secure, typically had the lowest interest rate of any type of local government debt.

Revenue Bonds

A second type of debt financing is the revenue bond. These bonds are not a general obligation of the property taxpayer, but rather are backed by revenue typically generated by the use of the capital project that the bonds financed. Revenue bonds must be approved by a simple majority of the votes, and thus authorization is easier to obtain than for GO bonds. Since revenue streams from projects are more difficult to forecast than property-tax rates, the interest rates necessary to attract buyers for revenue bonds are usually higher than those for general-obligations bonds. In California the most common use of revenue bonds has been to finance the construction of sewer and water plants and transmission facilities (McTighe 1979, p. II-4).

Lease-Purchase–Lease-Revenue Bonds

An increasingly common method of financing major capital improvements is through lease-purchase or lease-revenue bonds. This method does not necessitate voter approval and has become popular with elected officials who must finance needed facilities. It is sometimes argued that this method overrides public preferences, since the electorate is not allowed to vote on the project. This technique has been used to finance construction of general-purpose public facilities, such as office buildings and libraries. It involves debt issuance by a nonprofit corporation set up by the involved jurisdiction.[6] The proceeds from this debt are used to construct the facilities. The local government agency that uses the facility will then lease it from the nonprofit corporation, with the lease revenue being exactly enough to service the debt completely. This lease payment is a line-item payment in the operating (noncapital) budget of the jurisdiction. When the debt is finally retired, the title to the improvements and property passes to the government agency.

Federal and State Funding

As previously mentioned, large sums of money are available from the state and federal government. Much of this money is earmarked for capital construction, primarily for sewer and water facilities and highways. Taking this money obligates the jurisdiction to provide the facilities; but since the provision of many of them is already mandated by direct order, this source of revenue is helpful.

Many jurisdictions have also used at least part of their revenue-sharing money for capital improvements.

Special Assessments

In this method of financing, each land owner is assessed a share of the bonded indebtedness based on the proportionate amount of benefit his property receives from the improvements. In California, assessment bonds can be issued when the owners of 60 percent of the land in a district agree. In addition, under certain circumstances cities, counties, and some special districts can also initiate a special assessment, although it is difficult to implement without significant public approval. Because property owners usually do not realize the improvements (in dollar terms) to their property until it is sold, but are forced to pay the debt service immediately, assessment districts are considered difficult to arrange. In addition, there are difficulties in determining benefits and their allocation from some types of improvements. Local governments have not heavily relied on special-district assessments in recent years (McTighe 1979, p. II-8).

Subdivision Requirements

Cities and counties, under the California State Subdivision Map Act (Gov. C. 66410-66499.37, Cal. Stats. 1974, c. 1536), can require public improvements or fees in lieu of public improvements from developers as a condition of approval of a final subdivision map. Local government agencies are increasingly likely to use this law as justification for forcing builders to provide more of the infrastructure within their development. After Jarvis-Gann, this method of provision of urban capital improvements is expected to become even more popular.

Pay-As-You-Go

The last traditional method of financing public facilities is through a pay-as-you-go system, in which funds are appropriated for the improvement on a year-to-year basis as part of the normal budget process. This method is difficult to utilize except for small projects, since funds for any capital project are in direct competition for operating funds with city services.

   These are just the simplest methods of financing capital facilities within any jurisdiction. One of the ramifications of the passage of Proposition 13 is the proliferation of complicated and subtle ways of providing infrastructure.

Tax-Increment Financing

One additional way of providing capital facilities for areas within a jurisdiction that had been growing in popularity before the passage of Proposition 13 was tax-increment financing. Although this method was briefly mentioned in chapter 2, it is worthwhile to spend additional time examining this approach to urban redevelopment, as it may still have some limited use in the future.

California law provides for the establishment of a community redevelopment agency (CRA) for each city and county in California (section 33100 of the California Health and Safety Code). This agency can be established whenever the legislative body of the local community decides that there is a need for the agency and then creates it. The CRA designs and implements a program of redevelopment for the blighted areas of the local jurisdiction. It has the power to sue (and be sued); it acquires property through the use of eminent domain; it can assemble tracts of property, dispose of property, borrow money from both the private and public sectors, construct public improvements, issue debt, and engage in other government activities that can pertain to redevelopment. One of the activities it can engage in is the use of tax-increment financing as a means of providing revenues for redevelopment. Tax-increment financing is most useful in the redevelopment of areas that either have been poorly developed or are blighted and therefore show little promise of being developed in the future.

The process begins with the local government designating a project area and then adopting a redevelopment plan. At that time (a specific date), the total assessed value of the project area is determined and declared to be the "base assessed value" for the project. From this date, until the project is completed, the CRA can use any tax revenues that are generated by an increase in the assessed value of the project area above the project area's base assessed value. These increases come either from new private construction within the project area or from market pressures that drive up assessed value. These revenues are called tax increments.

The justification for this system is that any increase in tax revenues from the blighted area would not have been available to the usual taxing agencies without the establishment of the redevelopment project. The use of these revenues by the CRA, therefore, leaves the other taxing agencies no worse off than they were prior to the beginning of the redevelopment projects, since the CRA only utilizes the tax increments. Once all debt is retired and the redevelopment project has been completed, the entire base goes back on the tax rolls. It is argued that in the long run the improvements generated by the CRA will be so large that the ultimate tax rate will be lower than what it would have been if the district had never existed, although before completion residents of the jurisdictions that include the project area are paying higher rates, since not all of the base is included.

The basic tool the CRA used to attract private investment is some initial public investment in the area. This could involve improving the capital infrastructure, assembling land, or clearing larger parcels to allow for easier construction. In order to undertake this investment, the CRA needs immediate access to the money that would be received over the long period of time that the tax increments occur. To obtain this access, the CRA can issue tax-allocation bonds. Unlike general-obligation bonds or revenue bonds, these debt instruments can be issued without voter approval. They are not legal obligations of the city nor of any public entity other than the CRA. There is no guarantee that the payment of principal and interest will continue even if the project is unsuccessful.

There is a close connection between tax-increment financing and the state sales-tax-subvention formula. This formula returns sales-tax revenues to the jurisdiction in which the sale took place. Since tax-increment financing can be used to redevelop commercial and industrial sections as well as residential areas, cities and countries saw this as a useful way of encouraging development of large commercial centers. To some extent, the combination of these two institutional factors has had an impact on the development patterns of jurisdictions, as can be seen in the proliferation of shopping malls throughout the state.

Even though the California Redevelopment Law was enacted in 1951, tax-increment financing was not widely used until the early 1970s. Only twenty-seven developments in the state existed before 1966. From 1966 to 1972 about 115 projects were started; between 1972 and 1975 another 115 projects were begun (Anderson 1976, p. 43). The principal reasons for this increase were the drying up of federal funds for redevelopment and the increase in the rate of inflation, which almost guaranteed the success of any project. However, after the passage of Proposition 13, tax increments are limited to new construction plus 2-percent growth in property value. This makes many potential projects not economically feasible.

Land Use and Government Prior to Proposition 13

Federal and State Impacts on Planning

The federal government influences land-use planning only indirectly. However, this indirect influence is important because of the massive amounts of federal funding given to state and local agencies. Most federal assistance programs that affect the physical development of a locality require land-use planning by the recipient. For example, urban-renewal programs require an action plan for the establishment and preservation of a well-planned community; federal aid to highways requires a cooperatively determined state and local transportation plan; and the Open Space Program, which provides assistance to state and local governments for acquisition and development of open space, requires open space and urban plans. Also, most of the federal funding available for environmental programs (such as clean air, water pollution, and open space) also requires plans and guideline development.

The participation of the state government in planning—in California, under the supervision of the Office of Planning and Research (OPR)—tends to be in the area of developing long-run policies to assist local governments in meeting problems associated with growth and development in urban areas; to assist local agencies in planning; and to generate guidelines for the mandatory elements of the city and county general plans (Longtin 1977). The purpose of state-government participation in planning is not to act in a regulatory capacity, but rather to provide aid and assistance. However, as will be seen later in this chapter, the state does strictly regulate in the areas of building construction and environmental policies.

Local Impacts on Planning

Regional planning in California is somewhat disjointed. The state legislature recognizing that planning often spills over jurisdictional boundaries, has passed legislation that allows cities and counties voluntarily to establish regional planning districts, as well as specific legislation providing planning for specific geographical areas (San Francisco Bay Area and Lake Tahoe). Unfortunately, regional plans tend to be advisory in nature and have no binding effects. However, since some federal money passes through some of the regional planning agencies for review, they have implicit power to affect local planning by withholding funds.

Perhaps the most powerful law in California regarding urban development is the Subdivision Map Act, as recodified in 1974. This law regulates the subdivision of land in California. Before any subdivision can be sold, a tentative map of the subdivision must be approved by the relevant jurisdiction and a final map based on a survey of the land filed with the county recorder. As a condition for approval, the local government can require a major redesign of the subdivision. The redesign can include, for example, the realignment, widening, and construction of streets; the construction of public works for drainage, flood control, sewers, and sewage disposal; and any other matter that can reasonably be expected to affect the community's health, safety, and welfare. This act is a means of forcing the developer to provide a good portion of the public infrastructure that otherwise would have to be provided by the local government. Court and legal opinions have broadly defined the powers of the local jurisdictions under this act. In 1975 the California attorney general, in a formal opinion, argued that the act applied to more than the physical criteria of specific plans, but that it also could be used to examine social and economic criteria of plans (58 Ops. Cal. Atty Gen. 41, 43 [1975]). Thus local governments, through this act, now have almost unlimited powers to force developers not only to provide much of the infrastructure, but also to be concerned with the demographics of the community. They can, for example, ensure that enough low-cost or affordable housing is provided.

Every city and county planning agency in California must prepare a long-term comprehensive general plan for development. This plan must then be adopted by the legislative body of the jurisdiction (Cal. Gov. C. 65300). All general plans have nine mandated elements that must be considered: land use, circulation, housing, noise, seismic safety, fire and geologic safety, scenic highways, open space, and conservation. This plan is in a sense a "constitution" for future development, and it is binding on legislatures. However, it is subject to legislative change (Longtin 1977). As of November 1, 1978, 74 percent of California cities and counties had adopted plans for all nine elements. The highest completion rates were in the land-use and open-space elements (96 percent and 97 percent respectively for cities and counties); the lowest were for scenic highways (86 percent for cities) and safety (84 percent for counties) (OPR 1980).

Almost all the techniques discussed in chapter 2 have been used in California. But it is not clear that they had major impacts on development prior to Proposition 13. One study, done under contract to the State Assembly's Special Subcommittee on Community Development, discovered that planning departments, despite their legal charge to develop general plans for coordination of any development that is occurring, have had little impact on public activities in either physical or socioeconomic areas. The study also found that the local planning processes are not of much concern to local elected officials who are primarily concerned with budget planning (Waldhorn 1976, p. 19). Furthermore, chief management officials also play virtually no role in terms of general planning. Only the staff of the planning department devotes much time to the preparation of the general plan. The nine mandated elements of the general plan also caused problems. In particular, many jurisdictions claimed that these elements caused unnecessary work and were usually unrelated to each other or to the other planning documents produced by the locality. Finally, it was found that budget planning and the development of the general plan were not well integrated. This separation could well lead to fiscal land-use consequences that are undesirable in the long run. In the short run, this situation often could lead to the finance department imposing land-use fees that considerably harm the prospects of a successful general plan, while the planning department can ignore the financial consequences of the types of development allowed.

Any relationship between areawide functional planning and local general plans appears to be circumstantial. In a study of four functional areas (parks and recreation, water quality and management, air quality, and transportation), it was discovered that the majority of functional plans were prepared by area-wide agencies or special districts rather than by local government. Local general plans were prepared exclusively by cities and counties and were not concerned with these areawide-agency problems. This study discovered that there was virtually no relationship between the mandated functional plans and local-government plans (James King 1977, p. 20).

Functional Restrictions

Two major functional areas that affect local development in California should be highlighted: building and housing regulations and environmental controls. These cut across all levels of government in their impacts.

Building and housing regulations establish minimum standards for structural soundness and safety that are necessary before a building can be occupied. The responsibility for the establishment and enforcement of building and housing regulations has rested primarily with local governments. However, in 1961 the state passed the State Housing Law, which set forth a comprehensive set of regulations. This was later amended to mandate that cities and counties adopt regulations that imposed the same requirements as those contained in the uniform industry codes (with some exemptions). Enforcement of the uniform codes is the responsibility of the cities and counties.

The principal uniform codes now enforced throughout the state include the following:

The Uniform Building Code—this regulates the materials and methods of construction for buildings.

The Uniform Plumbing Code—this regulates the materials and methods of construction of plumbing in order to ensure the flow of clean water and the outward flow of sewage.

The National Electric Code—this regulates the materials and methods of wiring, including connection and insulation, so that there is adequate electric current and no shock or electrical-fire risks.

The Uniform Housing Code—this establishes minimum standards for space, occupancy, and maintenance of buildings.

In January 1970 the National Environmental Policy Act (NEPA) became law. Also in 1970 California passed the California Environmental Quality Act (CEQA). These acts (together with several other state and federal pollution-control acts) regulate air, water, solid-waste, and noise pollution. The net impact of these laws and regulations has changed the land-development process within the state. Some of the major laws that have had significant impact on the scope of land development in California are as follows:

NEPA–this federal law applies to all activities carried out, funded, or authorized by the federal government. Each federal agency is required to consider carefully the environment impact of proposed federal actions on projects before they are undertaken. CEQA–this act is patterned after the federal law (NEPA). It requires all state and local governments to consider the environmental impact of any project they might carry out and also to consider the environmental impact of any private projects that are subject to the agencies' regulating powers.

Federal Water Pollution Control Act and California Porter-Cologne Water Quality Control Act (FWPCA)–the FWPCA amendments of 1972 regulated the discharge of pollutants from point sources by establishing effluent levels and water-quality standards. They also give financial aid to state and local governments (through research, development, and construction grants) for sewage-treatment plants. The 1972 amendments to the Porter-Cologne Act implemented the FWPCA; this is the main law that regulates wastewater discharge in California.

Air, solid-waste, and noise pollution are the three other environmental areas that are regulated in California. Air pollution is regulated by agencies at all three levels–federal, state, and local. Solid-waste pollution control is carried out primarily at the local level. The state and federal governments have enacted regulations affecting solid wastes; but certainly in the pre-Jarvis-Gann era both recognized that the regulation, collection, and disposal of solid waste was a responsibility of local government. Noise pollution was also considered a responsibility of local government, with local jurisdictions using a variety of control methods (planning, zoning, subdivision controls, environmental controls, and design and construction standards for buildings) to minimize noise. The state role is limited to developing a noise-control program, conducting research into the health effects of noise and technological methods of monitoring noise, and providing ordinance assistance to cities and counties interested in noise-abatement programs. The federal government has controls over specific sources of noise, including railroad and aircraft.

The principal land-use implications of these functional regulations differ by type. Many of the regulations serve to ensure that developers will build safe homes and thereby protect consumers. This protection adds to the costs of development, and thus the consumer is paying for this additional safety. However, the building codes are developed by the industry and may reflect quality dimensions that consumers would not want if they were known.

The environmental restrictions are more important. They directly affect such growth problems as industrial siting and the extent of residential development. If either use, for example, causes an excess of pollution over the set standards, it cannot occur without entailing extensive new capital improvements.

Indirectly, by affecting new growth, the standards influence the formation of suburbs and the redevelopment of older areas.

Land use in California is complex. Developers must exist in an environment that involves satisfying several layers of government and several sets of regulations. When Proposition 13 passed and local government implemented new rules as well as new fees and charges, it added an overlay to this system that made it even more complicated and sophisticated. Interactions between the public economy and the private developer are now even more important to quantify.

Notes

1. These numbers are considerably higher than those reported by Shapiro and Morgan (1978). This may be either because their numbers come from more sophisticated calculations or because their estimates were calculated for a slow-growth period.

2. In the Northern California Bay Area counties, the rate is 6.5 percent, with the additional 0.5 percent going to help finance BARTD (Bay Area Rapid Transit District).

3. In many cases the lines between the categories in this section are far less distinct than the text seems to indicate.

4. There are actually no totally unrestricted grants in the United States, since all have, for example, equal-opportunity or citizen-input requirements.

5. For more detail on the use of these techniques see McTighe (1979) or McWatters (1979).

6. This type of financing is also used in joint-powers agreements in which two or more government entities cooperate to provide a service.

5 The Fiscal-Limitation Movement

The History of Limitation Movements

From the Boston Tea Party to Proposition 13, the history of the United States is full of examples of citizens rising up against perceived excessive taxes or government growth. The fiscal-limitation movement has its antecedents far back in American history.

Property-tax-rate limits originated in the late nineteenth century to restrain public-sector spending for roads and canals that were being operated for private benefits. However, the limits were not effective because they were set too high. The rate limits that appeared during the Depression of the 1930s were intended both to reduce property-tax burdens and to reduce the possibilities of foreclosure on individuals who had to make both house and tax payments. These limits were effective and caused local budgets to fall. At this time the first extensive use of the sales tax occurred for the purpose of restoring the local budget to previous levels (P. Ellickson 1979, p. 8). No new overall limitations on property taxes occurred until the early 1970s.

The recent fiscal-limitation movements arose primarily because of an increased tax burden. Between 1968 and 1973, growth in gross national product (GNP) averaged 8.3 percent; state and local taxes, however, went up by 12.4 percent; state income taxes went up by 20.1 percent; and local property taxes went up by 10.4 percent. Each of these increases was substantially larger than the average increase in the previous five years (Myers 1978). In 1971, if a state had a property-tax burden that was one standard deviation above the nationwide average, the probability of the state imposing tax controls was 12.3 percentage points higher than in a state with an average tax burden, whereas if a state had local expenditure growth one standard deviation or more above the national average, the probability of imposing controls was 12 percentage points higher than in those states with average expenditure growth (Ladd 1978). These limits seemed to work; since in the five years after 1973 the collections of total state and local taxes, state income taxes, and local property taxes all rose at a slower rate compared to the previous five-year period (Myers 1978).

The controls of the early 1970s illustrated a movement away from the traditional limits placed on property-tax rates to a broader limit placed on local property-tax collections.[1] By 1978 twenty-three states had placed limits on overall local property-tax revenues, while only four limits were enacted prior to 1970 (P. Ellickson 1979, pp. 8-12).

Since 1976 the fiscal-limitation measures can be classified into two loose categories: those that are aimed at restricting the future growth of the public sector and those that are aimed at cutting back the existing levels of government expenditure. The former generally do not attempt to reduce the size of government or to provide tax relief. Rather, they try to guarantee that the public sector will not grow faster than the general economy. Some limit government expenditures, others limit revenues. Some restrict local-government action and others limit state action. Finally, some limits apply to all revenues and expenditures, and some apply only to specific taxes (P. Ellickson 1979, pp. 2-4).

Cutback measures, as exemplified by Proposition 13, are more ideological and less pragmatic in nature than are growth limits. Their goal is immediate tax relief or reduced government expenditures. As of May 1979, there were three states with these types of limits: California, Idaho, and Nevada (although the Nevada law needs to be approved by the voters one more time before it becomes effective).

Of the four propositions similar to Proposition 13 on the ballots of various states in November 1978, two passed (Idaho and Nevada) and two were rejected (Michigan and Oregon). Although Idaho and Nevada had lower tax burdens than Michigan and Oregon, previous state limits on tax payments had had little fiscal effect in the two states, and the voters lacked the opportunity to choose a more moderate course. On the other hand, Michigan and Oregon had past histories of property-tax restraint, and the ballots in these states did allow the choice of a moderate course of action (P. Ellickson 1979, pp. 12-15).

Of the ten limits passed in November 1978, nine were constitutional amendments. In the past most such limits were statutory. Furthermore, most of the limits were placed on the ballot by initiative, rather than by the legislature (P. Ellickson 1979, pp. 12-15). Both of these trends seem to indicate that the citizens distrusted their elected officials. This potential antagonism between the citizen and the politician will almost certainly have an impact on the way the limits are implemented.

Since most of the significant controls are relatively recent, there is not much data on their effects. It is reasonable to assume that local governments will seek ways to stretch or circumvent them by finding additional sources of revenue or manipulating budgets. An example of this type of activity can be seen in the behavior of local governments in Arizona. Since 1921 cities and counties have been faced with a 10-percent growth limit on expenditures. However, because of appeals to either the legislature or the judicial system, 50 percent or more of the expenditures are now free of the limit. Most jurisdictions in Arizona utilize two budgets: a working budget that reflects the actual planned expenditures, and a public budget that contains artificial figures. The local-budget process in Arizona is extremely complex. It effectively prevents informed citizen participation; however, it does provide city management with flexibility (P. Ellickson 1979, pp. 14–15).

Controls do seem to have some impact. One study of the noncutback types of controls found that local-government expenditures in states with limits were between 6 and 8 percent below what they would have been if the limits had not been enacted. Furthermore, the same study discovered that limits were not associated with greater diversification in the local revenue system (Bell and Fisher 1977).

The California Experience

The Years before Jarvis-Gann

Modern property-tax reform began in California in 1965. In that year the two major San Francisco newspapers began a series about county assessors, some of whom were receiving campaign contributions in return for reviewing and adjusting property assessments (Levy 1979, p. 68). It appeared that some businesses were being assessed a percentage of market value significantly less than other businesses because of these adjustments.[2]

As the scandal unfolded, property-tax reform became an issue in the state legislature. Although in the past reform had been given low priority, by 1967 it had become a major consideration. In that year the Petris-Knox Bill (AB 80) passed. This bill required that within three years all property must be assessed at 25 percent of market value and that county assessors must ensure that the ratio was relatively stable. The California State Board of Equalization was given monitoring authority. Although this law seemed somewhat innocuous, it took almost all discretion away from the assessors. Ten years later, when property values were exploding, they had no choice but to allow assessed values also to explode. And since the assessors had to reassess every two or three years, the taxpayer was faced with periodic 40- to 60-percent increases in assessed value.

The immediate impact of the Petris-Knox bill was to hurt households. This was because many single-family dwellings were assessed at a lower percentage of market value than businesses. For example, in San Francisco the average single-family dwelling was assessed at about 9 percent of market value, but the average business was assessed at 35 percent; in Alameda County, across the bay, single-family households were at 22 percent of market value whereas businesses were at 28 percent. Because of this reform, households faced increases in their tax bills while businesses saw declines (Levy and Zamolo 1978, p. 5).

California is one of fourteen states that allows citizens to amend the state constitution through an initiative process. Since it is easy to meet the requirements for qualifying an initiative (the number of signatures necessary is only

8 percent of the number of voters in the last general election), there have been many initiatives in California history, covering a wide variety of subjects. There was soon an initiative to combat the assessment increase derived from Petris-Knox.

Philip Watson, the assessor of Los Angeles County, sponsored an initiative that appeared on the November 1968 ballot. This initiative would have amended the constitution to force the financing of "people-related services," typically education and welfare, from nonproperty-tax sources.[3] The property tax was to be limited to funding only property-related services, typically police, fire, and general government services, and limited to 1 percent of market value. The principal weakness of the Watson initiative was that it did not identify the source of funding for "people services."

The legislature waited until the last possible moment to come up with an alternative. This alternative, which also amended the state constitution, was the initiation of a $750 home-owner exemption and a 15-percent inventory exemption. Because the legislature waited so long to act, a pattern that was to be continually followed, there had to be a supplementary informational mailing to the voters and, at the election, a supplemental ballot for the proposition. In part because the legislature was able to present a "responsible" alternative, and in part because of a favorable economic climate (Levy 1979, p. 70), Proposition 9 lost, 2 to 1, and the legislature's alternative passed with 54 percent of the vote.

The next tax initiative appeared on the June 1970 ballot. This initiative, sponsored by the California Teachers Association, would have increased the state government's share of educational and welfare expenditures. It also would have increased the homeowners exemption to $1,000. Although it said nothing directly about property taxes, the strong implication was that these taxes would be reduced. However, a firm opposition, led by the League of Women Voters, resulted in a "yes" vote of only 28 percent. It was also in 1970 that Howard Jarvis failed to get enough signatures to qualify a tax-limitation initiative.

The second Watson initiative appeared on the November 1972 ballot. This initiative would have restructured the entire tax system. It placed a limit on the local property tax, raised excise taxes on specific products, and shifted more of the expenditures on welfare and education to the state. This initiative lost, with 34 percent of the voters giving it approval. It may be that the voters considered the impact of this proposition on local governments more seriously than their own tax liabilities (Beaumont 1979).

Again the legislature acted late. On the last day of the 1972 session, after the November election, the legislature passed SB 90, a major tax-reform bill. This bill expanded the home-owner exemption to $1,750 and expanded the inventory exemption to 45 percent. It also gave a tax credit to renters and limited city, county, and special-district property-tax rates to the rates in effect in either fiscal-year 1971 or fiscal-year 1972, whichever figure was higher. It also placed a limit on the rate at which expenditures for school districts could increase. SB 90 was to govern the tax structure in the state until the passage of Jarvis-Gann.

In November 1973 Governor Ronald Reagan attempted another initiative, Proposition 1. This initiative would have limited the growth in state expenditures to the growth in personal income. Since the proposition said little about property taxes, its opponents characterized it as leading to a potential shift of expenditures from the state to the local level, thereby increasing the property-tax rate. Proposition 1 was barely defeated, with 54 percent of the voters voting "no." Studies have since shown that self-interest played a more prominent role in this election than in the past (Beaumont 1979).

The Jarvis-Gann Initiative

The period from 1965 to 1976 might be characterized as one of incremental reform.[4] The electorate voted down any major change in the tax system and appeared to put faith in the legislature, which usually did something at the last minute. But for the next few years the legislature could not agree on property-tax reform. When the legislature convened in January 1977, reform was a primary item on the agenda. When the legislators adjourned without agreement on how much money the state should spend or who should get the relief, there was bitter disappointment. In late 1977 Howard Jarvis and Paul Gann began their drive to qualify the initiative, and within one month they had over 1.2 million signatures, more than twice the number necessary. Although the legislature once again proposed an alternative, this time it was too late; and Proposition 13 passed in June 1978 with 65 percent of the vote.

Three basic factors influenced the passage of Proposition 13: housing inflation, the California tax structure, and the inactivity of the legislature. Although these factors are interdependent, an examination of each is necessary in order to understand the initiative's success.

In October 1973 the average price of a home in Southern California was $35,800, or $1,100 less than the national average. But by April 1978 this average-priced home was worth $83,200—$26,200 above the national average. This translates to an average growth rate of over 20 percent per year (King and Kemp 1978). It was approximately the same for the San Francisco area, where prices of homes were rising at over 13 percent per year from 1973 to 1977 (Levy and Zamolo 1978). There were also indications that the rate of housing-price increases was accelerating. Because of this large and accelerating increase and because the assessor was continually forced to update the tax rolls as fast as feasible, home owners were wealthier in terms of housing assets but were also paying substantial taxes on those assets. For many this was giving rise to a large cash-flow problem, and Proposition 13 was seen by some as the only way they could afford to maintain their homes.

There were several reasons why the demand for housing rose in California during this time period. California's population-growth rate exceeded the average U.S. growth rate by more than 1.5 percent per year, indicating a large influx of in-migrants. At the same time, the average household size in California was growing smaller, from 2.95 in 1970 to 2.69 in 1978. These two factors together caused an increase of 18 percent in the number of households formed in California during this period (Connerly and Associates 1978). In addition, the California economy greatly accelerated after the 1973-1975 recession; by 1977 California had an unemployment rate lower than the national average. Although income distribution in California did not change during this period, the growth in personal income exceeded the national average.

In addition, there is the so-called California life style. California residents appear to look at housing as an investment, and there is an element of speculattion in the state's real-estate market. The number of families who could afford a house rose when banks were forced to count women's earnings as part of the qualification package. This investment psychology and the ability to participate in the market sharply increased the demands for homes in the state.[5]

But none of this would have been possible without the help of the California home-finance industry. Because the industry was willing to extend larger loans, prices were not as constrained. In part the loans were increased because total family income was counted, but there was also an institutional reason for the continued extension of credit. The home-finance industry in California uses trust deeds as opposed to mortgages, which are in common use elsewhere in the country (Kirlin and Chapman 1978). For the lender, trust deeds have several advantages compared with mortgages. They allow a lender to recover a property in default in a short period of time, 110 days, and then immediately to sell the property unencumbered to any purchaser. Unlike mortgages, trust deeds require no legal judgment to foreclose if a property is in default. Finally, there is no right of redemption after foreclosure. These three institutional factors reduced uncertainty and allowed the home-financing institutions to take greater risks in lending money.

According to construction-industry calculations (Construction Awareness Program 1979), labor and material both fell by over 17 percent in their contributions to the total costs of housing between 1970 and 1978. But land, as a percentage of total costs, rose by almost 28 percent; financing rose by over 47 percent; and other costs rose by over 13 percent. The price of a home that the industry was analyzing rose by 139 percent during this period.[6]

The primary reasons for the increase in importance of interim financing are the national economic effects combined with the increased land regulations and permit approvals that had to be obtained prior to construction. During this period inflation was beginning to accelerate. The GNP implicit price deflator rose by about 6.5 percent per year during the 1970-1978 period; it rose by an average of 2.5 percent in the 1960-1970 period (Economic Report of the President 1979). Since interest rates usually contain an inflation premium, the costs of borrowing money to finance development also increased in importance. Finally, increased government regulations increase uncertainty about the profitability of any development and therefore also likely to force an increase in the interest rates that financial lenders charge developers, since profitability and loan repayment are closely linked.

Perhaps as important as increased interest rates is the increase in the amount of time that the developer must hold the land while waiting for permit approval. The longer this period, the longer the developer must borrow money, and the higher the financing costs. One study has estimated that the costs of an average house go up annually between 9.4 and 26.6 percent because of delays caused by the California Environmental Quality Act alone (Connerly and Associates 1978).

The second largest increase in construction costs was for land. Part of this increase was caused by the same inflationary factors that affected the entire economy. However, growth moratoriums and the permit process also reduced the supply of land (or slowed down its rate of increase). With slow or zero growth in buildable lots, it was to be expected that the price of existing buildable lots would increase. In examining the impact of the California Coastal Commission on housing prices, one study tentatively concluded that simply because of the commission's creation of both positive externalities and an artificial scarcity of housing within the zone, there was an approximate $850 increase in the price of homes outside the Coastal Zone and a $1,590 increase for homes inside the zone (Frech and Lafferty 1980).

Despite these cost increases, the home-construction industry was in the midst of a boom immediately preceding the passage of Proposition 13. In June 1978 the seasonally adjusted annual rate of housing-permit issuance reached a record high in California of 432,400 units. Although this reflects a bias, since many of the permits appear to have been taking out in anticipation of increased regulations occurring because of Proposition 13, it did reflect a renaissance in construction (Gruen Gruen & Associates). However, since Proposition 13's passage construction has steadily slowed, in part affected by the increased fees, rules, and regulations, and in large part affected by increases in interest rates and the economic slowdown.

As discussed in chapter 4, California was a high-tax state, with tax revenues considerably above the national average. The California income tax is quite progressive, reaching a maximum rate of 11 percent on married-couple income greater than $31,000 or individual income greater than $15,000.[7] Married California residents paid 1 percent on income less than $4,000, while single Californians paid 1 percent on income less than $2,000. The California tax code is also stricter than the federal code. For example, California requires that one hold an asset for five years rather than one in order to obtain the full capital-gains deduction. During this same time period, the revenues from the California sales tax also grew quickly. Together with the income tax, these revenues led to a large state surplus. This surplus was to play an important part in the passage of Proposition 13.

With the possible exception of State Treasurer Jesse Unruh, no one appeared to know the extent of the surplus. In January 1977 the estimated cumulative surplus for fiscal year 1977-1978 (which would begin in July 1977) was $940 million, representing about 7.5 percent of anticipated revenues (Levy 1979, p. 80). Eighteen months later, by June 1978, the estimated surplus was about $5.9 billion. During this time and especially in the six months preceding the June election, there were continual estimates as to the magnitude of the surplus; and it may have been anticipated by the voter that this gigantic amount would be used to bail out the cities, counties, school districts, and special districts if the taxes were cut.

The increase of $5.0 billion can be attributed to three causes: The current surplus was higher than estimated; revenues were underestimated; and, because of the passage of Jarvis-Gann, the state was able to cut expenditures (primarily property-tax relief). Two of the reasons for the underestimates of the current surplus and revenues have already been discussed: the elastic tax system and the vigorous inflationary economy. Two noneconomic reasons are also crucial in explaining the growth. The first is institutional. As property-tax assessments rose, state funding for many school districts fell under a formula inversely relating funding and assessments. This led to a decreased amount of state expenditures. The second is political. Governor Brown was extremely cautious in his estimates of the surplus so that he could maintain as much flexibility as possible; at the same time, William Hamm, the new legislative analyst, was also conservative, perhaps because this was his first year in the position. These factors combined to enlarge the surplus beyond anyone's expectations.

The final reason for the magnitude of support for Proposition 13 was the inaction of the legislature between 1975 and 1978. It has been argued that this inability to enact anything more than small, incremental reforms—in a period of growing unrest, increasing assessments, and enlarging surpluses—was the direct cause of the passage of the proposition (Quinn 1978). Between 1975 and 1977, the only property-tax-relief measures passed allowed for more extensive tax relief for low-income senior citizens and home-owner exemptions for welfare recipients. These measures did not affect the majority of property taxpayers.

Three types of major reforms were considered during these two years—split rolls (allowing home owners to be assessed at a lower rate than businesses), a freeze on assessment, and increased home-owner relief. At least twenty-two reform measures were seriously considered between 1975 and 1977 (that is, they were proposed as either statutory changes or constitutional amendments, hearings were held, and bill numbers were assigned. These measures were all modest, and they all failed. These failures occurred in part because the legislature did not know how much money would be available for financing any reform, and in part because the legislature could not agree on the type of aid to be provided.

By January 1977 paralysis had given way to complexity. Everyone agreed that property-tax reform was necessary. Now, however, it appeared that incremental reform might not be enough to pacify California residents. Again, several bills were proposed, amended, and rewritten. The governor had proposed his relief bill, while the Senate had produced two additional bills of their own. All the bills were complex because of the features each contained: circuit breakers for home owners and renters, split-roll assessments, and relief for local governments for the costs of state-mandated programs. The bills differed only in the details of how these devices were to work. Because of their complexity and because some were oriented heavily toward income redistribution while others were not, none passed during the 1977 legislative session. Only after Jarvis-Gann had qualified did the legislature in early 1978 take action to produce a bill (SB 1) that would provide reform. This bill authorized a split roll; limited increases in the property tax to the GNP price deflator for state and local services; provided further property-tax relief through state assumption of some of the major county health and welfare costs; set aside future state revenues in excess of a personal-income growth index for taxpayer relief; and expanded renter, welfare-recipient, and senior-citizen tax relief. Because of the split-roll feature, this legislation required a constitutional amendment and appeared on the same ballot as Proposition 13. However, because the wording of the proposition did not mention tax relief, many voters thought that no substantial relief would occur; and this proposition failed as 13 passed.

The result of increasing home prices and of legislative inactivity was a dramatic increase in property taxes. Suppose, for example, that a home was purchased for $32,000 in 1973. At an average tax rate of $12.50 per $100.00 of assessed value, the tax bill for the family would be $781.25.[8] Assuming that the price of the house rose by a low 15 percent per year, by 1978 the market value would be $64,363. The taxes, assuming a constant rate and reassessment in 1978, would be about $1,793, an increase of almost 130 percent. If the house were financed with a 20-percent down payment, an 8-percent interest rate, and a thirty-year mortgage, the monthly payments, inclusive of taxes, would be $253 at the beginning of the period and $337 by the end of the period. To keep principal, interest, and taxes in the same proportion to monthly income would require an increase in income of over 33 percent. Although this was feasible for those in the work force, for home owners on fixed incomes (notably retired people), this led to serious cash-flow problems. The dilemma that these households confronted when voting on Proposition 13 was whether the promised decline in service would actually occur. And if services did fall, would it be worth the decline in their property-tax bill to 1 percent of the home's 1975 value—in this case, $423? For most, the choice was easy.

In this example it was assumed that tax rates were constant over the period. In reality, however, tax rates were declining, but by an average of only 1.3 percent per year. Local governments were partially reaping the benefits of the inflated housing prices.

But in real terms local governments were not as expansionary as the data seem to indicate. During the 1973–1977 period, California local-government expenditures grew by about 10.7 percent per year, while the state- and local-government price deflator rose by about 7.7 percent per year. If the national price deflator is applicable to California, there appears to be an average annual real growth rate of about 3 percent. This was less than the real growth rate of housing values.

There has been at least one case study of what actually occurred during this period. The Los Angeles city program budget was analyzed for the causes of its 65-percent growth from fiscal-year 1973 to fiscal-year 1978. It was discovered that about 75 percent of the increase in expenditures was caused by wage and expense inflation. The other 25 percent was caused primarily by a change in the labor mix. Over time, there were fewer lower-paid employees delivering services to city residents and more higher-paid city employees ensuring compliance with state and federal mandates or defending the city in the courts (Chaiken and Walker 1979). It may have been that city services were declining while some of the overhead expenditures were increasing.

The composition of the local tax base is also important in explaining why jurisdictions were unable to reduce the tax rate. Table 5–1 illustrates an example. In 1973 the total assessed value of this fictitious California jurisdiction was $100,000, divided into the typical California ratio of one-third residential and two-thirds commercial and industrial. Total taxes raised with the $10/$100 tax rate were $10,000. The bottom half of the table is for 1974, produced under the arbitrary assumptions that reassessment was immediate and that there was a 10-percent increase in the cost of living, a 15-percent increase in assessed residential-property value, and a 5-percent increase in the assessed property value of commercial and industrial properties. There are four cases to be noted. If rates remain the same, as in case 1, total tax collections increase by $830 (8.3 percent), and the tax bill on the residential sector increases by 15 percent. Total property-tax revenues have not gone up by the rate of inflation. Case 2 illustrates what occurs if the city desires to keep the home owner's tax bill constant. In this case the property-tax rate must drop to $8.70/$100, and the total tax revenue the city receives falls by about 6 percent. The jurisdiction may argue, as in case 3, that with a 10-percent inflation rate, the property-tax bill on the resident should also increase by 10 percent. In this case the tax rate must drop to $9.57/$100, and the city receives about a 3.5-percent increase in revenue. Finally, if the city decides that its workers deserve a cost-of-living

Table 5-1
Why Tax Rates Did Not Fall

1973

Type of Construction	Assessed Value		Taxes Paid[a]
Residential	$33,000		$3,300
Commercial-industrial	67,000		6,700
Tax base	$100,000	Taxes	$10,000

1974

Assume 10-percent increase in cost of living
Assume 15-percent increase in residential assessed value
Assume 5-percent increase in commercial-industrial assessed value

Type of Construction	Assessed Value	Taxes Paid			
		Case 1	Case 2	Case 3	Case 4
Residential	$37,950	3,795	3,300	3,630	3,855
Commercial-industrial	70,350	7,035	6,120	6,732	7,147
	$108,300	$10,830	$9,420	$10,362	$11,002

Notes:

Case 1: Tax rate remains the same: $110/$100 assessed value.

Case 2: Constant home-owner bill: Tax rate falls to $8.70/$100 assessed value.

Case 3: Home-owner payment rises by cost of living: Tax rate falls to $9.57/$100 assessed value.

Case 4: Total property-tax revenues rise by cost of living: Tax rate increases to $10.16/$100 assessed value.

[a]Tax rate = $10/$100 of assessed value

increase of 10 percent and attempts to finance this increase with an increase in the property tax, the rate, as shown in case 4, must rise to $10.16/$100 in order to raise enough revenue. Because the city must apply the same rate to all property, it is very difficult for it to reduce the property-tax rate significantly.

The campaign for Proposition 13 was based on two, not necessarily consistent, elements. The first was that the current property-tax situation was intolerable: Taxes were too high, the tax was inequitable, 1 percent was enough for necessary services, and the state had enough money so that services would not be cut. The second was that government spending must be reduced and the only way to show the politician who was boss and to send a message to Sacramento was to cut revenues. The campaign played on the emotions of the average voter, who may not have realized the many taxing jurisdictions to which property taxes are paid and the tremendous variation within the state in the degree of dependence on the tax, even among the same type of government agencies—for example, cities ranged from 0- to 60-percent dependence on the tax, and school districts ranged from 20- to 90-percent dependence (King and Kemp 1978).

Proposition 13 was never behind in the polls, although the percentage spread between those in favor and those opposed was only 3 points in the first week in May (Field 1978). However, in the middle of May 1978 the Board of Supervisors of Los Angeles County requested the assessor to release assessment data immediately instead of waiting until the usual release date in July. The assessor had recently been appointed by the board to fill out the unexpired term of Phillip Watson, and he decided not to resist. The results indicated an 18-percent increase in total assessed value in Los Angeles County, even though only one-third of the properties were reassessed (King and Kemp 1978). Typical increases were between 40 and 60 percent. The board then requested the assessor to roll back values to 1977 levels; although the assessor agreed, the damage to the anti-Proposition 13 campaign had been done. By the end of May, polls showed 57 percent in favor, 34 percent opposed, and 9 percent undecided. In the actual vote Proposition 13 passed by a 65–35-percent margin.

Voter polls seemed to indicate that the electorate did not accept the arguments of the opponents of the proposition. Most believed that the government could provide the same level of services with 10 percent less money, and almost 50 percent believed that the same level of services could be provided with a 20-percent cut in funds. Twenty-two percent believed that government was providing unnecessary services, and 69 percent named welfare as the service they would most like to see reduced (police and fire were named as the services that the voter would least like to see reduced). Finally, 73 percent believed that the state was inefficient, 64 percent believed it of the counties, 53 percent believed it of the cities, and 45 percent believed it of the school districts (Lipson 1980, pp. 6–7). Later studies showed that the principal opposition to the proposition came from government workers, whereas home owners and the elderly were the principal proponents (Magaddino, Toma, and Toma 1980).

In retrospect it appears that both elements of the campaign worked. Voters did want property-tax reductions and smaller government, and Proposition 13 provided both. Later, to ensure that government would not increase its share of the economy, Californians passed a government-appropriation limitation measure in November 1979 by an even larger majority.

Only about one-quarter of the benefits of the tax reduction went to owner-occupied residences. About 28 percent went to owners of commercial, industrial, or agricultural land; another 12 percent went to landlords. Thirty-six percent of the benefits went to either the federal or state government because of lower deductions (*Consumer Reports* 1979). In the future, the home owner will pay an increased share of the tax burden, since homes are sold more frequently than businesses and will therefore be reassessed more often. Because of the reassessment clauses, new buyers will also pay more in taxes for identical services than those who bought in the past.

Postelection Activities

The California State Legislature immediately faced a series of problems that had to be resolved between June 6, the date of the election, and July 1, the date when the constitutional amendment would become effective. Principally, they needed to determine how the remaining property-tax revenues would be allocated; they needed to determine to what extent and in what ways the state should help local governments; and they needed to do something to respond to the pressures to cut government spending. Only after these questions were resolved and the proposition declared constitutional could there be any stability in local planning.[9] Senate Bill (SB) 154, Chapter 292 of the 1978 Statutes, was enacted on June 23, 1978. This was the major fiscal-relief program for the first year, although there were to be eleven additional bills enacted before all the contingencies raised by Jarvis-Gann were answered. This bill attempted to answer the problems faced by the legislature.

Although the structure of SB 154 was primarily developed by the legislature, the role of the executive branch was also important. Governor Brown, determined to make Proposition 13 work, set the tone for the legislative deliberations. The administration played a key role in protecting the cities, in cutting back state expenditures, and in proposing no salary increases for public employees or increases for recipients of Aid to Families with Dependent Children (AFDC). However, the actual drafting of the bill was done by a Joint Conference Committee composed of the leadership (both Democratic and Republican) of both houses of the legislature. This committee utilized the expertise of the Department of Finance and the Health and Welfare Agency primarily for technical assistance and for negotiating with the counties in considering the state's role in providing health and welfare benefits. Within this committee the legislative staff played a major role, far greater than in the past, whereas the impact of special-interest groups was only marginal compared to that of the staff (Lipson 1980, pp. 20–21). The joint committee was affected by several key environmental factors. It was an election year, and in November all the members of the assembly and half the members of the Senate would have to stand for reelection. There was a large surplus, and it was expected that the state would not allow local-government expenditures to be cut significantly. Since there was little planning for implementation prior to the passage of the initiative, there was little time for the committee to learn about cities and special districts— those units of government that they knew least about. Compromise was necessary in order to avoid the embarrassment of doing nothing, since the whole state was watching the legislative activities. Finally, the legislature could read the polls that indicated citizens' priorities for how the aid should be spent—notably for police and fire protection (Lipson 1980), pp. 53–57). The end result, SB 154, contained four basic provisions: It set up the rules for the allocation of property taxes collected under the 1-percent limit, it established the amount and type of state aid, it tied strings to the aid, and it financed an emergency-loan program (which was never used).

In the rush to allocate the property tax that could still be collected, the legislature chose a relatively simple formula. It first mandated that each county had to levy the full $4 per $100 of assessed-value rate (the equivalent of 1 percent of market value). After this money was collected, it would be allocated to the jurisdictions on a pro rata basis, according to each jurisdiction's average percentage of all property-tax revenues collected within each county. School districts used the previous year to obtain their percentages; the cities, counties, and special districts used the previous three years to establish their percentages. For example, suppose that over the past three years the city of Santa Monica collected an average of 1 percent of the total property taxes collected in Los Angeles County. After the passage of SB 154, Santa Monica would receive 1 percent of the new tax revenues collected in Los Angeles County. This simple formula was meant to maintain stability until a longer-term formula was established. However, it did have one significant land-use implication that was not considered in the rush to enact the measure. Although any new development would always add costs to the jurisdiction in which it was located, under this allocation formula the jurisdiction would not receive all the new property-tax revenues of the development (although it would receive any sales-tax or other revenues generated). To continue the example, suppose a $1-million development was going to occur in Santa Monica. The development would generate $10,000 in taxes (1 percent of $1 million), which would go into the county pool. Santa Monica would receive 1 percent of this amount, or $100. If property-tax revenues were the only consideration, it would clearly be in Santa Monica's financial interest to encourage the new development to occur outside the city boundary, since the expected costs of service to the development would almost certainly exceed the property-tax revenues received. And Santa Monica would receive the $100 no matter where in the county the development occurred. This unintended consequence of SB 154 led to a bias against new housing construction, since few revenues were directly tied to this type of construction other than property taxes (although fees, charges, and other developer exactions could be increased).

The state legislature could choose among four alternative approaches to allocate state assistance to local jurisdictions (Kirlin 1979).

1. There could be a transfer of state revenue sources to local governments. For example, the state could give local governments a greater share of the sales tax than they were currently getting and allocate it on a different basis than point of sale (Brimhall 1979).
2. The state could bail out local governments by annually appropriating block grants. This would be riskier than the first alternative from the local jurisdictions' perspectives, since annual appropriations would have to be made.

3. The state could buy out specific services from local government. In this case the state would assume a greater fiscal responsibility for the specific service, but the local government would continue to provide it. There is also risk in this situation, since the state could mandate additional-service-delivery provisions without providing sufficient revenues for the local government to provide the augmented service.

4. The state could take over some of the locally provided financed services. In this case the state would assume full responsibility for the financing and the provision of the service.

The methods of assistance ultimately chosen by the state were combinations of bailouts and buyouts. Cities, counties, and schools were generally given enough assistance to reduce their revenue losses by about 10 percent in fiscal-year 1978-1979. Table 5-2, columns 4-8, illustrates the financial effects of the estimated and actual state bailout under SB 154. Of the total estimated revenue loss to local governments of over $7 billion dollars, the state budgeted replacement of $4.172 billion and ended up replacing $4.365 billion.

Cities received block grants. The legislature knew little about cities, since these governments had not traditionally served as administrative or delivery agencies for state services. They were also less dependent on the property tax than the other government agencies and thus received less state replacement aid.

Counties received far more assistance, with the majority of the aid used to buy out health and welfare programs, including Medi-Cal (the California version of Medicare), Supplemental Security Income/State Supplementary Payment (SSI/SSP), (income supplements to the poor and disabled mandated by the state and federal government), AFDC, and food-stamp administration. Of the $1.493 billion the counties received from the state, only $0.436 million was in block grants.

School districts (K-14) received the largest share of the bailout, since they were typically most dependent on the property tax. Schools also had no alternative revenue sources; they could no longer set tax rates, and they could no longer float general-obligation bonds. The over 1,000 local districts also had the largest number of employees who could be hurt by layoffs and were faced by a set of state rules that severely curtailed their flexibility. These rules not only included curriculum and teaching standards, but also financing constraints arising because of the *Serrano* v. *Priest* decision and labor constraints dictated by the state code.[10] School districts had 90 percent of their property-tax loss replaced by block grants.

Special districts were a problem to the legislature. They were numerous—almost 4,800 exist in California—and they did a variety of things and were financed in a variety of ways. Primarily because of time pressures and a general lack of knowledge about these districts, the legislature decided to give them $125 million in block grants, with $3.7 million more for unmet needs. Most

Table 5-2
Fiscal Effects of SB 154 and AB 8
(estimated review in millions of dollars)

(1)	(2)	(3)	(4)	(5)	(6) SB 154	(7)	(8)	(9)	(10)
Jurisdiction	Total Revenues, All Sources[a]	Property-Tax Loss Because of Proposition 13	October 1978 Estimate of Bailout	Estimated Loss as Percentage of Total Revenues (Net)[b]	Actual 1978-1979 Bailout	Actual Loss as Percentage of Total Revenues[c]	Property-Tax Loss Replaced by Bailout[d]	Estimated 1979-1980 Bailout under AB 8	AB 8 Increase over SB 154
Cities (except San Francisco)	5,292	806	250	10.5	221[c]	11.0	27.0	225	+1.8
Counties (including San Francisco)	7,740[f]	2,236	1,493[g]	9.6	1,503	9.5	67.2	1,619	+7.7
Schools (K-14)	12,125	3,539	2,267[h]	10.5	2,451	9.0	69.2	2,872[i]	+17.2
Special districts	5,368	463	162[j]	5.6	190[k]	5.1	41.0	206	+8.4
Total	30,165[l]	7,044	4,172	9.5	4,365	8.9	62.0	4,922	+12.8

Source: Calculated from Albert J. Lipson and Marvin Lavin, "Political and Legal Responses to Proposition 13 in California," RAND Report R-2483-DOJ (Santa Monica: RAND Corporation, 1980), p. 61; and Summary of Legislation Implementing Proposition 13 for Fiscal Year 1978–79, Assembly Revenue and Taxation Committee, October 2, 1978, table 10.

a Includes property taxes to repay prior voter-approved indebtedness, which are above the 1-percent limitation; property-tax figures also include state-property-tax subventions.

b Calculated as (column 3 – column 4)/column 2.

c Calculated as (column 3 – column 6)/column 2.

d Calculated as column 6/column 3.

e Owing to interpretation of bailout legislative provisions by the state controller, cities received $30 million less than the $250 million appropriated by SB 154. AB 8 clarifies the meaning of provisions affecting the use of local reserves to ensure that state assistance for cities and counties in 1978–1979 is distributed.

f Exclusive of $1.911 billion in federal aid attached to AFDC—a state buyout would shift this revenue to the state and thus lower the counties' total revenue base.

g The county "state surplus" entry includes $13 million in state mental-health money allocated to counties under SB 2212.

h Does not include funds added for county school superintendents by SB 260.

i Total bailout aid for schools has been reduced by $782 million, the amount of property tax shifted from schools to cities, counties, and special districts.

j The additional $30 million provided to special districts by SB 31 is not included.

k Special-district receipt of $30 million in added bailout from SB 31 is included in this figure.

l Numbers in Revenue and Taxation Committee document add to this strange total.

of this money was targeted for the nonenterprise districts (those that could not charge fees for service). Later, in March 1979, SB 31 added $30 million in bailout funds to the districts.

In addition to this aid, $900 million was appropriated for an emergency-loan fund. Of this, $30 million was for loans to prevent bond defaults, and $870 million was for general-emergency loans.

Finally, the state responded to the perceived demand for less government. In order to do this, several strings were tied to the state aid. There were four particular requirements to which local jurisdictions had to agree in order to receive the bailout money: They could not give their employees salary increases in excess of the state-employee wage increase, they had to use one-third of their surplus in excess of 5 percent of their budget to replace state aid, they had to provide the same level of police and fire protection, and they could not cut certain specific health programs disproportionately. For its part, the state gave no cost-of-living increases to AFDC recipients, the aged, the blind, or the disabled on SSI/SSP, although it did allow the 3.7-percent federal cost-of-living increase to be passed through. Furthermore, it gave no wage increase to state employees, thereby constraining all wage increases in jurisdictions receiving the state aid to zero.

In February 1979 the State Supreme Court struck down this last provision.[11] The court held that the provision violated both federal and state constitutional prohibitions against impairment of contracts, as well as home-rule guarantees of the California Constitution. The decision immediately allowed for about $1 billion in pay increases for about one million employees (Hager 1979, p. 1). However, this ruling had little practical effect since almost all local jurisdictions had put aside money to fund the increases (Comptroller General 79-88, 1979, p. 16).

In addition to the land-use implications, SB 154 had three other important ramifications. There was an implicit shift in funding from the local property tax to the state income and sales taxes, which made the California system of finance much more interdependent than in the past. Second, there was a great deal of functional and financial centralization at the state level. The legislature told cities that they had to spend money in certain ways, told special districts that they must raise more of their own money, and assumed responsibility for some county health and welfare services. The state had greatly increased its powers at the expense of local government. Finally, by eliminating property-tax differentials between areas (although some marginal differentials remained to pay off bonded indebtedness) by forcing all counties to tax at their Jarvis-Gann limits, they minimized any property-tax-rate-related impacts on land use.

The legislature, returning to session in September 1978, once again found a surplus larger than anticipated. This time they acted expeditiously. Before the November elections they passed a $1 billion tax cut, consisting of a one-time $675 million income-tax rebate for 1978; a partial indexing of the brackets to offset all inflation above 3 percent; and some additional tax relief for senior citizens, welfare recipients, and the disabled. A stimulus for this cut was to fulfill a promise that the Democrats had made to the Republicans during the SB 154 debate, that either a revenue or expenditure limit be placed on the state budget in return for Republican support. After SB 154 passed, no agreement could be reached, and the tax cut was a compromise face-saving act for both parties (Kirlin and Chapman 1979). Not all the cities received bailout money under SB 154. Fifteen cities declined to take the money for various reasons, mostly because of the strings attached. Thirty-two cities were ineligible to receive the state assistance, since they did not levy a property tax; and 50 cities were penalized their entire portion because they had too large a surplus. Thus, 97 out of 417 cities did not get the bailout (Comptroller General 79–88 1979, pp. 7–8). This explains why cities were the only element of local government to receive less bailout than budgeted. All the rest received more than originally planned.

With a full year of deliberations and the advice of a blue-ribbon committee established by Governor Brown, the state legislature was able to enact in July 1979 a long-term bailout bill, Assembly Bill (AB) 8, Chapter 282 of 1979 Statutes. This bill was complicated, all-inclusive, and had a major provision that allowed the state to reduce its obligation. It consisted of four major parts, although it also dealt with such concerns as contributions to the teachers retirement system and the amount of state aid that goes to the specifically named cities of La Habra Heights and Grand Terrace. The bill itself was over 100 pages long and came with a 4-page index. The last columns of table 5–2 show the estimated assistance under AB 8 for 1979–1980.

The first part of the bill guaranteed to cities, counties, and special districts that they would receive their previous year's allocation plus an adjusted amount of their block-grant aid. This constitutes a base that will be allowed to grow over time. The funding of this starting allocation came from a shift of about one-third of the school property taxes to other local governments. In addition to this base determination, revenues from assessed-value growth in a jurisdiction were allocated proportionally, based on where the construction occurred (situs) to local governments and schools. The $10,000 tax increase generated in the previous example would now go only to the jurisdictions in which the buildings were located.[12] This effectively eliminated the antidevelopment bias of SB 154. Included in this part of the bill is a $206-million grant to special districts (also funded by the tax shift), which was to be allocated to special districts by county Boards of Supervisors. This continued the allocation mechanism established under SB 154.

The second part of AB 8 concerned health and welfare provisions. The state will totally buy out the county share of costs of Medi-Cal, SSI/SSP, Aid to Adoptive Children, and the work and training expenses of a work-incentive program. It will partially buy out some of the AFDC costs and some health-services costs. It will also permanently waive the counties' match for some community mental-health programs and for alcohol and drug-abuse programs.

The third part of AB 8 relates to educational financing. State aid is increased to offset the movement of the school's property base to the other jurisdictions. Some money will also be given to education for capital improvement. The net result of this increase in aid is that by 1983–1984, 94 percent of the unified districts will be within a $150-per-average-daily-attendance expenditure range, which brings the state closer to the *Serrano* standards. Finally, school districts were authorized to establish nonprofit corporations as a way of financing school-facility construction. These nonprofit corporations could issue tax-free bonds backed by development liens against specific property within the school district. These liens would require the consent of all owners within the final boundaries benefited by the facility and would be in equal amounts on each acre. The school district would lease the facility from the nonprofit corporation.

The final part of AB 8, called the "deflator," describes a mechanism to cut state assistance if sufficient funds are not available. For fiscal year 1980–1981, if on June 10, 1980, the total of the general-fund revenues, transfers, and the beginning surplus is less than $20.5 billion, then the aid under AB 8 will be reduced by the amount of the shortfall. Fifty percent of the shortfall will be made up from decreased school-district aid, and 50 percent will come from reductions in the home-owner and business-inventory exemption reimbursements from the state. In future years this limit would be increased to the equivalent of the 1980–1981 limit in order to determine if cuts are to be made. The legislature has the opportunity to override this portion of AB 8.

There are a few important differences between SB 154 and AB 8. AB 8 is long term and far more complex. AB 8, aside from an audit provision, imposes no mandates for service provision on local jurisdictions in order for them to receive aid. AB 8 allows local jurisdictions to gain credit for development, although one provision says that no jurisdictional change can occur—including annexation and incorporation—unless each local agency agrees on a basis for revenue exchanges. This has caused problems for large-scale developers (Wolinsky 1980).

Table 5–2 shows that the same priorities that existed for the allocation of state aid under SB 154 also exist under AB 8. Schools and counties receive the most money, while cities and special districts do not fare as well. School districts did exceptionally well in the bargaining; nearly 90 percent of K–14 school operating costs are now funded by the state (Lipson 1980, p. 61).

Because of this overall increase in aid, it is now estimated that over 73 percent of the state budget will go for local assistance in 1979–1980. This represents an increase of nearly $7 billion in actual dollars spent over the last two years. At the same time, state operating expenses have risen by only $1.2 billion and capital outlay has increased by only $300 million (Lipson 1980,

p. 70). The state appears to be acting as a banker for localities collecting money through sales and income taxes and returning it through a combination of bailouts and buyouts.

Generally, AB 8 is much less detrimental to new development than SB 154. By including the "situs" provision rather than insisting on a proportional distribution among all jurisdictions, it allows communities to capture some of the benefits of the development projects. This should lead to fewer financial restrictions on new development. By allowing the use of school districts to form nonprofit corporations, it avoided placing all the responsibility for new construction on developers.[13] However, the necessity for agreement before any annexation or incorporation can occur might increase the difficulty of obtaining permit approval.

Local Responses

Cities, counties, and special districts imposed many new fees to offset real revenue losses. Counties are expected to raise about $27 million through new fees and user charges (about 2 percent of their property-tax loss). Cities are expected to gain about $103 million from new and increased fees and charges (about 18 percent of the property-tax loss). But there is a great deal of variation within the city category, with some cities expected to have no increased revenue from this source, whereas others, for example Oakland, anticipate replacing 38 percent of their property-tax revenues by utilizing new fees and charges. Enterprise districts are expected to raise $205 million in new fees and charges, and even nonenterprise districts believe that they will raise $6 million more from this revenue source (Comptroller General 79-88, 1979, pp. 12-13).

In real terms, local-agency expenditures will fall. Local governments are going to be far more careful in undertaking new activities, expanding old activities, and allowing new development. This care will manifest itself in several ways. The private sector will almost certainly be used to provide some new services. For example, in Los Angeles private summer schools are being provided, which are staffed by certificated personnel who rent school-district classrooms during the summer. This is in place of the now nearly vanished public summer school. Developers will have to provide far more and higher-quality infrastructure than in the past in order to secure development approvals. And careful fiscal-impact statements, which analyze the benefits and costs to developer and jurisdiction, will become sophisticated bargaining tools in negotiations over new development plans. There may be an initial tendency to slough off on the developer as many costs as possible; but in the long run, if communities wish to remain vital, some accommodations will be reached.

Finally, the growing fiscal pressures might cause both the state- and local-government sector in California to become less willing to participate in federal programs, particularly if these programs require new matching funds. There is concern over the ability and desire of local jurisdictions to participate in federally assisted capital projects (regardless of whether or not there is a matching requirement) because of the future operating and maintenance costs (Comptroller General 79-88, 1979, pp. 37-38). This may be important as the federal government continues to mandate an upgrading of both environmental and wastewater-treatment standards—both of which may imply large capital costs.

Are Controls Desirable?

If it is necessary to restrict government growth or limit specific taxes, are Jarvis-Gann cutback controls the best way to go about it? At least one analysis has indicated that rate or limit controls are not desirable, since they not only interfere with the local-government decision-making process, but they also probably do not work very effectively in containing costs, reducing waste, and reducing inefficiency. Furthermore, they may be expensive, causing in some instances large welfare losses and declines in service levels (Ladd 1978, pp. 6-9).[14]

But if controls are not to be used and a reduction in either property taxes or government is desired, what should be the instrument? If the state is wealthy, like California, the legislature could do exactly what it did after the passage of the initiative—give money to local governments. Studies have shown that in certain circumstances direct lump-sum state grants can reduce property taxes by as much as 90 to 95 cents for each dollar of relief. In this case controls are not necessary, although if there is a lag, the fall in taxes might be so slow that controls would act as an encouraging device (Ladd 1978, pp. 11-14). However, the California experience argues that this theory does not always work. In the face of a large and growing surplus, the California legislature acted too slowly and timidly to offset the increased property-tax burden. Unless there is a way of ensuring that the state grants will begin, the politics of the situation implies such long lags that controls may be the only expeditious way of forcing action. In this case, Proposition 13 acted as a stimulus for something that should have been done much sooner.

If limiting government is desired, there is a second suggestion that each government activity should have attached to it a specific tax or set of taxes. These should ensure that an adequate level of revenue is raised for the activity and would induce a complementarity between the base and the action (Brennan and Buchanan 1978). In effect, the taxpayer would know exactly what is being paid for and would act to ensure that overprovision would not occur. However, this method assumes that the voter is aware of the externalities that are associated with each particular government service and can thus make accurate decisions. This is unlikely to occur. And it also assumes that a government must be tightly constrained in its behavior. This minimization of flexibility might well force inefficient behavior on the part of government. Only if government is totally untrustworthy should this method be used.

In the short run, controls are probably unavoidable. They did reduce California property taxes and local-government growth quickly. The principal danger with controls is that they tend to be inflexible and, if not carefully thought through, may cause more harm than good. In California, with its large surplus, Jarvis-Gann was managed, at least in the short run. But the long-run effects, even in a wealthy state, might not be quite so desirable.

Notes

1. California was an exception to this; in 1972 the state legislature placed a rate limitation on cities and counties, with a levy limitation only on school districts.

2. In California the property-tax bill is based on the assessed value of the property, which in turn is equal to 25 percent of the market value.

3. If, however, such a service as education is capitalized into property values, then this distinction makes no sense.

4. Watson and Gann tried a property-tax initiative in 1976, but it did not receive enough signatures to qualify for the ballot.

5. The number of apartment dwellers remained approximately constant— at about 45 percent—from 1970 to 1976, so that with an increase in population, both segments of the housing market were affected.

6. As a percentage of 1978 costs, material was highest, accounting for 28.8 percent; then land, at 26.8 percent; labor at 17.2 percent; profits at 12.4 percent; interim financing at 9.6 percent; and other expenses at 5.1 percent (Construction Awareness Program 1979, p. 6). Part of the reason for the continued high costs of material was the sporadic lumber and cement shortages that occurred in California during this period.

7. These rates were in effect for year 1977. Beginning in 1978 there was partial indexing of the brackets to avoid inflationary movement into higher brackets.

8. This is determined by taking one-fourth of $32,000, subtracting $1,750 (the home-owner exemption) and multiplying this difference by $12.50 per $100.

9. Within four months of its passage, Proposition 13 was declared by the California Supreme Court to be constitutional in *Amador Valley Joint Union High School District* v. *State Board of Equalization,* 22 Cal. 3d 208 (1978).

10. School districts cannot lay off permanent employees because of revenue reductions (Education Code 44892), and certificated employees can be

laid off only after they have received notices of intent on two separate occasions and after hearings are held that affected employees can attend (Lipson 1980, p. 36). The *Serrano* v. *Priest* decision dictated that the expenditure-per-pupil gap between school districts be dramatically reduced.

11. *Sonoma County Organization of Public Employees* v. *County of Sonoma,* 23 Cal. 3d 296, 591 p. 2d 1, 152 Cal. Rptr. 903 (1979).

12. The actual mechanism for apportionment is complicated. See Senate Local Government Committee (1979).

13. AB 8 also restricted the amount of interim-facility fees that school districts could impose on developers to no more than five annual lease payments and gave the developer the opportunity to provide interim facilities at his own expense.

14. This argument has been challenged by Bell and Fisher (1978). Also, the conclusions were based on the less-stringent controls that predate Proposition 13.

Land-Use and Budget Changes in the Year after Proposition 13

This chapter analyzes some available data to illustrate what occurred in the year following the passage of Proposition 13. Much of this data is preliminary and should be interpreted as only the short-run responses of developers, consumers, and jurisdictions to the massive change in their economic environment. The long-run impacts may be quite different. The initial section of the chapter (after the data limits are discussed) will examine the postproposition changes that occurred in the local-government planning sector. After this, the revenue and expenditure changes that occurred in the various jurisdictions' budgets because of the impact of Proposition 13 and the state's response will be examined. This part will be intentionally brief, since much analysis has already been done in this area (see California State Department of Finance 1979). The emphasis will be on analyzing those revenue and expenditure changes that may significantly affect land use.

The second half of the chapter will be the specification and empirical testing of a simple model of land use. This model will be derived from the model in chapter 3. It will attempt simultaneously to relate the development, consumption, and jurisdictional sectors of California cities. Since the model is preliminary, some of the results are unanticipated; however, the simple model does offer some valuable empirical insights.

The Data

There are principally two data sources that were extensively used in this chapter. The first was a survey of city planners in California; the second was a state Department of Finance survey undertaken in the period immediately following Proposition 13's passage.

The City-Planner Survey

Two surveys of city planners were undertaken; the first in October-November 1978, the second in May 1979. Since the same individual usually answered

The data collection used in this chapter was funded by the Lincoln Institute of Land Policy, Cambridge, Massachusetts.

both surveys, which had similar questions, it is anticipated that the responses are consistent.

The thrust of the questions was to determine the impacts of Proposition 13 on city land-use planning and city financial policies. The methodology of the survey was simple. The planning directors of all of the incorporated cities in San Diego, Orange, Los Angeles, and Sacramento counties (130 in all) were each sent a questionnaire with a letter explaining the purpose of the study. The letter also stated that within a week a researcher would call and set up a telephone appointment. At that time either the director or a staff member would read the answers on the questionnaire to the researcher, who would record them on a duplicate copy. In this manner a high response rate was obtained. There were 108 cities that responded to both surveys.

The principal problem with this survey is that the sample may be biased. The preponderance of the cities were in Southern California, and thus it is difficult to generalize from the results. However, when revenue and expenditure data for 95 of these cities were compared to the data for 372 cities in the state, there were no significant differences between them.[1]

Revenue and Expenditure Data

As a condition of receiving state bailout aid under SB 154, local jurisdictions were required to report in September 1978 their actual revenues and expenditures for fiscal-year 1977–1978 and their budget revenues and expenditures for fiscal-year 1978–1979. The local jurisdictions also had to report funds from new and increased fees, charges, and levies enacted after Jarvis-Gann, as well as some miscellaneous personnel data.

Not all the cities responded to the state's questionnaire. Those cities that did not have a property tax or did not expect to receive money under SB 154 for other reasons had no reason to respond, since later in the year, by state law, they would have to report the same data. Data were only collected for 372 of the then 417 incorporated cities in California. However, all the major jurisdictions did respond, and the state claims that its sample represents 95.6 percent of total revenue for California's cities (California State Department of Finance 1979, p. 35).

It is expected that the estimates of new or increased fees, charges, and levies are probably incomplete and should be thought of as minimums. This is because the state survey was done only three months after the June election. As time passes, it is expected that these fees, charges, taxes, and levy increases will be more important. The actual data for local-government revenues and expenditures for fiscal-year 1978–1979 (which ended June 30, 1979) would normally be released by the state in March 1980, nine months after the end of the fiscal year. However, the actual data was not released until the end of June 1980.

This data set is subject to the usual caveats concerning budget data. It is assumed that the city treasurer or city clerk filled in the right numbers. It is assumed that the revenues actually came from the sources indicated and that the expenditures were made in the areas claimed. It is also assumed that the cities projected revenues and expenditures accurately.

Fortunately, the survey was done rapidly after the passage of Proposition 13. In November 1979 Proposition 4, the Gann initiative, passed. This initiative constrained all levels of government in California to spend no more than a 1978-1979 expenditure base adjusted for population and for income or cost-of-living growth. Since this qualified some time before the November ballot, city finance officers were aware that they should attempt to increase the fiscal year 1978-1979 base. The projected expenditures might thus be higher than the normal pattern would indicate. But because the state survey was undertaken more than a year before the passage of Proposition 4 and several months before it had even qualified, it is assumed that the predicted-expenditure figures reported are not artificially high.

Construction Data

The construction data used in the report come from Security Pacific Bank. This data have usually been considered accurate, although they are partially based on voluntary reporting of jurisdictions. Since the series is of long standing, it has become somewhat institutionalized. Response rates are good, and the data is used by many agencies for planning. The data used are the series of single-family dwelling-unit permits given by the jurisdiction. This overstates the construction that actually occurred; but given the opportunity costs of holding vacant land, it is unlikely that over time this bias is large.

Planning Analysis

One consistent theme underlying many discussions of Proposition 13 is that of increased citizen awareness of government. The citizen revolt was supposed to have been sparked by perceptions of government inefficiency. However, it may take even a greater stimulus to involve the population in local government. It is possible that citizens have become more active in local government; but if so, the city planners are not aware of it, since only 9 percent responded that citizens were more interested in land-use policy after the passage of the initiative. This could be a misperception on the part of the planners; but if it is accurate, it could mean that voters' interests do not extend past the revenue side of government.

Although 68 percent of the surveyed cities were looking for new revenue sources, only a relatively small percentage, in response to the proposition, were making modifications in their comprehensive plans (22 percent), or had implemented a controlled-growth strategy (25 percent). It may be that the latter are long-run projects and that the planners were waiting for the state legislature to write a long-term bailout plan. This plan turned out to be AB 8. An additional discovery was that debt financing has virtually disappeared as a tool of public-works finance, with only 17 percent of the sampled cities still engaging in new debt-finance activities. This was expected since the initiative made it extremely difficult to issue debt, and a move toward any lease–lease-back style of financing must be managed out of the reduced operating expenditures.

When jurisdictions were asked about the impact of Propostion 13 on their flexibility, the results were somewhat inconsistent. The vast majority of the sample (68 percent) believed that flexibility in maintaining existing levels of public services would be affected. Yet nearly equally large majorities believed that it would not affect flexibility in planning and zoning (62 percent), in providing services to new residential areas (60 percent), or in providing services to new commercial or industrial areas (67 percent). These results might indicate that planners would not want to say anything that could be taken to mean that growth ought to be severely restricted.

Question 4 of the survey was concerned with the jurisdictions' strategies toward various types of development. Proposition 13 appeared to have had a negligible impact on local strategies toward contiguous and multinucleated growth, with only 14 and 8 percent of the cities, respectively, claiming that the proposition had had an impact. Of the cities that did claim an effect, there was a 2-to-1 movement toward increasing contiguous development, whereas there was a 3-to-1 opposition to new multinucleated sprawl.

A large number of jurisdictions claimed that Proposition 13 had affected strategies toward service extension, park development, urban infilling, and new commercial development. However, the impacts were decidedly different. Thirty-two percent of the cities maintained that service extension was affected, and by a 10-to-1 margin they indicated that the proposition had had a negative impact. Forty-seven percent of the jurisdictions revealed that park and recreational development were affected and by about a 3-to-1 margin felt that the impact was negative. However, whereas 32 percent of the cities represented that their policies toward urban infill were affected, 100 percent of those felt that urban infilling should be increased. And of the 63 percent of the jurisdictions that felt that policies toward new commercial development were affected, a 12-to-1 margin believed that the policies now reflect a stronger commitment to commercial development.

These results seem to indicate three findings. The first is that when there are impacts, they tend to be toward decreasing new outlying growth and encouraging contiguous growth or urban infilling. There also appears to be a tendency toward encouraging commercial development, perhaps to take advantage of the sales-tax-subvention laws in California. Finally, the reactions seem to have been undertaken without consideration of other potential reactions, since there appear to be few clear patterns of responses to the questions.

Table 6-1 shows the responses to the fifteen sections of the question concerning specific actions taken by jurisdictions in response to Proposition 13. With one exception, part m, every single section of the question has the "no" responses predominating. These results are consistent with the responses to the other questions in the survey and generally indicate only a very small and slow movement of change. Furthermore, most of the change has occurred in areas in which the planning department either shares administrative jurisdiction or is not involved at all. Although 87 percent of the jurisdictions are not changing the types of residential and commercial development allowed, and 82 percent are not changing the comprehensive plan or zoning ordinances, a markedly

Table 6-1
Jurisdictional Actions after Proposition 13
As a consequence of Proposition 13, has your jurisdiction . . . ?

		Percentage		
		Yes	*No*	*Being Considered*
a.	Changed the types of residential and commercial development allowed?	6	87	7
b.	Changed the comprehensive plan and map?	4	82	13
c.	Changed zoning ordinances?	4	82	14
d.	Changed policies for extension of public services to new developments?	10	77	13
e.	Imposed more of the cost of public-service construction on developers?	28	61	11
f.	Transferred costs of what are often government services to residents or businesses in new developments?	18	72	10
g.	Changed user fees charged?	32	61	5
h.	Changed business-license fees?	26	66	7
i.	Established assessment districts for services and construction previously provided from general revenues?	11	69	19
j.	Changed annexation plans?	16	82	4
k.	Increased utilization of fiscal-impact statements for development?	15	75	11
l.	Changed building-permit policies?	7	92	1
m.	Changed fees for permits, variances, and so on?	48	44	8
n.	Changed staffing and/or budgets of departments involved with land use?	47	51	2
o.	Deferred land-use-related capital expenditures?	25	71	4

lower 61 percent have decided not to impose the costs of public services on developers or have not changed user fees. These latter decisions are made at least in part by the city finance officers.

Chi-square analysis was done to investigate whether there were any significant patterns of response. Responses to parts b (changing the comprehensive plan), d (changing public service extension policies), and k (strengthening the use of fiscal-impact statements for new developments) seem to be related to many of the patterns of response to other questions. At the other extreme, responses to parts e, f, m, and o (imposing new cost conditions on the developer, imposing new costs on the residents of the new developments, charging fees for building permits, and deferring capital expenditures) appear to be unrelated to other responses. These last results might indicate a lack of communication between the finance and planning departments, since they all deal with increasing charges—a subject usually not in the purview of planning departments.

Furthermore, most of the recommendations for change appear to come either from the staff of the planning commission or from the city council rather than from planning-commission members.

Redevelopment activities also appear to have been impaired by the passage of the initiative. Although only 42 percent of the cities claim that there has been a negative impact on redevelopment, this represents nearly 64 percent of the cities that are undertaking any redevelopment activities. The responses to this question might be biased since SB 154 was in place at the time of the survey and the allocation of the tax increment was quite uncertain. Under AB 8, this uncertainty will be removed. However, the future for most redevelopment projects is still dim.

A final set of results derived from the raw questionnaire responses indicates that there has been very little change in city reactions between the October-November 1978 results and the May 1979 results. Planners and finance directors appear to have reacted either quickly or not at all to the passage of Proposition 13. With the sole exception that an additional 10 percent of the cities were looking for new revenue sources, there were no major differences between the two sets.

In addition to facing numerous changes in the jurisdictions' attitudes toward development, the local builder must also contend with the large number of permits, procedures, and policies that are typically required for development to proceed. Although many of these steps in the development process were in place before the passage of the proposition, their enforcement has become more rigorous since its passage. Since many of these steps involve decision points, the likelihood of a smooth approval process is somewhat low (Pressman and Wildavsky 1973).

In Orange County, for example, to construct a single-family dwelling in an entirely new subdivision can require the developer to proceed through a minimum of the following 226 procedures, policies, and requirements (Californians for an Environment of Excellence, Full Employment, and a Strong Economy through Planning):

To obtain a general-plan amendment:
    7 county procedures
    7 County Environmental Management Agency policies
    <u>11</u> state requirements

    25

To change zoning:
    17 county procedures
    <u> 8</u> County Environmental Management Agency policies

    25

To form the subdivision (3 county and 2 state requirements before filing):
    9 county procedures
    16 County Environmental Management Agency policies
    <u>10</u> state requirements

    35

To get an environmental-impact statement approved:
    15 county procedures
    1 County Environmental Management Agency policy
    <u>19</u> state requirements

    35

To process variances, use permits, and conditional permits:
    11 county procedures
    7 County Environmental Management Agency policies
    <u> 2</u> state requirements

    20

To obtain grading permits:
    7 county procedures
    2 County Environmental Management Agency policies
    <u> 7</u> state requirements

    16

To begin building:
    8 county procedures
    2 County Environmental Management Agency policies
    13 state requirements
    <u> 3</u> separate additional plan checks

    26

Building inspection (after which the house can be occupied):
    1 county procedure
    4 County Environmental Management Agency policies
    <u>39</u> state requirements

    44

Although some of these requirements may be trivial, since the builder would be likely to meet them anyway, and although most were put in for consumer protection, this is still a large number of requirements. It might be noted that this process ignores any additional requirements imposed by the city in which the development occurs.

Although 30 percent of the cities and 52 percent of the counties increased planning and development fees in the wake of Proposition 13 (Cal-Tax Research Bulletin 1978), planning-department budgets did not escape unscathed from the impacts of the proposition. In many cases it appears that the new fees replaced revenues that were then transferred to other departments. Of 358 cities responding to a state survey of planning-department budgets of cities and counties, 187 jurisdictions increased the planner's budget and 171 decreased it. However, 59 percent of the increases occurred in cities of under 25,000 population, whereas 42 percent of the decreases occurred in cities larger than 25,000 (OPR). Approximately the same pattern holds for counties—a slight majority of the 56 county responses increased their planning-department budgets (29 counties); but most of the increases occurred in the smaller counties, whereas most of the decreases occurred in the larger counties [California State Office of Planning and Research (OPR) 1980].

The state survey also indicated that after the passage of Proposition 13 cities reduced their full-time professional staffs by an average of 6.2 percent. Counties reduced their staffs even more—the average full-time staff fell by 8.4 percent. In large part because of the staff reductions, 67 jurisdictions reduced or eliminated programs and projects, 43 reduced or eliminated advance planning, 15 reduced or eliminated zoning and subdivision updates, and 8 cut hours (OPR 1980, pp. 5-6).[2]

However, if the program and staff reductions were merely stripping away the bureaucratic fat, then perhaps they could be accomplished without affecting the jurisdiction's planning ability. This question was directly examined by still another survey—this one conducted by the Citizens Direction Finding Committee of Orange County. This survey discovered that of the surveyed cities that had reduced staff, most did not feel that their planning ability had been reduced.

There are several implications of these results for the model developed earlier. All three sets of actors—suppliers, consumers, and jurisdictional decision makers—are affected by these new planning directions.

Almost all the impacts on the developer are in the direction of increasing development costs. Cities will be providing less infrastructure and less service extension for new residential developments. To make these developments attractive to the jurisdiction, the builder must bear the additional costs of providing services that in the past had usually been provided by the jurisdiction. It also appears that more construction infill will occur, since it requires less new infrastructure and services. Infill also requires meeting fewer requirements. There will also be encouragement of more commercial development, which, with a fixed supply of land, will mean less land available for residential construction. Existing policies, procedures, and requirements are likely to be examined more closely; fiscal-impact statements are likely to become more important, and, combined with the decrease in planning-department budgets and staffs, this will mean longer delays for the developer; the opportunity costs involved with holding land will increase; and the costs of construction will rise. Most of these planning impacts will move the marginal-cost curve up, with resultant price increases and quantity decreases. In the year immediately preceding Jarvis-Gann (July 1, 1977–June 30, 1978), slightly over 159,000 new single-family dwelling units were authorized. In the year immediately following, the rate of construction fell by nearly 20 percent to slightly less than 128,000 units authorized (Security Pacific National Bank 1978, 1979). A large part of this decline might have occurred because of interest-rate increases and a slowing of the national economic recovery, but the increased development costs must surely have played a part.

The consumer faced more than a slowly growing market and these simple price increases. Since cities are looking for new revenue sources, there are likely to be increased fees and charges for services. These may be levied on all city residents, but potential movers into the city have the option of not moving and thus avoiding the new charges. Although consumers benefit from the property-tax savings, with the fixed (and perhaps even diminishing) supply of residential land, the tax reduction may be capitalized into the price of the homes, so that movers may not even see the benefits of the reduction. It might be noted that there are two distinct effects on the consumer's demand curve. The reduced services and increased fees will cause a downward shift in demand; the reduced taxes will cause an upward shift in demand. The ultimate location will depend on the relative strengths of these two impacts. But given the unambiguous shift in supply, it is likely that the final real equilibrium price will be higher than it was in the pre-Jarvis-Gann equilibrium. Of course, if the new development is homogeneous with the existing housing stock, there will be no short-run price effects because of these jurisdictional actions, although the slowdown in new construction will be large. Since there is a price difference between old and new single-family dwellings, it is likely that both price and quantity effects are occurring.

There may be less city planning on the part of jurisdictions since there are fewer resources devoted to planning departments. This could lead to a loss of flexibility and to greater work loads on the remaining staff. Of course, with the decrease in construction, these impacts may not yet have been felt. It also appears that most of the proactive responses to the initiative will be undertaken by other departments and will come in terms of lower service quality and increased or additional fees and charges. Finally, there appears to be less residential redevelopment in the future for jurisdictions. This will further constrain housing markets, especially for the middle- and lower-income city inhabitants.

Revenue and Expenditure Impacts

As can be seen from table 6-2, there was a wide variation in the impact of Proposition 13 and the state bailout on the various units of local government. While cities, nonenterprise special districts, and the various types of educational districts all saw a decline in the total revenues received, counties and enterprise districts actually saw an increase in total revenues. The total decline for all units of local government was 1.4 percent. This small decline demonstrated both the impact of the state bailout and the expansion of user fees and charges.

Property-tax dependence also changed dramatically: There is now no unit of government in the aggregate that is more than 45-percent dependent on the property tax, whereas in the past the range was from 15 to 74 percent. However, if housing turnover rates continue to be high, then over the long

Table 6-2
Local Government Revenues[a]

	Percentage Change in Revenue FY1978-FY1979	Property Tax as Percentage of Total Revenue	
		FY 1978	FY 1979
Counties	1.9	37.0	17.3
Cities	-6.4[b]	22.8	10.8
Enterprise districts	9.5	14.7	8.8
Nonenterprise districts	-11.7	73.5	44.9
Schools, K-12	-2.7	57.8	25.8
Community colleges	-11.5	52.2	24.2
Total	-1.4	41.3	19.2

Source: Calculated from California State Department of Finance, 1979, tables 1 and 2.
[a]Including all state aid
[b]Reflects adjustment made to reconcile federal grants. Reported totals show a 9.3-percent decrease.

run the ratios will gradually increase. This will occur because of the passage
of the appropriation limit in November 1979. The property-tax-dependence
ratio will have to increase because of limited expenditures, a slow increase in
state aid, and a fast increase in the property-tax base.

Cities varied widely in their dependence on the property tax. Some cities
did not collect any—for example, Lancaster; others—for example, Bradbury—
depended on the property tax for over 50 percent of their revenues. Table 6-3
shows the extent of the variation of the impacts of Proposition 13. Property
taxes did fall by an average of 49.6 percent, with a standard deviation of 22.5

Table 6-3
Reported City Revenues

Source	Percentage of Total Revenue 1977-1978	Percentage of Total Revenue 1978-1979	Total Change	Average City Change
Property tax	20.5	9.8	-56.5	-49.6 (22.5)
Sales tax	16.5	19.4	6.5	5.6 (53.3)
Total tax	47.4	41.8	-20.0	-19.8 (16.5)
Total license and permits	2.1	2.4	2.6	8.2 (63.5)
Total fines and forfeitures	1.7	1.9	2.4	-2.1 (53.1)
Revenue from money and property	3.0	2.8	-15.0	-19.0 (35.1)
Revenue from other government	32.1	33.6	-5.1	10.0 (58.6)
Total charges	7.8	9.4	8.6	10.8 (75.5)
Contributions from enterprise	2.4	2.9	5.8	18.7 (168.8)
Fund transfers	1.1	1.9	53.7	56.5 (1032.7)
Total other	2.3	3.4	34.7	55.9 (575.2)
Grand total	100.0	100.0	-9.3[a]	-5.5 (29.3)

Source: Adapted from Jeffrey I. Chapman and John J. Kirlin, "Land Use Consequences of
Proposition 13, *University of Southern California Law Review* 53 (1979). Used with permission.
Note: Standard deviations are in parentheses.
[a]See footnote b in table 6-2.

percent. However, because cities were forced to draw on their surplus (in order to get SB 154 bailout money and to continue to finance services), there was also an average fall of 19.0 percent in the revenues gained through money and property management (with a standard deviation of the changes of 35.1 percent). Particularly large standard deviations appear for average changes in sales-tax receipts, fines and forfeitures, charges, enterprise contributions, fund transfers, and other revenues.

One important revenue source should be singled out: the federal government. If there is no change in the revenue-sharing formula, in 1981 there could then be a decrease of as much as $70 million in revenues received from the program. Through other programs, however, counties can expect to receive $156 million more from the federal government. The amount of assistance to cities is unknown because most cities incorporate federal receipts into their budgets only as the funds arrive. Even though cities projected a decline of 23 percent in federal assistance, it will probably increase by about 10–15 percent (Comptroller General 79–88, 1979, pp. 13, 37).

In order to guarantee an adequate level of service expenditures, cities drew down their reserves to a remarkable degree. There was a fall of 35 percent in the unobligated reserves (all funds) and of 39 percent in the unobligated reserves (general fund). Obligated reserves also fell by nearly 10 percent (Chapman and Kirlin 1979b). These falls greatly diminished the flexibility of the cities.

One response to the fall in property-tax revenues was an increase in the fees and service charges implemented by the jurisdictions. Cities anticipated that increased taxes, fees, and service charges would add nearly $103 million to their revenue base (California State Department of Finance 1979, p. 28). Within five months of the passage of Proposition 13, 43 percent of the cities and 74 percent of the counties had increased some fees, with smaller cities increasing the fees more than larger cities (Cal-Tax Research Bulletin 1978). Thirty percent of the cities raised charges in areas that related to land use and development (California Commission on Governmental Reform 1978, pp. 2–3).

In August 1979 the Association of Bay Area Governments (ABAG) conducted a survey of cities and counties in Northern California. In this survey they identified a wide variety of fees and charges that jurisdictions imposed on developers. They classified these fees into four main types, each of which contained several specific fees (ABAG 1980, pp. 19–33). These may typify fees currently implemented in California.

Planning Fees: These included fees for general-plan amendments, rezoning, use permits, design review, site-plan review, tentative map plans, final map plans, an initial environmental study, processing of the environmental-impact report, and encroachment permits. For a 100-unit subdivision, these fees ranged from $175 to $20,475, with a mean of $5,326 and a median of $4,068.

Building Fees: These are fees for building permits, plan checks, plumbing permits, mechanical permits, and electrical permits. There was little variance in these fees among jurisdictions because most were based on the Uniform Building Code requirements. The range in building fees for a single-family dwelling was from $254 to $1,688 per unit, with a mean of $496 and a median of $401.

Growth-impact Fees: These are charges for parks, schools, residential construction, and other miscellaneous growth impacts. There was a great deal of variation in these fees; they ranged from $25 to $4,500 per unit, with a mean of $1,206 and a median of $900.

Utility Charges: These are payments primarily for sewers, storm drains, and water. Again there was a large range of $205 to $2,829; however, the mean of $1,448 is quite close to the $1,489 median.

The ABAG survey ultimately found that the total of the development fees for a single-family dwelling (on a per-unit basis) ranged from $800 to $5,919, with a mean of $2,804 and a median of $2,777. For a seven unit multifamily building, ABAG discovered fees that ranged from $982 to $25,482, with a mean of $10,102 and a median of $10,026 (ABAG 1980, p. 59). On a per-unit basis, these fees were less than those on a single-family dwelling.

Another conclusion of this study was that the slower-growing cities have lower fees and that faster-growing cities have higher fees primarily because of the differences in growth-impact fees. At one extreme, these were about 2 percent of the total fee package for the slow-growing older cities (for single-family dwellings), but they reached 38 percent of the total fee bill in the fastest-growing and most-distant suburbs. For the multifamily development, the range was from 3 to 33 percent (ABAG 1980, pp. 36, 60). It appears that high growth-impact fees were being used to finance the infrastructure.

Although the fees are high in absolute terms, it is not clear that they are high enough to cover the full costs of services, including extending the public infrastructure (Conservation Foundation Letter 1979). For most areas in California it appears that fees are no more than 2 or 3 percent of the total cost of the house. However, on the margin fees could be more important. As table 6–4 shows, some of the changes in percentage terms have been large. It is not unusual to see fee increases of over 100 percent, and there are instances of increases of over 1,000 percent. It was found in another study of Northern California cities that since 1976, 21 percent of the cities had increased their fees by over 50 percent in constant dollars (but 24 percent had actually allowed real fees to decrease over the same period) (Gabriel, Katz, and Wolch 1980, pp. 12–14). Unfortunately, not enough data have been collected to examine fully the impacts of these marginal changes.

Based on the ABAG survey and the wide variety of fee increases, it appears

Table 6–4
Some Fee Changes That Occurred within Three Months of Proposition 13

	Type	Pre-Proposition 13	Pre-Proposition 13	Percentage Change
City				
Bradbury	Building permit (average)	$937	$1,402	50
Concord	General-plan amendment	0	600	—
La Habra	Variance	40	120	200
La Mesa	Sewer connection	25	300	1,100
Navato	Parks (4 bedroom house)	120	325	171
Oceanside	Zone change	300	1,000	233
Sunnyvale	Subdivision map	15	300	1,900
County				
Alameda	Subdivision map	50	720	1,340
Conta Costa	Rezoning	200	670	235
Los Angeles	Conditional-use permit	375	730	95
San Diego	Rezoning	355	1,250	252
San Mateo	Subdivision map	250	500	200
Santa Clara	Rezoning	100	600	500
Siskiyou	Compliance certificate	25	50	100

Sources: Construction Industry Research Board, "Samples of Increases in Building Fees, 1978" Reprinted with permission; County of Los Angeles, Department of Regional Planning, "New Fees Effective," October 1978.

that the old, slow-growing cities, have not changed their fees significantly. The newer, faster-growing cities appear to be charging high fees. But some of them couple these high fees with a progrowth attitude, whereas others use the fees to prevent growth. Only over time, with case studies of specific jurisdictions, will the full impact of fees be discernible.

It is possible to test the hypothesis that cities increased other revenue sources to make up for the loss in property-tax revenues. Using regression analysis, it was discovered that for every dollar decline in property-tax revenue, there was a 20-cent increase in total city charges or a 21-cent increase in the other tax revenues obtained by the city. Although these are preliminary results and are based on projected changes, the estimates are quite precise and indicate an active response to the loss of revenue by the city departments.

Although the growth of local-government expenditures was less than in previous years, it was still positive in nominal terms. The average budget increase was about 6.8 percent, although the range was from 0.7 percent (schools, K–12) to 27 percent (enterprise districts, including capital outlay). Counties increased their expenditures by an aggregate 9.5 percent; cities, taken separately, increased expenditures by 3.8 percent. However, this may well mask actual declines in service levels. Authorized position changes for full-time personnel dropped by 4.9 percent for counties, 3.1 percent for cities, and 8.2 percent for nonenterprise districts (and rose 0.3 percent for enterprise districts) (California State Department of Finance 1979, pp. 18-20). It has been estimated that 26,500 individuals initially lost their jobs (although later 9,500 were rehired); and there was an additional decrease of 90,000 workers through attrition (Comptroller General 79-88, 1979, p. 27). Cities that were dependent on the property tax for 25 percent or more of their revenues did not plan to hire a single additional employee in the fiscal year following the initiative's passage (Cal-Tax Research Bulletin 1978). The morale of government employees was significantly depressed and many high-caliber people left to join the private sector (Comptroller General 79-88, 1979, p. 30).

There was a great deal of variation in the ways that cities responded to Proposition 13 cutbacks in terms of allocating money to various services. Libraries (-9.2 percent), parks and recreation (-7.9 percent), and contribution to enterprises (-4.0 percent) were the only expenditure categories that in the aggregate showed large expenditure cuts. Building regulation (3.2 percent), public safety (8.3 percent), and public works (7.6 percent) showed the largest total increases. But again, the standard deviations of the average city changes are immense. For example, the standard deviation for libraries was 53.1 percent; for parks and recreation, 201.9 percent; and for contributions to enterprises, 85.9 percent. For public safety and public works, the standard deviations were 24.5 and 85.1 percent, respectively. The standard deviation of the average change in expenditures for cities was 42.9 percent.

Jurisdictions used several methods to deal with the revenue shortfalls that affected their expenditures. The Economy and Efficiency Commission of Los Angeles County identified six specific actions that the county took. The county imposed a hiring freeze, held wages down, tightened control of the benefits that the employees were receiving, engaged in a civil-service reform (making some county department heads ineligible for civil-service protection), increased productivity in various departments (particularly in the Department of Public Social Services), and reduced service levels (not one new library book was purchased during the fiscal year) [Los Angeles County Economy and Efficiency Committee (EEC) 1980, pp. 6-12]. Many of these responses were typical of many jurisdictions and indicated the variety of ways in which the jurisdictions muddled through the first year after Proposition 13.[3]

As observed in chapter 4, the first-year state bailout caused an increase in the centralization of power. Service-level mandates for police and fire were expressed in the bailout legislation. At the county level, at least for Los Angeles County, the proportion of resources allocated to health and welfare actually increased after Proposition 13 because of state legislation and because cuts were made only in county-run programs (EEC, p. 5). It was found that most localities had attempted to maintain the preproposition level of local funds allocated to federal-aid programs in order to ensure that the federal aid remained unchanged (Comptroller General 79–88, 1979, p. 33). This would necessarily distort the local-expenditure allocation process toward what the federal government considered important.

Some expenditure items specifically relate to land use, typically those in the areas of public works and capital-improvement plans. Although the aggregate public-works portion of the budget showed an increase of 7.6 percent, aggregate city public-works full-time employment fell by over 1,000 authorized positions (4.7 percent). These cuts have typically led to reduced levels of maintenance of landscaped areas, streets, lighting equipment, and buildings—levels that are unlikely to be sustained for long periods of time.

Perhaps even more significantly, all types of city debt showed a decline. Lease-purchase agreements fell by 6.1 percent, other bonds fell by 3.3 percent, and other long-term debt fell by 4.3 percent. This appeared to be a consistent phenomenon across cities, because the standard deviations of the average changes in each of these categories were all remarkably small. Since much of this debt is used to either replace or extend the infrastructure necessary for development, this trend implies that future infrastructure will have to be privately financed. The state Department of Finance found in a field survey that 90 percent of the cities were cutting capital-improvement programs (California State Department of Finance 1979, p. 33).

As in the case of the cutbacks in planning, there are also revenue- and expenditure-change implications for the three sets of actors.

The developer must now build in jurisdictions that face sharply lower locally raised revenues. This could well mean that additional fees and charges will be imposed. Because the local jurisdiction will find it difficult to incur debt, it is likely that the infrastructure that had in the past been provided by the public sector will now have to be provided by the private sector. Debt expenditures fell in the year after Jarvis-Gann, and there is every likelihood that they will continue to fall. One implication of the expenditure cutbacks involves the drop in personnel available to serve the community. To the extent that developers need to deal with public personnel in order to obtain permits, determine rule changes, or get specific services delivered, they will find it slower as they must now wait in longer queues. Both revenue and expenditure factors tend to move the developer's marginal-cost curve up.

If it is assumed that property-tax reductions are capitalized, and that the price of the house thus increases to reflect the decreased tax liability, it is unlikely that the new resident will capture much of the benefits of Proposition 13. It is also unlikely that the new fees and charges that the resident faces will be capitalized, since they are similar to benefit taxes. These charges should increase over time as the public sector shifts some of its functions to the private sector. Nonmovers benefit if the present value of their tax reduction exceeds the present value of their service loss.

The financial role of government in the lives of private individuals may be decreasing, since in real terms government expenditures fell in the year after Proposition 13. Service quality also probably deteriorated. Since jurisdictions were unequally affected by Proposition 13 because of their unequal dependence on the property tax, it is likely that the various bundles of goods and services that the jurisdictions can afford to offer will begin to diverge. This divergence will be slowed if the state continues to mandate how localities can spend their money, but at least some strings have been loosened since the passage of AB 8. As the property tax becomes less important and state funding becomes more important, the diversity of revenue packages will diminish.

Local jurisdictions will become more interested in the fiscal characteristics of new development. Developers will be forced to defend their projects on budgetary grounds. This will probably mean, at least in the short run, an intense desire for commercial development to generate sales-tax revenue, with residential development given a lower priority.

Although this analysis has attempted to separate the three actors, a great many interactions are occurring between the sectors. In order to examine fully some of the empirical magnitude of these interactions, a more formal specification of the activities occurring in this scenario must be undertaken. The next section attempts to do this.

Empirical Estimates of the Land-Use Model

A theoretical model of the residential land-use market and the public sector was developed in chapter 3. This model can be used to generate a series of hypothesized relationships that can be tested. This section will specify some of these relationships.

The Private Sector—Supply

Although the California developer tends to build in large quantities, he still faces considerable competition. It is assumed that competitive behavior exists and that there are attempts to maximize profits, subject to the usual market constraints. Specifically, the developer faces a given construction technology and fixed input prices. His marginal-cost curve is defined as the additional costs incurred for a one-unit increase in output, and profit maximization occurs when marginal costs are equal to the market price. To the extent that the market price increases, with all else equal, the developer will attempt to supply more output. If the marginal costs of development increase, at the same output price, the developer will supply less.

The principal inputs that a developer utilizes are land, labor, and capital. It can be assumed that the prices of labor and capital within California are fixed and do not vary significantly across city boundaries. This is a strong assumption; but since the construction industry is unionized by region, it is probably not terribly inaccurate for new developments. The price of land does vary by jurisdiction. Usually land prices are a function of the alternative uses that the land may have. If a parcel of land is capable of being used for higher economic purposes, its price will be higher. Jurisdictions can affect land price by using zoning or other rules to restrict artificially the supply of land to be used for any particular economic purpose. This artificial restriction would cause economic rents to accrue to the landowner, and the price would increase.

The jurisdiction can also have an impact on development costs through the imposition of development-restricting rules and charges on the developer. To the extent that these rules and charges are increased, the costs of development also increase.

The supply curve of the developer relates the quantity of new single-family development supplied to the price of the development, the price of the land, and the rules and charges (which affect development costs). This supply function can be written:

$$Q_{sj} = f_1(P_{Qj}, P_{Lj}, C_{xj}, R_{uj}) \qquad (6.1)$$

where

Q_{sj} = quantity of single-family development supplied in jurisdiction j

P_{Qj} = output price in jurisdiction j

P_{Lj} = price of land in jurisdiction j

C_{xj} = charges in jurisdiction j

R_{uj} = rules in jurisdiction j

The Private Sector—Demand

Consumers gain utility from the consumption of goods and services, subject to income constraints. If housing is considered a consumption rather than an investment decision, then housing services are also included in this bundle.[4] Government services are also included in this potential-consumption set. The consumer maximizes utility by trading off purchases of goods and services, with the tradeoff terms being set by relative prices.

The demand curve for new single-family development relates the quantity of development demanded to the price that the consumer must pay for the development. Furthermore, the consumer's income is also important since it sets the constraints for the decision. If there are substitutes for the new development, the consumer should also take them into consideration.

Local-government expenditures and taxes vary by jurisdiction. If the Tiebout model is accurate, these variables must have an impact on the demand for development in a specific jurisdiction. To the extent that expenditures are high in a jurisdiction, the demand for development in that jurisdiction should increase. However, if the tax price is the cost of those expenditures, then the higher the tax price, the less desire for the new development. Equation 6.2 illustrates these relationships:

$$Q_{dj} = f_2(P_{Qj}, Y_j, S_j, E_j, T_j) \tag{6.2}$$

where

Q_{dj} = quantity demanded in jurisdiction j

P_{Qj} = output price in jurisdiction j

Y_j = income of consumer in jurisdiction j

S_j = substitutes for new development in jurisdiction j

E_j = expenditures for public services in jurisdiction j

T_j = local taxes in jurisdiction j

Despite the appearance of expenditure and tax terms on the right-hand side of the equation, this model does not address the capitalization questions discussed in chapter 3. This is because the left-hand variable is not property value but rather new single-family development. The interpretation of the right-hand variables is that a potential consumer must "buy into" the jurisdiction by confronting these variables, and that in this manner they have an impact on the quantity demanded. The model implies only that consumers do take into account local fiscal variables as they shop for new development.

Private Equilibrium

It will be assumed that the market will clear at a unique equilibrium price. At this price, the quantity supplied of new development precisely equals the quantity demanded of new development; that is:

$$Q_{Sj} = Q_{Dj} \tag{6.3}$$

The equilibrium solution serves another purpose. Because of severe data limitations, structural equations 6.1 and 6.2 cannot be estimated in the specified form. In particular, selling-price data for new developments are almost always unavailable by city. But because of the equilibrium assumption, a reduced form of the system of equations can be utilized. This would be accomplished by solving equations 6.1 and 6.2 for price, and then, by using equation 6.3, determining a reduced-form equation in which the price variable has disappeared; that is:

$$Q_j = f_4(P_{Lj}, C_{xj}, R_{uj}, Y_j, S_j, E_j, T_j) \tag{6.4}$$

with all the variables having been previously identified, and Q_j being the equilibrium quantity of development. When this equation is estimated, the coefficients are of reduced form and therefore have no direct supply-and-demand interpretations. They reflect the combined impact of a particular variable on the amount of equilibrium construction. No price elasticities can be calculated; therefore, it is impossible to determine the ultimate incidence of the rules and charges imposed on the developer.

The Public Sector

The third set of actors in this model is the jurisdictional decision makers. There are three interdependent decisions that they make that are of specific concern in the model. They determine the extent of rules and charges that the developer faces; they determine the expenditure level and service quality within the jurisdiction; and they determine the locally raised revenues. This model argues that all these decisions are made simultaneously.

Rules: A decision must be made concerning the rules that are imposed. If too many rules are imposed, they could dramatically reduce the amount of construction that occurs; if not enough are imposed, too much construction may take place in the city, and the demands on the city's budget may be excessive. To some extent rules and charges may be substitutes for each other; if a jurisdiction imposes many charges on a developer, it may be reluctant to impose rules. Finally, the decision makers realize that with the loss in property-tax revenues, they must be careful in promising additional expenditures for any particular development. The following relationships can thus be hypothesized:

$$R_{uj} = g_1(Q_j, TL_j, C_{xj}) \tag{6.5}$$

where

T_{Lj} = property tax loss in jurisdiction j because of Proposition 13

It is hypothesized that if a community has a great deal of development, it will most likely impose rules so that the activity can be easily regulated if desired. Furthermore, if the community is anticipating a loss because of the passage of Proposition 13, then it should also be willing to impose more rules on the developer. Finally, if rules and charges are regarded as substitutes for each other, then as charges increase, rule use should decrease.

Expenditures and Revenues: Decisions must also be made concerning a jurisdiction's level of expenditures and revenues. There has been a long debate about this problem (Scott 1972). The basic point of disagreement is over the determination of the level of expenditures. One side maintains that the budget predominantly reflects internal negotiation strategies, and that the ultimate expenditure levels and patterns reflect the previous strengths of the agency department heads. Revenues are typically ignored in this model. At the other extreme, it is postulated that the external environment drives the formation of the budget. Revenues are important since they act as a constraint, but the various strengths and weaknesses of the participants are unimportant. The importance of community variables—a set of influences that is only implicit in the previous system—is crucial to this model.

There is no particular reason to believe that either way of thinking about the budget is unique. A city budget must reflect both internal negotiations and external pressures. This model will use a combination of the two schools of thought. Equation 6.6 illustrates the postulated relationships.

$$E_{tj} = g_2(E_{t-1j}, TR_j, Y_j, Q_j, OR_j) \qquad (6.6)$$

where

E_{tj} = expenditures of jurisdiction j in time t

TR_j = local tax revenues of jurisdiction j

OR_j = other revenues received in jurisdiction j

The lagged expenditure variable refers to the argument that the budget is determined internally, reflecting nothing more than an increment over the previous year's budget. The income variable represents the community demographics that are argued to be the crucial variable. The new-development variable is specified in order to determine the impact of new construction on city expenditures. The revenues are in the equation since it is believed that they act as spurs to city expenditures, although local tax revenues might well have different impacts than nontax revenues.

The final relationship concerns the jurisdiction's tax revenues. After the passage of Proposition 13 these are few, but those that remain become crucial since they represent the last vestiges of local autonomy. The concern is to raise revenues that are a function of local taxes. Most of these revenues are constrained since the property-tax rate and sales-tax rate are set by the state. However, the jurisdiction does have some control over these bases. Since this model is concerned with the impact of construction on the local budget, it is postulated that the amount of construction that occurs has an impact on the revenues that are received by increasing the relevant base, whereas an increase in population also increases the revenues received through local taxes, again by increasing the base.

$$TR_j = g_3(Q_j, POP_j) \qquad\qquad (6.7)$$

where

$$POP_j = \text{population in jurisdiction } j$$

Equations 6.4, 6.5, 6.6, and 6.7 form a model that loosely corresponds to the graphical analysis done in chapter 3. This is a simultaneous system, since construction is influenced by rules and expenditures, rules by construction, expenditures by tax revenues and construction, and tax revenues by construction. As any one of the exogenous variables changes, the equilibrium in both the private and public sectors should also change.

Specification of the Variables

Equation 4: Q_j, the quantity of new residential development, appears in all the equations. It is defined as the number of single-family dwelling units authorized per jurisdiction during fiscal-year 1978–1979.[5] Unfortunately, data are not available for the price of undeveloped land by jurisdiction. However, intensity of development might be correlated with land prices, with higher intensity reflecting greater economic use of the land. Housing density will therefore be used as a weak proxy to reflect land prices. This should be negatively related to the amount of construction that occurs. The income variable is defined as median household income and should be positively related to construction, reflecting the belief that higher-income people are more likely to demand new construction. Substitutes for new construction are assumed to be the existing housing stock, which, correcting for city size, is once again measured by housing density. The coefficient on this variable will reflect both price and substitution impacts—both of which should be negatively related to construction. Expenditures are defined as the total budgeted expenditures of the jurisdiction. Taxes in this equation are defined as the local tax burden facing the mover. This includes property taxes, sales taxes, and other taxes, divided by personal income. This definition reflects the tax payment that a mover must make to live in the jurisdiction, as well as the constraint on disposable income.

There exist charges on both the developer and the consumer. For example, the developer must pay filing fees, zoning variance fees, and so on. The consumer may be forced to pay refuse-collection and fire-service charges. The former raise development costs; the latter are additional expenditures for the consumer in the jurisdiction. The total-charge variable will be negatively related to construction for both these supply-and-demand reasons.

Two separate indexes of rules were derived from the land survey. The first was derived from the jurisdiction's overall development strategy after the passage of Proposition 13. The jurisdiction was awarded one point for each type of development that it would restrict because of Proposition 13. Since six types of development were mentioned (contiguous, satellite, service extension, infill, parks, and commercial), the maximum development-cutback score was six; the minimum score, if the city did nothing, would be zero. Table 6-5 shows the frequency distribution of rules-1 for the ninety-five cities.

Forty-two percent of the cities did not restrict any specific type of development because of Proposition 13. None of the cities reacted by restricting all types of development, and nearly 95 percent of the jurisdictions restricted two or fewer types of development, with a mean of less than one restriction.

A second series of questions asked planners about specific actions that the jurisdiction might undertake in order to deal effectively with the Jarvis-Gann impacts. The fifteen specific actions presented in table 6-1 were identified as potential activities undertaken as a consequence of Proposition 13. For these questions the value 0 was given for a "no change" response, while the value 1 was given for "being considered" or "yes" responses. This coding slightly biases the results toward an indication of more activity than may have actually occurred. Scores on this index, rules-2, could range from 0 to 15, with higher

Table 6-5
Rules-1

Number of Responses Detrimental to Development	Number of Juris- dictions	Cumulative Frequency	Percentage	Cumulative Percentage
0	40	40	42.1	42.1
1	32	72	33.7	75.8
2	18	90	19.0	94.8
3	4	94	4.2	99.0
4	1	95	1.0	100.0

Mean = 0.88.
Standard deviation = 0.93.

scores indicating more restricting activities. Table 6-6 shows the frequency distribution of the responses.

At one end of the scale there were eight cities that did nothing. At the other end, no city did everything. The average number of actions that a jurisdiction either accomplished or considered was between four and five. Only three cities took more than ten actions in response to Proposition 13.[6]

If restrictions are important to developers, both of these indexes could be negatively related to construction. It is thus possible to respecify equation 6.4 as follows:

$$\overset{(-)}{} \quad \overset{(-)}{} \quad \overset{(+)}{} \quad \overset{(-)}{} \quad \overset{(+)}{} \quad \overset{(-)}{}$$
$$Q_j = \alpha_{04} + \alpha_{14} C_{xj} + \alpha_{24} R_{ukj} + \alpha_{34} Y_j + \alpha_{44} HD_j + \alpha_{54} E_j + \alpha_{64} T_j$$
$$+ \mu_{4j} \qquad\qquad (6.4a)$$

where

α_{04} = constant

α_{i4} = estimated coefficients (with hypothesized sign written above) for equation 6.4a

μ_{4j} = stochastic error

HD_j = housing density

R_{kj} = rule index k, $k = 1, 2$

Equation 5: The revenue equation is specified in a similar manner. Rules, construction, and charges are defined in the same manner as in equation 6.4a. Property-tax loss is defined as the difference between the estimated property-tax revenues for 1978–1979 and the actual revenues received for 1977–1978 (and thus it is always negative, because of the initiative). Equation 6.5a will be estimated (with the hypothesized signs above the coefficients):

$$\overset{(+)}{} \quad \overset{(-)}{} \quad \overset{(-)}{}$$
$$R_{ij} = \alpha_{05} + \alpha_{15} Q_j + \alpha_{25} TL_j + \alpha_{35} Cx_j + \mu_{5j} \qquad\qquad (6.5a)$$

Equation 6: The expenditure equation relates the expenditures for fiscal-year 1978–1979 to the expenditures in the previous fiscal year, tax revenues received, the income level of the community, the amount of new construction that occurred in the community, and the other revenues that the jurisdiction receives. Tax revenues received are the sum of the property-tax and the sales-tax revenues with some small other sources included. These taxes are all derived

Table 6–6
Rules-2

Number of New Activities Undertaken	Number of Jurisdictions	Cumulative Frequency	Percentage	Cumulative Percentage
0	8	8	8.4	8.4
1	10	18	10.5	18.9
2	9	27	9.5	28.4
3	10	37	10.5	38.9
4	12	49	12.6	51.6
5	13	62	13.7	65.3
6	12	74	12.6	77.9
7	8	82	8.4	86.3
8	6	88	6.3	92.6
9	3	91	3.2	95.8
10	1	92	1.1	96.8
11	1	93	1.1	97.9
12	0	93	0	97.9
13	2	95	2.1	100.0

Mean = 4.51.
Standard deviation = 3.1.

from the local tax base. Other revenues are defined as equal to the difference between the total revenues that the jurisdiction received and the tax revenues. Income is again defined as median household income, and construction is the same variable that has appeared in equations 6.4a and 6.5a. Equation 6.6a thus reads (with the hypothesized signs above the coefficients):

$$\ln E_{tj} = \overset{(+)}{\alpha_{06}} + \overset{(+)}{\alpha_{16}\ln E_{t-1,j}} + \overset{(3)}{\alpha_{26}\ln TR_j} + \overset{(+)}{\alpha_{36}\ln OR_j} + \overset{(+)}{\alpha_{46}\ln Y_j} + \alpha_{56}\ln Q_j$$
$$+ \mu_{6j} \qquad (6.6a)$$

where

$$\ln = \text{natural logarithm of the variable.}$$

Equation 7: The final equation relates tax revenues to construction and population. It is also solved simultaneously with the private-sector equation and the other two jurisdictional equations. Equation 6.7a can be specified:

$$\ln TR_j = \overset{(+)}{\alpha_{07}} + \overset{(+)}{\alpha_{17}\ln Q_j} + \alpha_{27}\ln POP_j + \mu_{7j} \qquad (6.7a)$$

In equations 6.6a and 6.7a total revenues and expenditures are specified rather than per-capita amounts because budget decisions are always made by decision makers examining the totals. Specific functional forms for the equations were chosen on the basis of fit. Two-stage least squares was the technique utilized to estimate the four equations simultaneously.

Results

The two rule indexes and two disaggregations of the charge variable result in four combinations of variables for equation 6.4a. Table 6-7 shows these results.

The regressions in the first two columns of table 6-7 use the first-defined rule index. Column 1 uses the aggregate of charges in the jurisdiction. Column 2 disaggregates total charges by subtracting fire-service charges and refuse charges from the total and introducing them separately.

The aggregated results are the best. Total charges are negatively and significantly related to the amount of construction—for every $100,000 increase in charges, new construction falls by nearly nine units. Previous years' expenditures are positive and significant; the local tax burden is negative, although not significant. Housing density is also negative. Income is negative and significant, and the rule index is positive and significant.

Total charges were disaggregated into those that were designed to be placed on the consumer (fire and refuse) and those that were designed to be placed on the supplier. These disaggregated results are somewhat less precise. Interestingly, the only charge variable that appears to be significant is fire-service charges. Developer and refuse charges are very imprecisely estimated. Columns 3 and 4 present results obtained when the second rule index is used. The overall results are slightly better. In column 4 refuse charges are negative but still not significant; income is negative but not significant; expenditures are negative (in column 4) but not significant; and housing density is negative and significant. All other results are very similar. For example, a $100,000 increase in total charges reduces new development by eight units. Column 5 of table 6-7 shows the results of estimating the construction equation without the rule index. This was done because it might be argued that if rules and charges are substitutes for each another, then perhaps only one should be included. These results have the same tenor as those in column 1.

Some conclusions can be drawn from these results. In all the equations there was at least one negative charge variable that was significant. However, in the disaggregated equations, when the charges that can be specifically placed on consumers are separated from those that are specifically placed on builders, it is the fire-service charge that is significantly different from zero, whereas the others seem to have little impact. It may be that builders assume that the charges can be passed on (whether they are or not) and thus do not take them into account.

Table 6-7
Construction Regressions

Left Hand Variable: Single-Family Dwelling Construction Permits

Right Hand Variables:	(1)	(2)	(3)	(4)	(5)
Intercept	129.18 (177.23)	219.83** (131.43)	23.4 (156.0)	9.28 (179.43)	283.96** (99.09)
Total Charges	-0.000089** (0.000035)		-0.000078** (0.000023)		-0.000055** (0.000019)
Developer charges		0.000032 (0.00011)		0.000054 (0.00012)	
Fire-service charges		-0.00032 (0.00017)		-0.00034** (0.00016)	
Refuse charges		0.000013 (0.000071)		-0.000042 (0.000079)	
Rules-1	318.38* (177.72)	201.75 (132.35)			
Rules-2			55.78** (23.79)	69.65* (35.39)	
Income	-0.044* (0.027)	-0.036* (0.021)	-0.0076 (0.013)	-0.011 (0.014)	-0.011 (0.012)
Housing density	-0.012 (0.041)	-0.043 (0.035)	-0.058** (0.023)	-0.061** (0.028)	-0.068** (0.021)
Expenditures	0.000011** (0.0000032)	0.0000062 (0.0000091)	0.0000099** (0.0000021)	-0.0000012 (0.000011)	0.0000079** (0.0000018)
Tax burden	-317.06 (1453.25)	-337.64 (1245.85)	-383.49 (1027.57)	75.33 (1243.18)	-491.89 (928.42)
SSE	7552089	4536353	3785228	4170316	3143189
MSE	114425.6	70880.5	57351.9	65161.2	46913.4

Standard errors are in parentheses.
*Significant at 5 percent.
**Significant at 10 percent.

In almost all the equations, expenditures have a positive impact and are significant. Furthermore, in almost all of the equations, the local tax burden is negative but is never significant. This may mean that movers are more aware of city services than of local taxes. Or it may indicate the consumer's perception that it really does not matter where he lives, since sales- and property-tax rates are invariant across jurisdictions. However, since fire-service charges are important, it may be that citizens are more concerned with some of the specific fees that do vary by jurisdiction. In any case, these results indicate that movers are at least somewhat concerned about fiscal variables.

The rule index is continually positive and significantly related to construction. There are several explanations for this unanticipated result, all of which require future work. The first is that the index is not measuring rules. Rather, it might well be measuring the degree to which localities become involved in the development sector, and indicating that those cities that react probably understand the problems of developers better than the cities that ignored the land-use effects. If this is so, the active jurisdictions might also be more amenable to allowing variances to their regulations, or not implementing or enforcing their rules and thereby actually encouraging development to take place. In this case development becomes an explicit decision by the jurisdiction. Only in the absence of this decision will the rules constrain. A second explanation might be more indirect. If local developers initially understand the jurisdiction's rules better than nonlocal developers, then they might construct quickly, since in the long run the rules and loopholes will become more generally known. A third explanation for the perverse sign is that there are other interactions that the model still has not accurately taken into account. In any case, it is clear that more work needs to be done in defining this variable.

Median family income also has an unanticipated sign and is significant in one of the equations. This may mean that wealthier households are not as interested in new developments when they look for dwelling places. More analysis also needs to be done for this variable.

The rule-equation results are quite robust (see table 6-8). In virtually every case the sign is exactly as anticipated, and in most cases the estimated coefficient is either significant or nearly so. The greater the amount of construction in the private sector, the greater the rule use in the public sector, the greater the property-tax loss, the greater the likelihood of imposing more restrictions.[7] Finally, there does appear to be a tradeoff between having a high level of charges on the one hand and rule use on the other.

Table 6-9 presents the results for both the expenditure and revenue equations. Both previous years' expenditures and revenue sources are significant and positive, as predicted. Previous expenditure patterns seem to have the highest elasticity, although the sum of the two revenue elasticities is larger, which may imply that revenues are more important than previous expenditure patterns. The other revenue elasticity is larger than the local-tax elasticity,

Table 6-8
Rules Regressions

Right-hand variables:	Left-hand variable: Rules-1		Left-hand variable: Rules-2	
	(1)	(2)	(3)	(4)
Intercept	0.48**	0.50**	3.15**	3.11**
	(0.16)	(0.16)	(0.48)	(0.52)
Construction	0.0016**	0.0012	0.0052**	0.0056**
	(0.00075)	(0.00089)	(0.0023)	(0.003)
Property-tax loss	-1.4×10^{-7}**	-2.12×10^{-7}**	-5.08×10^{-7}**	-4.48×10^{-7}**
	(4.71×10^{-8})	(8.50×10^{-8})	(1.46×10^{-7})	(2.76×10^{-7})
Total charge	-5.75×10^{-8}*		-1.94×10^{-7}**	
	(2.98×10^{-8})		(9.21×10^{-8})	
Developer charges		-3.59×10^{-8}		-2.11×10^{-7}
		(3.99×10^{-8})		(1.30×10^{-7})
Fire-service charges		-3.27×10^{-7}		-1.67×10^{-7}
		(6.66×10^{-7})		(2.16×10^{-6})
Refuse charges		-2.51×10^{-7}		5.27×10^{-8}
		(2.09×10^{-7})		(6.80×10^{-7})
SSE	51.5	47.16	491.42	495.57
MSE	0.75	0.70	7.12	7.40

*Significant at 5 percent.
**Significant at 10 percent.

Table 6-9
Revenue and Expenditure Regressions

Left-hand variable: LnE			Left-hand variable: LnLT		
Right-hand variable:	(1)[a]	(2)[b]	Right-hand variable:	(1)[a]	(2)[b]
Intercept	1.24*	1.24**	Intercept	7.05**	7.05**
	(0.63)	(0.63)		(1.21)	(1.21)
LnE_{t-1}	0.45**	0.45**	Ln Construction	0.66**	0.66**
	(0.12)	(0.12)		(0.15)	(0.15)
LnLT	0.19**	0.19	LnPOP	0.49**	0.49**
	(0.09)	(0.09)		(0.12)	(0.12)
LnOR	0.34**	0.34**			
	(0.05)	(0.05)			
LnY	-0.066	-0.066			
	(0.056)	(0.056)			
Ln Construction	-0.019	-0.019			
	(0.024)	(0.024)			
SSE	1.51	1.51		105.41	105.41
MSE	0.02	0.02		1.51	1.51

*Significant at 5 percent.
**Significant at 10 percent.
[a]Using rules-1, total charges (other results virtually identical).
[b]Using rules-2, total charges (other results virtually identical).

which indicates that other revenue sources stimulated expenditures more. Once again the median-family-income variable has the wrong sign, but it is not significant. Interestingly, the amount of new construction does not seem to have much impact on the level of city expenditures, since it is never significantly different from zero (in fact, its sign is consistently negative). An explanation of this may be that it is total expenditures that are represented by the left-hand variable in the regression. This relationship might well be demonstrating that the quality of service has fallen in order to keep total expenditures constant. This would be the equivalent of a downward shift in the A locus derived in figure 3-4D of chapter 3.

The local-taxes-collected equation, 6.7a, is also quite good. All the variables are significant and in the postulated direction. Construction is positively related to local taxes, and local-tax revenue also increases as population increases. It is interesting to note that in this simple model new construction does not seem to have much impact on expenditures, yet is quite important for revenues.

With the exception of the rules and income variables in the first equation, the system does quite well. Nearly all the other signs are as anticipated, and the levels of significance are generally quite high. As a first approximation, this model seems to indicate that there are significant simultaneous relationships between the private and public sectors. It indicates that by imposing charges on consumers and developers, a jurisdiction can significantly lower the amount of new construction that occurs. But as the revenue and expenditure equations demonstrate, this new construction might have added to the revenues while not affecting the expenditure levels much at all (although service quality might have fallen).

Several extensions of this model are possible. Actual revenues and expenditures, as opposed to those budgeted, might be a better measure. More research must be done to establish either better measures of rule use or better interpretations of the measure used in this study. Another way to extend the model would be through the development of data on selling prices for residential construction. If these prices could be determined, then the structural equations could be estimated and the specific impacts of rules and charges on both demand and supply could be determined. Another result of this structural estimation would be the calculation of the extent of forward shifting of the charges by the developer.

An additional enlargement of the model would be to include multifamily construction as well as commercial and industrial development. An enlarged model would be more useful for the purpose of determining the impacts of development and the local budget on each another.

Notes

1. Ninety-five cities in the sample also reported their revenue and expenditure data to the state. The state sample consisted of 372 out of 417 cities. Test results for this and all other tests are available from the author.

2. One jurisdiction responded by eliminating the planning commission.

3. Other case studies replicate these results. Walker et al. (1980) have found definite cutbacks in prosecution and law-enforcement activities, ranging from not prosecuting certain types of crime (nonviolent misdeamors in San Joaquin County) to having police ignore "minor stuff." Chapman (1980) has found deterioration in support services for the Los Angeles Police Department, which has led to an increase in response time to nonemergency calls.

4. In any case, cross-sectional expectations about appreciation are unlikely to vary across jurisdictions.

5. All data are reported for the fiscal year immediately following the passage of the Jarvis-Gann initiative.

6. The simpe correlation between rules-1 and rules-2 is 0.45.

7. Since property-tax loss is defined as a negative number, the negative sign in the estimates is consistent with the theory.

Some Long-Run Land-Use Problems: Rent Control, Development, and Debt

This chapter will examine in detail three areas related to land use that appear to have been affected by Proposition 13: rent control, local development, and local debt. Because these phenomena take time to unfold, there are incentives for decision makers to defer analysis of their implications. Yet their long-run impacts may be important.

Rent control was never explicitly mentioned in the text of Proposition 13. If anything, at times the campaign for the initiative explicitly promised renters that they would receive some of their landlords' tax savings. But after the initiative's passage there were few cases of this, and apartment rents continued to rise. In response, cities began to consider rent controls. The first section of this chapter will examine this phenomenon.

Development was seriously affected by the initiative. With a lowering of property-tax revenues that could be generated from any particular type of development, the incentives appeared to change in favor of growth slowdown. The second section of the chapter will analyze the future of residential and commercial development in California.

The third section will examine the new role of debt finance for California municipalities. Included in this section will be an analysis of the immediate impact of the proposition on existing debt, followed by a discussion of new ways of financing capital projects.

The last section of the chapter will focus on the land-use implications of these three topics. It will draw on the previous analysis to offer predictions concerning the impacts of the present course of events.

Rent Control

The California rental market has been characterized by large imbalances over the last twenty years (Capozza 1979, p. 64). At times the market for apartments has been tight and rents have increased rapidly, as was true in the early 1950s and the late 1970s. However, there have also been extraordinarily long stretches of time in which rents have increased quite slowly. For example, between these two time periods in Los Angeles County, rents rose by less than 2.5 percent per year (Capozza 1979, p. 60). This was slower than the rate of increase of construction costs (4.7-percent-per-year growth during this time) and is probably the result of an excessive supply of apartments. Since a large proportion of rent increases can be traced to construction-cost increases and vacancy rates (Capozza 1979, p. 77), it was only a matter of time before this excess was absorbed by the increasing California population and rents began to rise. Between 1976 and 1979 they rose between 6 and 10 percent a year.

It was in this atmosphere that the campaign for Proposition 13 was conducted. Renters were led to believe that if the initiative was successful, landlords would reduce rents and pass on the tax savings to tenants. At one point during the campaign, Howard Jarvis advocated that apartment owners promise to lower (or maintain) rents in order to convince tenants to support the measure (Kirlin and Frates 1979, p. 1).[1] But after the proposition passed, rents continued to increase and in some cases rose dramatically. It is useful to attempt to explain what went wrong.

Tenants may have made two fundamental errors in their analysis. The first was that they ignored the effect of the tax reduction on the price of buildable vacant land. To the extent that this tax reduction was capitalized into the price of land, so that its selling price rose, new apartment construction would become more expensive. At equilibrium the rents charged for new apartments would be the same as those charged for comparable old apartments. On the margin, rents would not change.

However, the analysis is different for landlords who had already owned apartments. If they had been shifting the property tax to their tenants, then their profit margins increased after the initiative passed. However, if this tax reduction was capitalized into their property value (which then increased), their rate of return would remain the same even with the increased profits. There would be no incentive to reduce rents.[2]

In any case, neither rent reductions nor stability materialized. Tenants coalesced into powerful political-action groups and put pressure on local politicians to implement rent-control ordinances. Within eighteen months of the passage of Proposition 13, nine jurisdictions had implemented rent controls, eighteen additional jurisdictions were considering them, and they had been defeated in an additional twenty jurisdictions (Kirlin and Frates 1979, p. 4).

The traditional textbook case of rent-control analysis assumes a competitive market with a homogeneous unit of housing service. With downward-sloping demand and upward-sloping supply, the imposition of a rent ceiling below the equilibrium rent would lead to a fall in the number of rental units supplied. In figure 7-1, if rents are controlled at price P_1, which is below the market-equilibrium price P_0, there will be a fall in the number of units suppled to level Q_1 from Q_0, and an excess demand of $Q_3 - Q_1$ will exist. Over time either non-price rationing of apartments will occur (with such factors as "who you know" becoming more important that the traditional price mechanism). If there is an increase in marginal costs of apartment provision, then the supply curve will shift upward (to S' in figure 7-1); the number of dwelling units supplied will fall (to Q_4); and excess demand will increase.

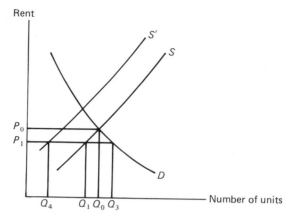

Figure 7-1. The Market for Apartments

However, if landlords have the option of allowing the unit to deteriorate, then the output of housing services will fall, although the price per unit of housing services will increase. It is possible to reach an equilibrium with no excess demand or nonprice rationing, since quality variance will take the place of price as an allocation mechanism (Frankena 1974; Arnault 1975). If demand increases or costs increase, there will continue to be a decline in quality (reflected in a fall of maintenance expenditures). It is possible for landlords to make a short-run profit in this case if the fall in the output of housing services reduces costs by more than the amount the rent-control constraint reduces revenues. A typical response to this reaction is to enforce housing codes strictly, which reduces landlords' profits and thus reduces incentives for other investors to enter the market. Note that if decontrol is allowed after a voluntary vacancy, landlords have the incentive to reduce maintenance so that tenants will vacate and the unit will be returned to the market (Eastin 1979, p. 33).

There are two important second-order effects. The tenants, in the aggregate, purchase less housing and more nonhousing services because of artificially low rents. This leads to an inefficient resource allocation in the economy, with too many inputs being allocated to the nonhousing sector (Eastin 1979, p. 48). Furthermore, the composition of apartment construction may not follow consumer preferences, since with the large excess demand landlords can easily rent units (Edelstein 1979).

Most of the empirical work seems to support the theoretical argument (for example, Eastin 1979; Moorehouse 1972). Maintenance does seem to fall in most cases, and when there is decontrol upon a vacancy, attempted evictions tend to occur for rather small contract violations.[3] The one contrary study (Gilderbloom 1978) discovered that the ratio of maintenance expenses to rents did not fall in New Jersey under rent control; however, this finding could as easily reflect an increasing maintenance-cost figure being divided by a frozen rental base. Furthermore, his work uses a definition of rent control that is more moderate than the types of controls that appear to be enacted in California. Even Gilderbloom admits that more stringent controls are probably harmful and that his analysis is basically short run (1978, pp. 1-2).

Equity issues of rent control are not always straightforward. A true evaluation of the income-distribution impacts of controls should consider not only the tenant and the landlord but also present and future apartment dwellers, lenders, construction workers, home owners, and apartment dwellers.

Although rent control is a straightforward redistribution of income from the landlord to the tenant, even this conclusion is subject to qualification. Tenants are locked into their apartments, since they must continue to live in them in order to receive the benefits of the lower rents. Tenant mobility may be diminished. Furthermore, if there were the possibility of controls being implemented when the building was being sold, the selling price was likely to reflect this risk and the original owners might have borne part of the burden.

Since rent controls reduce the landlord's rate of return and make the apartment sector less attractive to investors vis-à-vis other sectors, it is likely that less investment in apartment construction will occur compared to what would have occurred without controls. Present apartment dwellers are not necessarily hurt by this (unless they wish to move), but future apartment dwellers are significantly disadvantaged. These new dwellers are likely to be either new in-migrants to the region or young people leaving their parents' homes. There is no reason why these individuals should be forced to bear the burden for those already in apartments.

Lending institutions face riskier loan opportunities if they lend to developers interested in apartment construction in rent-controlled areas, since developers' profits are squeezed. If they do loan, the interest rates developers face (and perhaps those faced by all borrowers if the institution desires to spread the risk) will be higher. This makes the project less profitable and less likely to be undertaken.

Construction workers also bear some of the burden if apartment construction slows down and if there is not a complete offset into new residential construction.

Finally, there are long-run impacts on the jurisdictional budget. With less apartment construction, the tax base grows more slowly than it would have if the controls had not been implemented. Furthermore, if the income method of assessment is utilized, the value of the current property-tax base value grows more slowly than anticipated.[4] To raise the same amount of revenue, the city must then impose higher property-tax rates on the entire base. For Fort Lee, New Jersey, a rent-controlled community, after five years of controls, it has been calculated that single-family dwellings were paying over 14 percent more in property taxes than they would have had to pay if there had been no controls (Sternlieb and Hughes (1979).

The principal gainer under rent control is the present tenant. The losers under rent control are the present landlords, the past owner, future apartment dwellers, individuals who take out loans from lending institutions, construction workers, and the single-family home owner. It is legitimate to ask if this is a reasonable situation.

Horizontal equity argues that economic equals should be treated equally. Rent control fails miserably in this case. A landlord who receives income from apartment rentals is treated quite differently from a worker who receives income from labor. Renters are treated differently from home owners in the same economic situation, since the renters are paying below-market prices for the same bundle of housing services for which home owners are paying (imputed) market prices. There is also no guarantee of vertical equity; people in different economic circumstances are not treated differently. High-income tenants may well benefit as much as low-income tenants under controls, because rents may vary by age of building or length of tenancy, rather than by income.[5]

One phenomenon in the post-Proposition 13 California economy that is associated with the potential or actual imposition of rent controls is the conversion of apartments into condominiums. These conversions grow out of two trends: the fall in profitability of apartment ownership and the increase in demand for home ownership.

Rent control, as previously noted above, severely cramps the operating profits of landlords. If these controls exist during a time of rising operating expenses, the profits are constrained even more. In California, with increases in fuel, utilities, and maintenance occurring rapidly during the past few years, and with rent control becoming more and more likely in major urban areas, it became rational for owners of rental units to consider the option of converting rental units to condominiums and selling them.[6] Because the demand for home ownership has increased in California, as described in chapter 5, there has been a ready market for these condominiums. A rising percentage of retired persons, families whose children have grown and moved out to their own dwelling units, rising housing costs, and changing tastes and preferences are also reasons for the increase in demand for condominium ownership (Ishino 1979, pp. 34-35).

Just as rent controls reflect conflicts between present tenants, landlords, and future tenants, condominium conversions reflect conflicts between present renters and present potential home purchasers. At the state level California regulates condominium developments through the Subdivided Lands Act and the Subdivision Map Act. The first is a disclosure measure designed to prevent fraud and misrepresentation by developers. The relevant sections of the Subdivision Map Act ensure that approval be given by the local authorities and that no conversion approval be given until the tenants receive 120 days written notice, and that the tenants have the first right of purchase. In addition to the state laws, local governments have also enacted condominium-conversion ordinances to protect renters. For example, over two-thirds of the cities in the San Francisco Bay Area have either ordinances, proposals, or policy statements regarding conversions. This is in part a response to the yearly increase of converted units from the over 500 converted in 1975 to about 7,400 converted in 1979 (Ishino 1979, pp. 21, 52–55).[7] Typically, local ordinances are concerned with six substantive areas: tenant protection, tenant relocation, provisions to upgrade the apartment building, consumer-protection provisions, provisions to facilitate home ownership, and provisions to protect the rental stock. The constraints are usually severe. In at least one instance, these types of ordinances have had some effect. In Los Angeles only twenty new applications for condominium conversions were filed in all of December 1979 and January and February 1980 (*Los Angeles Times,* Feb. 24, 1970, p. 1).[8] However, it is still too soon to evaluate the impact that these ordinances will have on the housing stocks of jurisdictions.

Empirically, there is still not yet enough data to permit an adequate examination of the impact of the rent-control ordinances in California in anything more rigorous than a case-study method. It is useful to look at four cases to attempt to discern the effects of the various control ordinances.

In 1973, Berkeley, California enacted a Neighborhood Preservation Ordinance that effectively stopped the destruction of older single-family dwellings and two- or three-unit apartments. Since there is little properly zoned land in Berkeley still available for new apartment construction, this ordinance stopped the construction of larger apartment units. Berkeley had also enacted a rent-control ordinance in the mid-1970s, but it was invalidated by the courts as being too confiscatory of landlords' property rights. In November 1978 a second rent-control ordinance was passed. This initiative was directly linked to Proposition 13, since it forced apartment owners to pass 80 percent of the Proposition 13 tax savings to the tenant for 1979. After January 1, 1980, rents can increase, but any increase greater than 5 percent must be justified. There are some exceptions, and the tenants administer the controls by withholding rents and forcing the landlord to go to court to justify increases.

The controls had no apparent effect on apartment construction, since this had been drastically cut back because of the 1973 ordinance. However, there was a rapid increase in condominium conversions from approximately five units per year preceding the ordinance to eighty-one units in the ten months following its passage. The city has recently enacted a conversion moratorium (Kirlin and Frates 1979, p. 6).

The Beverly Hills City Council enacted a rent-control ordinance in September 1978. Rents were initially rolled back to May 1978 levels, but were allowed to be raised if there were voluntary vacancies, as well as by a fixed percentage each year. Units with rents greater than $600 were exempted. Again, there appears to have been little initial effect of the ordinance. There have been no applications to build apartments since the ordinance was passed, but applications have averaged less than two a year over the last five years (Kirlin and Frates 1979, p. 7). Furthermore, since 1975 there have been virtually no condominiums converted from apartments. In that year Beverly Hills enacted a conversion ordinance that forced major structural modifications to be made in order for the conversion to be undertaken.

The Los Angeles City Council, under pressure from tenants who had expected rents to fall, enacted a rent-control ordinance in August 1978. This ordinance initially rolled back rents to May 31, 1978 levels, but it was later amended to allow for a percentage increase that varied according to when the last rent increase had occurred. Voluntary vacancies exempted the apartment from controls for the initial rent of the tenant. Although it was enacted for one year, the ordinance has since been annually renewed with modifications. It is administered by the city council and a landlord-tenant mediation board. Unfortunately, Los Angeles does not differentiate between types of multifamily construction, and thus there is no way of knowing whether apartment construction has increased or decreased. However, it does appear that there was a rush to convert apartments to condominiums after the passage of the controls. Table 7-1 shows that there was a significant increase in both the number of apartment units converted to condominiums and the number of applications for conversion in 1979, the year after the ordinance.[9]

A study at the University of California at Los Angeles, undertaken one year after the Los Angeles ordinance was put in effect, discovered that about 25 percent of tenants in the city moved during the past year and thus about 25 percent of the apartments were decontrolled. The rent increases in the decontrolled units were between two and three times higher than the ordinance allowed for nonmovers (7 percent). Because of this, Los Angeles considered eliminating the decontrol feature of the ordinance. However, the feature was maintained for one more year. Slightly less than 5 percent of the tenants were evicted, with the tenants reporting that the principal cause for eviction was

Table 7-1
Condominium Conversions in Los Angeles

	1977	*1978*	*1979*
Apartment units converted to condominiums	88	1190	1701[a]
Applications for conversion	184 (11,705 units)	94 (3,909 units)	213 (7,259 units)

Source: John J. Kirlin and Steven B. Frates, "Impacts of Rent Control upon the Housing Stock of Selected California Cities" (Sacramento: Sacramento Public Affairs Center, 1979). Reprinted with permission. "Conversions Slow, City Officials Believe," *Los Angeles Times,* February 24, 1980, p. 12.

[a]Through September, 1979.

that the landlord wanted the unit or that there was to be a condominium conversion. However, the landlords reported that the principal reason for eviction was nonpayment of rent. Vacancy rates in Los Angeles are currently less than 1 percent (Institute for Social Science Research 1980).

The Santa Monica rent-control ordinance, enacted through the initiative process in April 1979, is by far the strictest in the state. With virtually no loopholes, it froze and rolled back rents, limited rent increases, stopped condominium conversions, and forbid demolition of any rental units for any purpose. There was no vacancy decontrol, and the removal of any rental unit from the market was virtually forbidden. The law is administered by a rent-control board, with an annual budget in 1979-1980 of over $600,000, an amount that is expected to increase by several hundred thousand dollars in the next fiscal year (Baker 1980, p. 7).

The Santa Monica rent-control ordinance passed on a second attempt by a 54-46 margin. However, landlords were well aware of the possibility of rent control, and in the year preceding its passage they took dramatic actions. Tentative agreement was given in that year for the conversion of over 3,000 apartments to condominiums (whereas in 1977 70 units were converted) (Mitchell 1979, p. 1). Furthermore, nearly 900 units were demolished in the fourteen weeks prior to the passage of the ordinance, and new apartment construction appears to have virtually stopped. It has been estimated that prior to the passage of the initiative, nearly 7.5 percent of the total city population was affected and perhaps displaced (Kirlin and Frates 1979, pp. 18-19). The key to the Santa Monica ordinance is the rent-control board.

Any landlord who wants higher rents must file a formal application and convince one of the board's examiners that the increase is justified. The case must be heard within 65 days of application; if there is an appeal, it must be decided within 120 days of the original filing. The rent-control board has broadly defined its own powers. For example, the board has insisted that illegally constructed apartments are covered by the rent-control law and has threatened to sue other city departments if attempts are made to close them down without board approval (Baker 1980, p. 7). A *Los Angeles Times* survey of the landlord's applications indicates that while slightly more than two-thirds of the landlords have been successful in applying for a rent increase, the average increase granted was less than one-fourth the amount asked. Appealing the hearing examiners' findings to the board as a whole did little good, since over 80 percent of the hearing examiners' findings were upheld (Baker and Specht 1980, p. 1). In order to be at least partially successful, the rent increases had to cover higher property taxes, utility bills, and building improvements, although since the examiners typically ruled that the costs of improvements must be collected over several years, some rent increases of only $1 per month have been allowed. Rent increases because of negative cash flows (over 70 percent of the applications) are usually not granted (Baker and Specht 1980, p. 1).

Typically, the enactment of these controls can be traced to the rising expectations of renters concerning the benefits of Proposition 13. When rents went up rather than down, the rent-control response became important.

But even if rent controls are considered to be false promises, it is still necessary to be concerned with the impacts that the unbridled market might have on certain segments of society. In particular, the elderly are often hard hit by raises in rents. Unless society is willing to say that the elderly should automatically move if rents go up, some help for them must be enacted.

The typical theoretical responses to this problem take two forms: Treat income-distribution problems as separate from housing problems, or stimulate more housing so that in the long run housing costs will not increase so fast. Neither is a short-term panacea.

Income-distribution schemes at the local level are nearly always doomed to failure. If taxes are imposed on firms or workers can move away, and if there are no barriers to entry into the jurisdiction, then the principal reaction to these plans will be to drive the wealthy out and encourage the poor to enter— a counterproductive situation. The obvious place for income-distribution activities to occur is at the national level, for in this case it is difficult to avoid the effects. This means that such policies as more progressive tax rates or higher allowances for age or handicaps provide a more appropriate method for aiding the elderly. If local governments feel the necessity for implementing some redistribution plan, they should investigate such a program as a voucher system, in which the city gives the benefited groups vouchers to use for rental payments and then redeems them from the landlords. This, or other types of rent-subsidy programs, gives a more efficient allocation of resources.

However, a typical problem of these types of programs is that they cost money, and after Proposition 13 governments in California are far more likely to attempt to have the private sector pay for programs then to take over the programs themselves. Under rent control (exclusive of administration costs) most of the costs of the program are borne by the private sector, in terms of reduced landlord income and reduced construction. If rental increases are to be minimized in the future, it appears likely that additional private-sector development must be encouraged. This encouragement can come from the relaxation of many of the constraints that now face development. In particular, zoning restrictions might be modified; and rent control, condominium conversion ordinances, and other controls on the profitability of construction must be reduced. In addition to relaxing the constraints, proactive legislation, such as awarding density bonuses to developers or carefully waiving some environmental considerations, might well encourage construction of additional rental units. Finally, if inflation rates can be curtailed, construction costs will not rise so rapidly perhaps profitability of apartments will increase, leading to more construction. Eliminating rent control, will not in itself stimulate enough construction to solve the apartment problem. But it is a major step along the way.

The Future of Development

In this section general-development issues will be analyzed, with particular emphasis on some of the practical questions that jurisdictions face. It should be considered as an extension of the analysis of chapters 3 and 6.

New development affects the revenues of a jurisdiction in at least three ways. By directly increasing the property value of a piece of land, it increases the property-tax base of the city. Even after Jarvis-Gann, new construction is initially placed on the rolls at market value and then is increased at the 2-percent rate each year until it is sold. The convergence of the total property-tax revenue in any jurisdiction toward a level based on the market value depends on the turnover rate in that jurisdiction. The average turnover rate for California counties in fiscal-year 1976–1977 was 0.183, which indicates that on a statewide average, property turned over about once every five and one-half years.[10] However, this aggregate masks a wide variation in rates, which ranged from 0.091 in Imperial County to 0.357 in Humboldt County (Balderston et al. 1979). A second way in which development influences revenues is through its associated economic activity. Sales-tax revenues and fees and charges are examples since they typically increase as development increases. A third way in which new development affects revenues is by increasing the size of the jurisdiction. For example, revenue sharing has as part of its formula the population of the recipient jurisdiction; as the jurisdiction grows, these revenues increase.

Public expenditures and growth are also linked. With a greater population to serve, city departments need more inputs to provide constant levels of service. These inputs increase expenditures. Furthermore large developments can necessitate the establishment of additional capital infrastructure. Of course, if there is slack within the city, the marginal development will impose few costs. But often the fear of future expenditures for the development plays an important role in the jurisdiction's willingness to allow the development to occur.

What is important is an accurate forecast of the expected revenues and costs of any particular development. A new generation of local fiscal-impact models is now used in analyzing development in California. These models, typically computerized, forecast future revenues and expenditures for developments as the jurisdictions attempt to quantify development impacts.

Unfortunately, the current levels of fiscal-impact analysis leave something to be desired. Although there have been no retrospective tests of their accuracy in California, a nationwide study of 140 different fiscal-impact statements found that 20 percent were either incomplete, incomprehensible, or incorrect; 50 percent could not be evaluated for accuracy; and 60 percent could not be replicated without using the same staff that did the initial study. The models also often contain a built-in bias: They exaggerate future service costs, since they tend to project the number of children per household based on 1970 census data. They also tend to ignore the indirect revenue flows that accrue because of development. In these cases most studies show that residential development does not pay. However, until a track record of proven accuracy is established, fiscal-impact statements should be considered as only one dimension of the development's evaluation.

Residential Construction

Given the growing and changing California population, new residential housing is needed if California is to continue to grow without forcing firms to relocate where the price of housing is cheaper. Yet there are currently economic incentives on both the developer and the jurisdiction to restrict the supply of housing. With an increasing demand and a decreasing supply, the market for new development will reach equilibrium at a high price and at a quantity that is smaller than that hoped for by many citizens.[11]

Many residential-housing concerns surround the possibility of a slowdown in the supply of housing. This issue was highlighted by the May 1979 report of the California State Office of Planning and Research (OPR) (OPR 1979), entitled, "New Housing: Paying its Way?" This report examined the fiscal-impact statements of ten housing projects in ten different cities and discovered that each of the projects would either lose money or would force a reduction in city-service levels. The implication of the results was that only very expensive housing would provide enough revenues, or that infilling of vacant land was the most effective type of development for the city to encourage.[12] If this conclusion was accepted by cities, strong barriers would be erected against residential developers and there would be a drop in home construction.

Within months the construction industry responded with a series of critiques of the study.[13] Although the criticisms were numerous, they fit into four basic categories:

1. OPR had managed to select only those studies with a negative fiscal impact. The construction industry was able to identify several projects that did have positive fiscal impacts on the local jurisdictions. Furthermore, the industry argued, old developments pay even less of their way than new developments.

2. OPR ignored problems in the methodology of the studies. Some of the studies apparently included all capital cost in the first year of operation, with no amortization. Others ignored revenues that accrue with growth, such as state subventions, reimbursements, charges, federal revenue sharing, some types of federal block grants, and specialized revenues (from, say, golf courses or stadiums). Also, some of the studies did not allow for resale appreciation of the homes, and several of the studies assumed continuation of SB 154, a logical but inaccurate assumption.

3. OPR implicitly assumed that new development should pay its way. If this is true, then very little new housing should be built, but commercial and industrial construction should be encouraged. OPR has little to say about where the workers should live.
4. OPR ignored the economic reality that infill areas are vacant because they are expensive to build on or because there are government-imposed constraints on the type of construction allowed. Furthermore, since industrial and commercial developments need large amounts of land, they will still occur on the fringe. With only infill residential construction, transportation costs will increase and there is likely to be a degradation of air quality.

In any case, cities are concerned about the fiscal payoff of development. Table 7-2, derived from the city-planner survey used in chapter 6, indicates that revenue-development potential and costs are crucial considerations for permitting development, although political considerations were the most mentioned factor. It is also interesting that service provision was not considered particularly important by many cities, although the costs of provision were.

In order to guarantee that the fiscal payoff is positive, local jurisdictions have been imposing new and increased fees, infrastructure requirements, and planning pressures on the developer. When these don't make the development "profitable," they attempt to sit down with the developer and negotiate terms of the development. Under these conditions it is possible to force development to be fiscally sound.

As discussed in chapters 3 and 6, California local governments are increasing development fees. However, the fees' revenue-raising capability is quite limited, since many of the activities are not easily priced and the fees are limited to the costs of the services.[14]

Table 7-2
Major Factors Influencing Cities' Land-Use Policies

Factor	Number of Cities Mentioning Factor	Percentage of Cities Mentioning Factor
Politics	50	44
Revenues	47	41
Development	43	38
Cost	34	30
Laws	32	28
Conservation	30	26
Service provision	17	15
Staffing	3	3

$N = 111$; cities could name more than one factor.

Even before Proposition 13, local governments were finding it difficult to finance capital infrastructure. Whereas in the past local governments provided a large share of the financing of public improvements, a trend toward shifting of the financial responsibility for the improvements to the developer had been occurring even before 1978 (McTighe 1979, p. I-1). Proposition 13's passage accelerated the trend since it virtually eliminated debt financing. To provide infrastructure, local governments were forced to pressure developers to provide such items as parks, school facilities, and streets and utility lines constructed to extremely high standards. These pressures increase the marginal costs of the developer. Marginal costs also increased because these front-end financing costs are similar to an excise tax on land that is changing in use, since the tax is paid only if the land use is changed. Marginal land will not be developed, but will be held off the market until it becomes more profitable to develop (Shulman 1979). This restricts supply and will cause land prices to rise faster than in the past.

The third pressure that the jurisdiction imposes on the developer is that of increased uncertainty arising in the permit and planning process. This uncertainty arises in at least three areas: the planning stage, the setting-of-development-standards stage, and the regulation phase. In each, effective reforms could be implemented to reduce developer risks while protecting consumers (Kolis 1979, p. 4).

Although it may be argued that binding comprehensive plans minimize uncertainty in practice, they may not have this effect. This is because they may be administered in terms of "spirit" rather than substance. They may be immutable in ways that the developer might not like, yet undependable for the establishment of a permanent set of development rights (Kolis 1979, p. 5). If development standards are written precisely so as to minimize risk, they may become obsolete over time, yet difficult to improve or update. But if the standards are vaguely written, then enforcement may be unpredictable (Kolis 1979, p. 5). The only feasible solution may be the establishment of a set of procedures that allow for local governments and developers to establish standards. Procedural fairness may also be a problem in the regulatory process. If new regulations can be added after the construction process has begun, the developer is again faced with increased uncertainty.

These planning pressures, together with the increased fee and infrastructure demands, lead to the conclusion that the normal development process in California will be slow. More and more people will be bidding for homes that are increasing in supply at a very slow rate.

The state has attempted to ensure that housing will be available for low- and moderate-income families. The state Department of Housing and Community Development argues that the local jurisdiction must attempt to satisfy the housing needs of the community and that the community can force a developer to provide a specified amount of low- and moderate-income housing

(Connerly and Associates 1979). Although this argument is resisted by many jurisdictions, a large number have enacted programs to do this. Called inclusionary housing programs since they include rather than exclude low- and moderate-income residents, these programs may force the developer to sell some of his units at substantial discounts from the market price. Typically, the buyers must have an annual family income of 80 to 120 percent of the median California or regional income (which translates into an income from about $16,000 to about $24,000); and prices must be between two and one-half and three times income, or between $40,000 and $72,000 (Hill 1980, p. 29).

However, this program has some unforeseen impacts. For most projects, if the developer wishes to maintain the same profit margin, prices or rents will have to be increased on the units not included in the program. Some examples of price increases necessary for the same profit margin range from 10.6 percent for a single-family detached unit in a 100-unit total development to 3.2 percent for a single-family detached unit in a 30-unit total development. Rent increases attributable solely to this program would be about 4 percent (Connerly and Associates 1979, pp. 57–74).[15] Note that the increment to the property-tax base might be lower under this program than otherwise, because of the lower selling prices.

There are at least five effects of an inclusionary program. In addition to the price of the market units increasing to compensate the owners, and the property tax base of the city not being as high, there are three potential income-distribution effects. The families that buy or live in the below-market-rate units benefit at the same time that families that may make slightly more than 20 percent above the mean income are squeezed out of the housing market; families that purchase the more expensive units subsidize families that purchased the below-market units; and many low-income households (those with income below 80 percent of the median) will not be helped at all (Connerly and Associates 1979, p. 99).

In order to encourage development where there are inclusionary laws, jurisdictions must find a way for the developer to enjoy profits at the same time that he is selling housing at below-market prices. The principal ways in which local California governments are attempting to do this are by speeding up the approval process and by granting density bonuses (that is, allowing developers to build more units per acre than the general plan would have permitted).

Speeding up the approval process probably has fewer negative effects than almost any other action that the local jurisdiction can undertake. Its principal drawback is that sloppily drawn plans might be approved, especially with the current cutbacks that are occurring in planning departments since the passage of Proposition 13. However, by lowering land-holding opportunity costs, this incentive could be quite powerful.

Assembly Bill 1151 mandates that local jurisdictions must provide a 25-

percent density bonus or other significant incentives for any development containing 25 percent affordable housing.[16] This density bonus is valuable only if land is scarce. If land is plentiful, density bonuses do not help very much. Increased density does have some negative effects, however, especially if the density is far above what was previously planned. The preexisting infrastructure may be too small to handle the increased population cases, and regional problems such as air quality or wastewater treatment might be aggravated (Connerly and Associates 1979, pp. 76-77).

Inclusionary programs are rapidly becoming more important in California. The Coastal Commission has an inclusionary program; and as the commission is phased out, it plans to pressure the fifty-three cities and fifteen counties within its jurisdictions to implement similar programs. Orange County in Southern California has also implemented an inclusionary program that calls for the eventual construction of 45,000 units (Hill 1980, p. 1). At least forty-four towns and counties are drafting inclusionary programs. About 2,500 units were built in 1979, and the trend is increasing.[17]

Builders have varying reactions to the programs. Those that have made profits under the programs are not antagonistic; those that are less successful think that the programs do not really work (Connerly and Associates 1979, p. 101). It does appear that the density-relaxed construction standards and approval speedups play an important role in encouraging the developer to participate.[18]

Commercial-Industrial Properties

Although most of the discussion in California has been concerned with residential construction, Proposition 13 should also have an impact on other types of city development. Because of the reduced revenues from the property-tax system, cities and counties are even more dependent on the types of revenues that arise from commercial and industrial development.[19] The principal tax revenue from these sources is the sales tax.

Since 1957 the California sales tax has been collected by the state, and 1 cent out of every dollar of sales is returned to the jurisdiction in which the sale occurred. This puts a premium on the type of development that both add to the property-tax base and increases sales-tax revenues. Proposition 13 increased this premium. The principal question for the jurisdictions now is how to encourage this type of development.

In the past the principal means of encouraging commercial development has been the use of tax-increment financing (see chapter 4). However, this technique is now less useful. The new ways of stimulating private economic development must be different from those of the past.

The first key to new development must be an awareness of the multiplicity of federal grants. For example, Urban Development Action Grants or general revenue sharing might be used to help improve the urban infrastructure to attract commercial enterprises. Low-cost loans to businesses from the local jurisdiction are also useful in attracting development.[20] A third factor (and major change from the past) is that an incremental approach to revitalizing commercial districts may be undertaken (Williams 1978), with careful analysis of individual developments. Finally, there must be greater reliance on the initiative of private entrepreneurs. The jurisdictions will have to stimulate interest by offering unique incentives for each project.

This last strategic element appears to have a great deal of promise. Local jurisdictions have regulatory powers to use in bargaining with developers. Developers can promote projects that can lead to an increase in jurisdictional revenues. There is room for bargaining around development. There are at least three examples of this occurring (Kirlin and Chapman in press, pp. 5–8).

Santa Monica was in the midst of a downtown-renewal plan in a redevelopment district when Proposition 13 was passed. The projected revenue loss was about $650,000, and the entire project could have collapsed. However, an agreement was reached between the city, the general partners in the development, and the department stores in the development, which rescued the project. According to this agreement the city will receive an amount approximately equal to the lost tax increment, to be paid annually until the tax-allocation bonds are retired. The developers get the opportunity to complete the project and will end up paying less in contributions to the city than what their tax payments would have been, as well as knowing that in the future their additional payments will end as the bonds are retired.

In Napa, a municipality in the Northern California wine country, the city had assembled land and was about to construct two parking garages and to reorient streets for a project when Proposition 13 was passed. After some bargaining, the developer agreed to build a large department store and satellite shops in the project area. The city will receive 10 percent of the excess of rents over costs on the satellite shops, and 10 percent of the proceeds of any refinancing within the thirty-year term of the agreement. Revenues to fund the bonds issued for the garage construction and street work were pieced together from the remaining tax-increment funds and increased parking fees. Finally, much of the increased sales-tax revenues and business-license fees generated by the development will go to bond retirement rather than to service provision.

A regional shopping center was the subject of negotiations in Fairfield, California. The city undertook public improvements to improve access to the site, solved site-drainage problems, and relocated an elementary school away from the project area. It also constructed a freeway interchange without any state or federal funds. In addition to the property-tax increase and new sales taxes and business-license fees, the city also gains revenues in other ways. A special-assessment district that encompasses the project area and adjacent areas was formed to issue bonds, and the developer will pay up to $350,000 annually in assessments for up to twenty-five years. The developer also paid the city more than $1 million over the city's land-acquisition costs and has agreed to pay the city 10 percent of any net annual cash flow of between $250,000 and $500,000 and 15 percent of net annual cash flow of over $500,000. This agreement runs in perpetuity and binds any future holder of the developer's present interest.

Not all jurisdictions can deal successfully with a developer. The city must be able to use its land-use-control powers to negotiate meaningfully and enter into contracts that are enforceable. The jurisdiction must also have the capacity to undertake capital-improvement projects; and, most importantly, there must be some private-sector interest in development within the city (Kirlin and Chapman in press, p. 12). Without this last item, there is little the city can do to entice developers.

There is a further complication for both residential and commercial development. This complication involves the regional-government planning agencies in California, which take state and federal guidelines and develop specific plans to ensure that local construction meets them. In Southern California, for example, there are three regional plans that are expected to affect both present and long-run building activity: the official population growth forecast (SCAG-78); the Air Quality Management Plan (AQMP); and the Areawide Waste Treatment Management Plan (208 Plan). Each has a major impact on the building industry (Beam 1979, pp. 1-6).

The Southern California Association of Governments (SCAG) has projected population, housing, and land use for six Southern California counties. These projections form the basis for the timing and sizing of all major capital facilities and for the review of any private development proposal. The current projections (they are adjusted on a periodic basis) seem to be consistent with location and growth trends and, properly used, will provide greater certainty to builders and developers since they indicate where development is expected to occur. However, since capital facilities will be sized to the forecasts, they may end up being de facto growth controls. The AQMP, which is based on the SCAG-78 population forecasts, recommends activities so that the area will attain federal quality standards by 1987 and avoid severe federal sanctions, such as the cutoff of federal construction grants. Unfortunately, the state Air Resources Board did not accept the recommendations of the AQMP, and after some negotiation it was decided that the region would have until 1982 to amend the plan. Since the plan is designed to lessen air pollution rather than control growth, it does not include land-use-control measures. And since it was developed with the wastewater-treatment-facilities plan and with the SCAG-78 forecasts, the regional plan is coherent. However, it does not prohibit local governments from adding land-use and population controls. Finally, the 208 Plan focuses on non-point-source wastewater problems and projects correct sizing of facilities to be consistent with the population forecasts.[21] All that local governments must do under this plan is maintain current street sweeping, water control, and catch-basin and storm-drain clearance programs.

There are three nonexclusive ways for jurisdictions to brighten the future for development after Proposition 13. If commercial infill construction, which is small and incremental, is encouraged, fewer new facilities will have to be provided and the jurisdictions will be able to place fewer demands on developers. For large developments the jurisdiction might be willing to share some of the profitability risks, perhaps through a relaxation of constraints. In both cases a logical action for the jurisdiction to undertake is to delay the fiscal-impact statement until after final project approval and issuance of the tentative tract maps. At this point, any additional charges that the jurisdiction might want to impose can be rationally calculated. The third proposal involves helping local jurisdictions gain more revenues than they are currently receiving (Misczynski 1979; Gruen Gruen n.d.). Having the state guarantee capital-improvement bonds, allowing for user fees to be used for purposes other than those for which they were collected, allowing local governments to bank the state revenue entitlement, allowing borrowing against future bailout revenues, and increasing the use of assessment districts are examples of small proposals that may work to generate enough revenue to allow the jurisdictions to ease some of the burdens on developers.

Future of Local-Government Debt

Chapter 4 previously discussed the basic debt instruments that were available to local government prior to the passage of Proposition 13: general-obligation bonds, revenue bonds, lease-purchase agreements, and tax-allocation bonds. The particular type of instrument used depended upon such factors as how the money was to be used and the ease of obtaining voter approval. Thus general-obligation bonds, which necessitated a two-thirds vote of the voting population, was seldom used in the immediate past by local jurisdictions, whereas lease-purchase agreements, since they required no vote, had become increasingly popular. Revenue and tax-allocation bonds, which depended on the revenue streams that occurred because of the financed investment, are in the middle. Into this complex world the passage of Proposition 13 introduced further uncertainty because the traditional financial sources of credit were no longer available. In particular, the risk of default on various types of instruments was changed so that some debts become virtually unsalable.

The factors that affect the risk of default depend primarily on the bond's security, which in turn is directly affected by the legal and economic constraints that determine the cash flow available for debt service and retirement. At one extreme, the general-obligation bond is secured by the cash flow of the municipality and is not tied to any specific project. This bond is backed by the full faith and credit of the community and, prior to Proposition 13, paid the lowest interest rate of all debt. At the other extreme, there is a pure revenue bond that is secured only by the revenue generated from the financed project, with the security of the bond totally independent of the cash flow of the jurisdiction.

Although the average annual rate of growth of debt in California during the five years preceding the passage of the initiative was 11.05 percent in real terms, the per-capita increase in debt was only 1.7 percent per year. Cities financed only 3.1 percent of their capital outlays through the use of GO bonds, revenue bonds, or other long-term debt during this time; they financed 96.9 percent from operating revenues.[22] Counties during this same period financed 14 percent of capital outlays from the bond market, 17.4 percent from state and federal sources, and 68.6 percent from operating expenditures (McWatters 1979, pp. 7–11). Pay-as-you-go financing was obviously quite popular, although since lease-purchase agreements appear on the expenditure side of the jurisdiction's operating budget, these numbers probably overstate the amount of current funding of capital projects. In the year before Jarvis-Gann, $58 million of GO bonds were issued by cities, $509 million of tax-allocation bonds were issued by community-redevelopment agencies, and $101 million of GO bonds were issued by special districts. No GO bonds were issued by counties. It appears that the GO bond was not seriously used as a debt instrument by cities in the year preceding the passage of the initiative.

Proposition 13 affected different types of debt in different ways, and thus complicated the financial markets. Although the state is not dependent on the property tax as a source of revenue, because of increased uncertainty about the extent of the state's responsibility for helping localities and therefore increased uncertainty about the state's expenditure patterns, the rates that the state must pay to market its bonds might increase. Since California has a strong economy (outperforming the rest of the United States over the last several years), most California state debt typically sells for a lower interest rate than debt issued by other states. Yet after the passage of Proposition 13, this gap closed, from 37 basis points below the national rates in 1977 to 11 points below by March 1979.[23] This is a statistically significant decrease in the interest-rate spread. State revenue bonds were issued far less frequently, and thus it is more difficult to determine any impacts. However, in the six months prior to the passage of the initiative, the one bond issue sold for 3 points above the national average, whereas in the nine months after the passage, eleven issues sold for an average of 75 points above the national average (Beebe 1979, p. 248). In January 1980 Standard and Poor demoted California state general-obligation bonds from AAA to AA+ because of their belief that there had been a substantial curtailing of the ability of the state to continue to be in unquestioned financial health over a long period of time (Cottman 1980, p. 1). This downrating reflected the expenditure constraints of Proposition 4 and the potential halving of the state's income tax (which was defeated in June 1980); although largely symbolic, it did cost the state between 5 and 10 basis points (Cottman 1980, p. 3).

Jarvis-Gann most affected debt financing at the local level. The initiative had little effect on GO bonds issued prior to July 1, 1978 (since they were specifically exempted) or on revenue bonds. However, it dramatically affected future GO bonds, lease-purchase financing, and tax-allocation debt. Local capital financing has drastically fallen since the passage of Proposition 13. Prior to its passage, for example, new California local debt issues accounted for 10 percent of total United States issues; they now account for about 2 or 3 percent. In California schools alone, there was a backlog of more than $740 million in maintenance work (Sansweet 1979, p. 1).

Because Proposition 13 specifically exempts tax increases needed to service old GO bonds, the impact of the initiative on them was slight since their security was unchanged. There was a slight increase in their yield in the secondary (resale) market (about 50 basis points), but this is almost entirely explained by term-structure changes (that is, national interest-rate policy) (Beebe 1979, p. 254). Local revenue bonds went up by about 100 points, but only 10 points of that increase can be attributed to the passage of the proposition. It is the other areas that are affected by the Proposition.

There is a de facto limit on the sale of new general-obligation bonds in Proposition 13; they must be funded out of the 1-percent property-tax limit. This means that the full-faith-and-credit commitment for the bonds, which was in turn based on the unlimited powers of a jurisdiction to increase property taxes to fund the bonds, has disappeared. GO bonds as a source of revenue have vanished from California. This means that the public capital projects that are truly public goods and are not funded by other levels of government do not have a secure source of financing and will not be provided by the public sector.

Lease-purchase or joint-powers-agency agreements revolve around the establishment of a nonprofit corporation that sells the debt, constructs the facility, and then leases the facility to the jurisdiction with the lease payments providing the debt service. The rental payments by the city appear in its current budget as an operating expense. To the extent that Proposition 13 reduces the available revenue for operating expenditures, it adds an element of risk to the chances that the city will not be able to make its rental payments. Although lease-purchase agreements are still viable (and may well be the only way for municipalities to finance capital construction under the current set of political and economic constraints), the passage of Proposition 13 has caused an increase of between 40 and 75 basis points.

Aside from the elimination of GO bonds, Proposition 13 affected tax-allocation bonds the most severely. These were already risky since their implicit collateral was the redevelopment that occurred in the blighted area, and their rates were already high. After the Jarvis-Gann initiative was passed, only those projects that had a significant amount of new, expensive construction would be economically feasible. The bond market realized this; by the time of the election, California tax-allocation bonds were 300 basis points above Moody's Aaa rate, compared with 90 in 1977. After the election, there was an additional increase of 229 basis points, with a minimum of 175 points of the increase resulting from the passage of the proposition (Beebe 1979, pp. 249–254). Rating agencies were averse to rating new tax-allocation bonds, but without the rating no underwriter would take the responsibility for marketing them. For many potential new issues, the market has disappeared (Sansweet 1979, p. 35). Of the approximately $1.1 billion in outstanding tax-allocation bonds, at least $79 million, covering thirteen redevelopment projects, is in danger of defaulting by 1983 (Sansweet 1979, p. 35).

Overall, there may be a shortfall of about 27 percent in the availability of capital financing (about $427 million), if per-capita capital expenditures are to be kept constant (McWatters 1979), But of the cities surveyed, 82 percent reported that they are not engaging in debt financing of public infrastructure construction.

Without state assistance either in providing funds or in passing enabling legislation, there are only a few ways of financing new capital. For the immediate future, the following methods might be used to ensure that adequate capital improvements will be possible (McTighe 1979).

Local improvements for new development, such as streets, curbs, gutters, lights, water, and sewer lines can be made as conditions of development by private developers. Of course, by frontloading on the developer, the community removes the local-debt interest subsidy provided by the state and federal governments, so in the aggregate costs will increase more than in the past. This technique will not work for the replacement of the existing public capital stock.

Flood-control and other drainage facilities should be financed by special-assessment districts, assuming voter approval can be obtained. Police, fire, libraries, roads, and parks could be financed by an earmarked, fixed percentage of general-fund revenues, developer contributions, or a fee related to the amount of construction that occurs. Of course, some combination of these methods of financing is also possible.

Sewers and wastewater-treatment facilities are candidates for revenue bonds, since fees based on usage can be charged. Also in this area there are possibilities for the use of federal and state grants as financing instruments.

Finally, public buildings and public-works facilities might be financed through the use of lease-purchase agreements or the establishment of an earmarked general-revenue sinking fund for their financing.

But these are short-run solutions to the financing problems. In the long run there will have to be additional state involvement. The problem is to ensure that this involvement does not subtract from the now limited amount of local autonomy that exists after Proposition 13, but that it rather allows local jurisdictions to maintain as much control as possible over their capital decisions. Some of the following ways for the state to help have been suggested (McWatters 1979, pp. 28–40).

The state could pass enabling legislation to allow for the possibility of special tax bonds. Upon a two-thirds vote of the voting population, local non-property taxes could be raised that would be earmarked for debt service. This would provide enough security to the bond market so that the bonds could be sold. Furthermore, since it is within the spirit of Jarvis-Gann in that it requires a two-thirds vote, it would also be politically feasible to implement. A variant of this is the linked-obligation bond, which would guarantee that a fixed percentage of the property tax that the city does receive would be used for bond repayment rather than going into the general fund.

The state could act as an insurer of the debt. Presently, for a premium of 1.5 to 0.5 percent of principal and interest, it is possible to get private debt insurance. An obvious advantage of this activity would be that the state would closely examine the bonds for their financial feasibility before they were issued. This might eliminate wasteful projects.

The state could act as a financial intermediary. In this case the local district could sell debt to the state, and then the state would sell the debt in the open market. This would help small jurisdictions that may not have as easy an access to the capital markets as does the state.

The state could also give debt subsidies, guarantees, or grants to the local jurisdictions to help them solve their infrastructure problems. In the short run state grants might be expedient, but in the long run it is unrealistic for the state to provide both operating and capital bailout funds. Furthermore, the marginal cost of obtaining debt credit increases since the financial markets recognize the total debt outstanding. If the state sold debt to provide financing for local jurisdictions, within a short time the expenses of the additional state debt would be quite high. Furthermore, since the state is on the same economic cycle as its jurisdictions, neither state guarantees nor subsidies will in the long run reduce risk enough to significantly affect interest rates.

Finally, the state legislature has proposed an amendment to the constitution that would allow the issuing of GO bonds upon approval of two-thirds of the voters voting on the proposition. This proposition will appear on the November 1980 ballot.

Some Conclusions about Development

In the near future there will be a continuing shift of responsibility to the private developer for providing the necessary infrastructure. This shift will occur for the ostensible reasons that fiscal-impact statements indicate that resident development does not generate enough revenues to offset its costs. However, when the debt constraints that face local jurisdictions are considered, it can be seen that they really have very little choice in forcing the developer to undertake the construction of the urban facilities. If the development is to occur, someone has to finance the infrastructure, even if forcing the developer to do so is more expensive.

A legitimate question concerns whether this situation is equitable. The benefits of capital expenditures are spread out far beyond the time period of the construction costs; perhaps future home owners or residents of the jurisdiction ought to pay for these benefits. However, it is difficult to ensure that this intergenerational equity is obtained. If the developer provides the amenities, the present purchaser may pay for part of them in increased housing prices, while the developer pays part of them in reduced profits. To the extent that future home owners also pay a higher price because of the capitalized value of the benefits of the infrastructure, the costs are passed on. However, if the infrastructure is financed through property-tax charges, this shifting to future generations might not occur. If the tax is capitalized into the price of the home, the present owner will bear the full tax.

The situation is further complicated because people who live in already developed areas have probably had their infrastructure publicly financed and provided. It may not be equitable to have some private financing and some public financing in the same city, since new residents of areas where the infrastructure was privately financed end up paying more for identical services than new residents of areas with publicly financed infrastructure.

In any case, if developers are forced to provide facilities, their profits will fall. Given alternative areas in which they can develop without having to provide the extra services, they will relocate. Unfortunately, many developers may not be large enough to relocate out of state and may face financial distress in the near future.

There are other pressures on residential developers' profits. Inclusionary housing programs further constrain developers, especially if market conditions do not allow them to shift the subsidy to the other buyers. Rent controls make apartment construction far riskier. Finally, the national economic climate, with its high interest rates, also forces profit margins to shrink as holding costs increase.

At the same time, commercial construction in undeveloped areas appears quite attractive. Because the sales-tax-subvention formula rewards cities that can attract construction, it is likely that commercial builders will continue to receive incentives for locating in particular jurisdictions. Negotiated settlements to everyone's benefit will continue to occur.

It appears that in the future there will be a shift of land use away from residential construction and toward commercial or industrial construction. But this is an untenable situation since without people there can be no industry or commerce. Only when it is realized that reducing the opportunities for developers, consumers, and jurisdictions is counterproductive to almost any goal that society wants, will a solution be found. If this occurs, there may be hope that at least risk and uncertainty can be lowered, profit opportunities restored, consumer choices expanded, and necessary development begun again.

Notes

1. The assumption that both tenants and Jarvis made was that landlords were shifting the full amount of the tax forward.

2. If the tax were not passed on before the initiative, then there would be no reason for the Proposition 13 savings to be passed on after the initiative.

3. The *Los Angeles Times* (Merl 1980, pp. 1, 3) reports the eviction attempt of a 78-year-old widow because she violated the nonsubletting clause in her rental agreement by allowing the city to pay her for using her apartment as a polling place. Her rent was the lowest in the building. Her landlord backed down under the publicity and denied that rent control had anything to do with the attempted eviction, but her lawyers estimated that about 140 attempted evictions a week occur because of the decontrol provision of the Los Angeles ordinance.

4. The income method of assessment uses the net revenue flow from a building to calculate the property value of the building. The higher the net revenue, the greater the property value. This is only a long-run effect in California since Proposition 13 defines assessed value. However, the selling price will reflect this reduced income stream, and in this way rent controls will affect assessed values.

5. At least one empirical study shows that rent controls do slightly affect income distribution, with lower-income tenants gaining. However, there is a great variation in impact. Furthermore, this study also found that although the total benefits under controls were $270 million, total costs were $521 million (Olsen 1969).

6. Tax-law changes lowering depreciation allowances in the Tax Reform Act of 1969 also reduced the profitability of owning or constructing apartments.

7. In this region conversions represented about 2.5 percent of total rental units, although in some cities, the percentage is much higher. It might be noted that between 30 and 35 percent of all multifamily construction in the area is of condominiums (Ishino 1979, pp. 26, 30).

8. It is also difficult to borrow money for new apartment construction in Los Angeles, and thus developers are building condominiums and thereby easing the conversion pressures. See table 7-1 for previous years' figures.

9. The large 1977 condominium-application figure might be derived from the announced (but later rescinded) change in the number of parking spaces required per condominium conversion.

10. This turnover rate is defined as (Sales + New Parcels)/(Existing + New Parcels).

11. It has been estimated for the California building industry (assuming the price of a house is equal to three times income, there is a 10-percent down payment, and the transaction occurs after Proposition 13's passage), that for every $1,000 increase in the price of a house worth between $42,555 and $52,500, 79,000 households are eliminated from those able to afford the house (Connerly and Associates 1978, p. 5).

12. OPR did not do the work, but rather used the city's own analysis.

13. See, for example, McDermott (1979), Construction Industry Federation (1979), Bartolotto 1979, or the California Council for Environmental and Economic Balance (1979).

14. Frieden argues that fees are also enacted to protect the fiscal interest of already established residents and to emphasize no-growth trends (Frieden 1979), pp. 9–10).

15. The assumptions were that 25 percent of the units be inclusionary, sales price be no more than 2.5 times local mean income, and 25 percent of the units be sold for no more than twice mean income.

16. Roos, AB 1151, Chapter 1207, 1979 Statutes.

17. The only two programs outside California in early 1980 were in Boulder, Colorado, and Montgomery County, Maryland.

18. There is another solution that might help provide low-income housing. It is currently legal under both state and federal law for the state or local jurisdiction to issue tax-free housing bonds and use the proceeds to finance middle- and low-income housing. The state has used this technique to finance 10,000 homes and 5,000 multifamily units, and has given commitments for an additional 3,000 units (Bry 1970, p. 3). However, this law is in the midst of being constrained by both the federal and state governments; and given the current high rates of interest, except for some isolated cases, it will probably not make much of an impact in the future.

19. California will be a lower-than-average property-tax state, so there may be some interstate migration of business. However, the property-tax differentials within California are likely to be so small that they will have only marginal impacts.

20. Los Angeles, for example, has a successful neighborhood-business revitalization program, which provides low-interest loans and loan guarantees to small and medium-sized businesses (City of Los Angeles Economic Development Office 1978).

21. So named because it is the SCAG response to section 208 of the Federal Water Pollution Control Act of 1972 (see chapter 4).

22. Included in operating revenues for city data is federal revenue sharing.

23. One hundred basis points are equal to 1 percentage point of the bond interest rate.

8 The Future in Perspective

This chapter will put in perspective the preceding analysis of Proposition 13 and its land-use implications. It will do this by first developing some preliminary conclusions concerning developers, consumers, and jurisdictional decision makers. Then some events that have occurred since the passage of the initiative will be examined, the predictions will be made about future budgeting and land-use problems in California. Finally, some recommendations concerning future policies will be made.

Some Conclusions

Developers

Residential developers will be far more constrained in the future. Since jurisdictions will be implementing many more fees and charges, developers' costs will be forced up. At the same time, developers will find that jurisdictions will be less willing to provide the typical preproposition urban infrastructure and that this will add an additional increment to development costs. In the short run some of the costs may be successfully shifted forward, and there will be a decline in new construction.

In addition to the new and increased fees, there will also be an increase in the types and intensity of enforcement of rules relating to new development. After Proposition 13 was passed, many jurisdictions did impose new rules and many claimed to be enforcing existing rules more vigorously. If the end result of these jurisdictional activities is to increase the time it takes to finish a development, they will also add to development costs.

Apartment construction will probably decrease. Rent-control ordinances seem to be growing in popularity; with the defeat of the statewide rent-control-limitation measure in June 1980, it is likely that rent controls will be in existence for a long time. This hinders potential profits and makes apartment construction much less likely (although it may encourage condominium construction). Although the repealing of all rent-control ordinances will not necessarily stimulate apartment construction, it would certainly be a step toward that goal.

Finally, because of the importance of the sales tax, development that involves commercial possibilities is much more likely to be approved than development that is residentially oriented. As development projects are analyzed, commercial developers should be prepared to negotiate over such things as profit sharing, infrastructure provision, and contributions to the local treasury. In the long run, if all jurisdictions want only commercial development, there will be fewer places for workers and shoppers to live; and housing prices will increase.

Consumers

Consumers will be living in a world in which aggregate revenue and expenditure patterns of local jurisdictions will be similar. Because of mandates, court rulings, and centralized financing and control for some services (such as education, health, and welfare), expenditure trends are likely to coincide. Because sales- and property-tax rates are invariant across jurisdictions and because the state and federal governments are providing large shares of the local budget, most of the revenue variance occurs in the non-property- and non-sales-tax fees and charges. However, jurisdictions do have some control over the tax base, and revenue patterns can be affected indirectly. Even so, consumers will have fewer fiscal choices.

Present home owners benefit from the large property-tax reductions. Their disposable income increased and their consumption probably increased as well. Of course, the public-service expenditures of the jurisdiction have fallen in real terms; but since the electorate voted for this cutback, the present home owner has probably experienced a net gain in welfare.

New development consumers are likely to be confronted by higher prices in the residential market. Because of development restrictions and increased development costs, the marginal costs of construction will increase, resulting in an upward shift in the supply curve. The home owner will now be partially funding the development infrastructure over the life of the mortgage. Unfortunately, there may be few alternatives for this consumer. Since apartment construction may be partially deterred by the rent-control ordinance, it will be increasingly difficult to find vacant apartments. Furthermore, these apartments are likely to be allocated on a nonmarket basis. There is likely to be more income inequity in apartment allocation than before the rent-control ordinances were passed.

Consumers will also be facing increased fees and charges for services. These are not likely to be capitalized into land values and will be similar to benefit taxes. If properly instituted, they will lead to an increase in economic efficiency, although they are regressive with respect to income.

One bright spot for the consumer is that with the increased emphasis on commercial activity, there will be a greater degree of competition among sellers, perhaps leading to lower consumer prices.

Jurisdictions

Since jurisdictional decision makers face reduced revenues, they will be forced to take very careful steps as they examine potential new construction in their localities. They will certainly evaluate any new development projects in terms of economic as well as social concerns. If residential construction does not pay for itself, these city officials will be increasingly unfriendly toward it. Because of revenue reductions, these same decision makers have cut, in real terms, many of the planning departments. This will make evaluations more difficult. Poor city planning is also likely to affect private development costs since it increases the time needed for reviews.

There will also be conscious decisions to cut service quality in both the operating and the capital budgets of jurisdictions. These cuts may take the form of slowing service response time or of not providing needed capital improvements. Furthermore, if real wages are held down, public decision makers will discover that the better-qualified workers will leave the California public sector. This will affect service delivery.

Public leaders will be more interested than ever before in attracting commercial development. Negotiations between commercial developers and public officials will center around changes in zoning, facility provision and planning, and other land rules in exchange for tax contributions and perhaps profit-sharing plans. But areas in which developers show little interest will find it difficult to offer enough financial incentives.

Finally, jurisdictional decision makers will find that they are living in an increasingly interdependent world, with many of their decisions being made by the state and federal governments either through mandates imposed on the local government or through the local government voluntarily distorting its expenditure patterns to gain additional grant revenues. This interdependence may be the hallmark of future local public finance.

Post-Jarvis-Gann Activities

Two important events occurred after the passage of Proposition 13. In November 1979 the Gann expenditure-limitation initiative (Proposition 4) passed by an even larger percentage than Proposition 13 (76 percent voted for Proposition 4, compared with 65 percent for Proposition 13). In June 1980, however, a second Jarvis initiative, designed to halve the state income tax, was defeated, with only about 40 percent of the electorate voting in favor. Both events have significant implications for the future of state and local finance in California.

Proposition 13 was designed to cut the property tax and to limit government through the removal of this revenue source. Proposition 4 limited overall government expenditures but did not constrain any particular type. Although this was a complicated initiative, it contained six major provisions (Cal-Tax News 1979):

1. Expenditure appropriations of state and local government from tax sources are limited to a formula based on population changes and the lower of either the consumer-price index or the growth of per-capita personal income.
2. The limitation can be adjusted by a majority vote of the relevant electorate.
3. Any surplus revenues must be returned to the taxpayers within two years.
4. Local governments must be reimbursed for new programs or higher levels of services mandated by the state.
5. Fees and charges not in excess of the cost of service provision are not limited.
6. Provisions are made for debt service, for emergencies, and for other miscellaneous changes in government or taxes. An example of one of these provisions is that it is not legal to switch to a fee to avoid the appropriation limit.

Proposition 4 has at least two immediate implications for land use. Even if new developments are extraordinarily "profitable" to a jurisdiction, they still may not be worthwhile. For example, a new shopping center might generate a sales-tax-subvention increase far in excess of the population growth and of either per-capita income or consumer-price growth. This excess revenue would have to be returned to the taxpayers of the jurisdiction, perhaps leaving little to pay for the increased services the shopping center would require. The second implication is that fees and charges that do not exceed costs (and do not replace existing taxes) are not subject to the limit. An expanded use of development fees will probably occur; and to the extent that they did not previously include overhead, they may now do so, which again should lead to even higher fees.

The results of the second Jarvis initiative (Proposition 9) in June 1980 might indicate that the electorate desires an opportunity to examine some of the long-run implications of the two previous constitutional amendments. Although the initiative's ultimate defeat was not expected six months before the election, the "no" campaign was able to convince voters that the cut in state revenues would be shifted to revenue cuts along the entire system of government. Because of this defeat, the state bailout will continue under the conditions of AB 8. This should result in an improvement in the climate for development.

Future Problems

Public-Finance Problems

The most important problem from the local government's perspective is that the electorate has decided that government is adequately financed at a lower real level of revenues. Many of the traditional services and capital facilities that were once provided by the public sector can now no longer be provided. If development is to occur or services are to be provided at past levels, the private sector must help. Any solutions to development or land-use problems that are based on additional government aid will not work since government does not have the money. This means, for example, that housing or infrastructure subsidies are not viable in the current environment. Furthermore, it may be unrealistic to argue for major increases in federal aid to the construction industry or for new federal income supplement programs that allow households to afford dwelling units more easily.

Because most new services and infrastructure will be financed by the private sector or through the jurisdiction acting as a private entrepreneur and selling the services, there may be greater economic efficiency; but it will be accompanied by greater societal costs of increased regressivity in the service-delivery system. This regressivity will continue to be a legitimate concern of local decision makers. It is likely that they will attempt to use nonfiscal measures such as intervention into the land market to offset this problem indirectly.

Land-Use Problems

Because of the problems in the financial sector, there will also be increased problems with land-use regulations. In particular, because of the potential fiscal loss associated with particular types of development, local jurisdictions will resort to an increased use of their land-control powers to restrict development and minimize service extensions. Those developments that do not generate enough revenue to pay the increases in costs that they generate will find it especially difficult to obtain the necessary clearances to proceed. Those developments that more than pay their way will be approved. Developers will be more willing to provide inducements so that their development will be perceived as being "profitable."

A second land-use problem is the attitude of the jurisdiction toward expansion of service boundaries. Jurisdictions are now more hesitant to annex because of the potential of increased costs of services. If this trend continues and local jurisdictions continue to be cautious in allowing new development and new annexations, then the owners of existing dwellings will accrue windfall gains at the expense of potential movers or residents of unincorporated areas, who will find it more difficult to find housing or receive services.

Other Problems

At least two additional local problems and one additional state problem exist. The local problems revolve around energy costs and jobs; the state problem revolves around the extent of the surplus available for the continuation of the bailout.

Energy costs affect land use in a wide variety of ways. The gas and electricity necessary to allow development to take place have already been implicitly discussed as an infrastructure problem. The costs of transportation are also important. If households locate far from employment or amenities, thereby incurring large transportation costs in order to own homes, this will have an impact on their housing-consumption decisions. It may be that these increased costs will be capitalized into reduced land prices. However, if they are not, then in the long run they, more than any other factor, will determine land-use patterns.

Historically, jobs have moved to the suburbs, so that employment opportunities exist away from the central city. As long as this occurs, transportation problems will not be critical. However, because of the decreased amount of residential development, fewer workers will be able to live in the jurisdiction in which they work. If workers cannot follow jobs, industry will be reluctant to move; and in the long run, residential development is closely tied to commercial or industrial development.

Finally, the state surplus is important in analyzing the impact of Proposition 13. The deflator clause in AB 8 forces the state to cut back on its aid when there is a revenue shortfall. Although estimates of the future surplus have varied widely (Oakland 1979; Kirlin 1979), the most recent have indicated that the surplus will be much smaller in the future. In fact, the state legislative analyst has argued that without a $500 million cut in the present state budget, it will be necessary to increase future taxes (Rood 1980). Since tax increases must be passed by two-thirds of the legislators, this is unlikely to occur; and the bailout's future might be dim.

Some Recommendations

Opportunities seldom arise for massive changes in the public-finance and land-use systems. The passage of Proposition 13 may give rise to one of these rare moments. Traditional methods of financing public services adequately will not be sufficient; in the long run change must occur in these methods or in the types of services delivered. Narrowly considered land-use interventions might also have long-run impacts; again, Proposition 13 may indirectly provide incentives for a major restructuring of this system.

Revenue Policies

The revenue restrictions of Proposition 13 make it necessary for jurisdictions to develop different tax policies. This probably means that there will be a movement toward benefit taxation, with the costs of many of the services being covered by recipient and user charges. Since citizens are sometimes forced to consume services by the local jurisdiction because of the negative externalities that would exist if there were underconsumption (for example, garbage collection) or because of public-good problems, a minimum amount of the service should be provided to all. This minimum amount should be financed from the general revenues of the jurisdiction. However, if a household desires a higher level of service, then it should pay for this increment. The charge for the increment should be the marginal cost of providing the service (Break 1980). The entire community would be covered by this plan—not just new developments. The marginal-cost price of the increment will lead to a level of service provision that will reflect a more efficient allocation of resources. This method also helps to ease at least some of the equity concerns, since the wealthy will have to pay more for additional services while the poor will have a guaranteed minimum service level.

It is difficult to use marginal-cost pricing for large infrastructure investments. However, the benefit principal can still be used. There are at least two ways of doing this. The first would be to impose all the costs of facilities that benefit only the development on the developer and the households in the new development. There is an obvious inequity in this recommendation. Those residents who moved into the jurisdiction in the past and for whom the jurisdiction provided the infrastructure may be advantaged, although they probably paid higher property taxes then the new residents.

A second and more intriguing way of financing the infrastructure would be the adaptation of the Incremental Budget Cost Pricing with Payback (IBPP) Plan (McDermott 1979). Under this plan, the developer pays the entire capital cost for all increases in the service-system capacity. The jurisdiction tells the developer what the capacity of the infrastructure should be and usually forces the developer to provide the entire amount. However, as other new developments occur in the area, their creators are charged a fee that is returned to the original developer who installed the excess capacity. The first developer incurs the risk that other developers will not have to face. But if the price scheme ultimately compensates the initial developer for both costs and risks, then the infrastructure will be provided and the costs will be shared by all the residents in the new development area.

Development and Land-Use Policies

The fact that there may be revenue shortfalls and growth controls does not in itself necessarily mean that demand pressures will stop: The single-family dwelling is a vital part of the American consciousness; the members of the post–World War II baby boom have reached the prime age for home purchases; and in-migration to California shows no sign of ceasing. It will be very difficult to restrict growth in the long run. Land-use policy should be used to deal efficiently with these pressures, rather than merely to attempt to stop development. In order to do this, local and state planners must embark on a series of steps that will allow as much logic and flexibility in planning as possible.

The first steps must be to reduce uncertainty. Decisions concerning the worth of a particular project must be made expeditiously. Developers must be given some vested rights in the development and must be allowed to sue the jurisdiction to enforce those rights. This is especially true if the developer is also forced to take additional risks in providing infrastructure.

A second step that the local planner can take is to rely more on market-allocation principles than on direct rules and regulations. Price incentives force efficient behavior. Rules should be used primarily to establish a clear system of property rights, including development rights. Within this system, the principal regulatory tool should be changing relative prices through fees and charges.

Finally, it should be emphasized that the rules that guide development do not have to be based entirely on the financial implications of that development. Social and political factors might be far more important than the particular costs and revenue flows from a particular development. Once the rules are ascertained, the fee structure can be set, depending on the preferences of the jurisdiction, to ensure that only "profitable" developments are established.

Some Final Conclusions

The basic thrust of this book has been to show the interrelationships between public budgeting, land-use controls, and the private-sector market for construction. The effects of Proposition 13 demonstrate this interrelationship. Because the interrelations were not carefully considered when rules, fees, and mandates were instituted in reaction to the initiative, some of the results were unexpected. However, when this complex relationship was unraveled, some of the occurrences are easily explained.

More work needs to be done. The relationships sketched have been tentative; the analysis of the proposition has been short run and preliminary. Furthermore, additional fiscal limits have been placed on some jurisdictions within the state, and the environment is still in a condition of flux. It is hoped that this book will add to the understanding of the impacts of government intervention into this particular area.

Bibliography

Anderson, Ralph, and Associates. "Redevelopment and Tax Increment Financing." Sacramento, January 1976.

Arnault, E. Jane. "Optimal Maintenance Under Rent Control with Quality Constraint." *American Real Estate and Urban Economics Journal* (Summer 1975): 67-82.

Assembly Revenue and Taxation Committee. *Summary of Legislation Implementing Proposition 13 for Fiscal Year 1978-79.* Assemblyman Willie L. Brown, Jr., chairman, October 2, 1978.

Association of Bay Area Governments (ABAG). *Development Fees in the San Francisco Bay Area: A Survey.* Berkeley: ABAG, 1980.

Baker, Bob. "Rent Board Rulings—Called Tough, Fair, Confiscatory—Fan the Storm." *Los Angeles Times,* April 20, 1980, "The Westside," part 11, pp. 1, 7.

Baker, Bob, and Specht, Jim. "Santa Monica Rent Control Takes Firm Grip—and Landlords are Hurting, Study Shows." *Los Angeles Times,* April 20, 1980, "The Westside," part 11, pp. 1, 6.

Balderston, Frederick, I., Heyman, Michael, and Smith, Wallace F. "Proposition 13, Property Transfers and the Real Estate Markets." Institute of Governmental Studies Research Report 79. Berkeley: Institute of Governmental Studies, 1979.

Bartolotto, Ben. "Notes: New Development and Proposition 13." Los Angeles: Construction Industry Federation, 1979.

Baxter, Cheryl. "The Impact of Government Policies and Programs on Land Value." *The Real Estate Appraiser and Analyst.* (May–June 1979): 42- 45.

Beebe, Jack H. "Proposition 13 and the Cost of California Debt." *National Tax Journal* Supplement vol. 32, no. 2 (June 1979): 243-259.

Beaumont, Marion S. "Proposition 13: A Decade of Development in California." *1978 Proceedings of the National Tax Association-Tax Institute of America* (1979): 153-162.

Beam, James. "A Discussion of the Impacts on the Southern California Building Industry of the SCAG Regional Growth Forecast, SCAG 208 Areawide Wastewater Treatment Management Plan, and the South Coast Air Quality Management Plan." Presentation to Real Estate Research Council of Southern California, August 16, 1979.

Bell, Michael, and Fisher, Ronald. "State Limitations on Local Taxing and Spending Powers: Comment and Reevaluation." *National Tax Journal* vol. 31, no. 4 (December 1978): 391-396.

——. *State Limitations of Local Taxes and Expenditures, A-64.* Washington, D.C.: Advisory Committee on Intergovernmental Relations, U.S. Government Printing Office, 1977.

Benton, Bill Browning. "The Implementation of P.L. 93–647 Title XX of the Social Security Act." Photocopy, Washington, D.C., 1980.

Black, David E. "Property Tax Incidence: The Exercise Tax Effect and Assessment Practices." *National Tax Journal* 30 (1977): 429–436.

Break, George. *Intergovernmental Fiscal Relations in the United States.* Washington, D.C.: Brookings Institution, 1967.

Break, George F. "After Proposition 13—Chaos or Reform." Photocopy, University of Southern California Law Center, Los Angeles, 1980, pp. 163–180.

Brennan, Geoffrey, and Buchanan, James M. "Tax Instruments as Constraints on the Disposition of Public Revenues." *Journal of Public Economics* 9 (1978): 301–318.

Brimhall, Grant. "Sales Tax Reallocation as a Response to Local Government Revenue Losses." Dissertation presented to the School of Public Administration, University of Southern California, Los Angeles, 1979.

Brueckner, Jan K. "Property Values, Local Public Expenditure and Economic Efficiency." *Journal of Public Economics* 2 (1979): 223–245.

Bry, Barbara. "Soaring Interest Rates Slowing Output of Tax Free Housing Bonds." *Los Angeles Times,* April 21, 1970, part 4, pp. 2, 3.

Buchanan, James M. "An Economic Theory of Clubs." *Economica* February 1975): 1–14.

Buchanan, James M., and Tullock, Gordon. "Polluters' Profits and Political Response: Direct Controls versus Taxes." *American Economic Review* 65 (1975): 139–147.

Burrows, Lawrence B. *Growth Management.* New Brunswick, N.J.: Center for Urban Policy Research, Rutgers University, 1978.

Cal-Tax News, August 1–14, 1979. Insert on Proposition 4.

Cal-Tax Research Bulletin. "Local Government Profile, November 1978.

California Commission on Governmental Reform. *Task Force Project Report on Local Non-Property Taxes, User Fees, and Services.* Sacramento, 1978.

California Council for Environmental and Economic Balance (CCEEB). "The Fiscal Impact of New Residential Development after Proposition 13." San Francisco: CCEEB, 1979.

California, State of. *Annual Report of Financial Transactions Concerning Cities of California.* Sacramento: State Controller's Office, fiscal years 1967–1968 through 1977–1978.

California State Department of Finance. *A Study of Local Government Impacts of Proposition 13.* Vol. 1. Sacramento: State Department of Finance, January 1979.

California State Office of Planning and Research (OPR). "New Housing: Paying its Way?" Sacramento: OPR, May 1979.

California State Office of Planning and Research (OPR). "Local Government Planning Survey, 1978." Sacramento: OPR, January 1980.

California State Senate. Local Government Committee. *Implementation of Proposition 13,* vol. 2. *Long Term Local Government and School Financing.* Sacramento: Senate Local Committee, 1979.

Californians for an Environment of Excellence, Full Employment, and a Strong Economy through Planning. "Local Government Permit Process." Undated wall chart.

Californians for Environment, Employment, Economy through Development (CEEED). "Government Fees Force Housing Costs Higher." Undated news release.

Capozza, Dennis R., "A Simple Structural Model of Rent Increases, in Los Angeles County." In *An Analysis of the Los Angeles Rental Housing Market,* edited by Richard V. Eastlin. Los Angeles: University of Southern California, 1979, pp. 59-77.

Carliner, Geoffrey. "Income, Elasticity of Housing Demand." *Review of Economics and Statistics* 55 (November 1973): 528-532.

Chaiken, Jan M., and Walker, Warren E. "Growth in Municipal Expenditures: A Case Study of Los Angeles." RAND Report N-1200-RC. Santa Monica: RAND Corporation, 1979.

Chapman, Jeffrey I. "L.A.P.D. in the Wake of Proposition 13." In *Managing State and Local Government: Cases and Readings,* edited by Fred Lane, pp. 481-506. New York: St. Martins Press, 1980.

Chapman, Jeffrey I., and Kirlin, John J. "Changes in Government Land Use Policies—An Unforeseen Response to the Jarvis-Gann Initiative. *Urban Interest* 1 (1979a): 81-86.

——. "Land Use Consequences of Proposition 13." *University of Southern California Law Review* 53 (1979b): 95-124.

City of Los Angeles. City Economic Development Office. "Third Annual Report for Period October 1, 1977 to December 31, 1978." Photocopy, City of Los Angeles, n.d.

Comptroller General. Government Accounting Office (GAO 79-88). *Proposition 13—How California Governments Coped with a $6 Billion Revenue Loss."* No. 79-88, September 28, 1979.

Connerly and Associates, Inc. "The Housing Crunch." California Building Industries Association, October 1978.

——. "The Implications of Inclusionary Housing Programs." California Building Industry Association, April 1979.

Construction Awareness Program. "The California Construction Story." Los Angeles: Construction Awareness Program, 1979.

Construction Industry Federation (CIF). "Critique of Office of Planning and Research Report Entitled 'New Housing Paying Its Way.'" San Diego: CIF, 1979.

Construction Industry Research Board. "Samples of Increases in Building Fees." Los Angeles, 1978.

"Conversions Slow, City Officials Believe." *Los Angeles Times,* February 24, 1980, part II, pp. 1, 5.

Cottman, Effie M. "Financial Instability Affects Bond Ratings." *Public Administration Times,* February 15, 1980, pp. 1, 3.

County of Los Angeles. Department of Regional Planning. "New Fees." October 19, 1978.

Dale Johnson, David. *GVRD Land Use Regulation Study.* Study prepared for the Regulation Reference of the Economic Council of Canada, March 1980a.

———. "Hedonic Prices and Price Indexes in Housing Markets: The Existing Empirical Evidence and Proposed Extensions." Working Paper no. 85, Real Estate and Urban Economics Program, Institute of Business and Economic Research, University of California, Berkeley, 1980b.

Davis, Otto A. "Economic Elements in Municipal Zoning Decisions." *Land Economics* 39 (November 1963): 375-386.

Doti, James, and Barakaszi, Linda. "The Composition of Orange County's Unsold Single Family Housing Units." Report no. 6, Center for Economic Research. Orange, Calif.: Chapman College, 1979.

Dyer, James C., IV, and Maher, Michael D. "Capitalization of Intrajurisdictional Differences in Local Tax Prices: Comment." *American Economic Review* 69 (1979): 481-484.

Eastin, Richard V. "A Survey of the Theoretical and Empirical Findings." In *An Analysis of the Los Angeles Rental Housing Market,* edited by Richard V. Eastin, pp. 24-55. Los Angeles: Center for Study of Financial Institutions, Graduate School of Business Administration, University of Southern California, 1979a.

Eastin, Richard V., ed. *An Analysis of the Los Angeles Rental Housing Market.* Los Angeles: Center for Study of Financial Institutions, Graduate School of Business Administration, University of Southern California, 1979.

Economic Report of the President. Washington, D.C.: U.S. Government Printing Office, 1979.

Edel, Mathew, and Sclar, Elliot. "Taxes, Spending and Property Values: Supply Adjustment in a Tiebout-Oates Model" *Journal of Political Economy* 82 (1974): 941-954.

Edelstein, Robert H. "An Evaluation of Rent Control as a Housing Policy Instrument." In *An Analysis of the Los Angeles Rental Housing Market,* edited by Eastin, pp. 81-106.

Ellickson, Phyllis. "The Fiscal Limitation Movement: Present Context and Outlook." RAND Note N-1160-FF. Santa Monica: RAND Corporation, May 1979.

Ellickson, Robert C. "Suburban Growth Controls: An Economic and Legal Analysis." *The Yale Law Journal* 86 (January 1977): 385-511.

Ellson, Richard. "Fiscal Impacts on Intrametropolitan Residential Location: Further Insights on the Tiebout Hypothesis." *Public Finance Quarterly* 8 (April 1980): 189-212.

Ervin, David E.; Fitch, James B.; Godwin, R. Kenneth; Shepard, W. Bruce; and Stoevener, Herbert H. *Land Use Control: Evaluating Economic and Political Effects.* Cambridge, Mass.: Ballinger, 1977.

Field, Mervin. "Sending a Message: Californians Strike Back." *Public Opinion.* (July/August 1978): 3-7.

Fisher, Ronald C. "Local Sales Taxes: Tax Rate Differentials, Sales Loss, and Revenue Estimation." *Public Finance Quarterly* 8 (1980): 171-180.

Frankena, Mark. "Alternative Models of Rent Control." *Urban Studies* 12 (1974): 303-308.

Frech, H.E., III, and Lafferty, Ronald N. "The Effect of the California Coastal Commission on Housing Prices." Working Paper in Economics, no. 152, University of California, Santa Barbara, 1980.

Frieden, Bernard J. "Allocating the Public Service Costs of New Housing." Report. Washington, D.C.: National Association of Home Builders, 1979.

Gabriel, Stuart; Katz, Lawrence; and Wolch, Jennifer. "Local Land Use Regulation and Proposition 13: Some Findings from a Recent Survey." Working Paper no. 80-4. Program in Real Estate and Urban Economics, Institute of Business and Economic Research, University of California, Berkeley, 1980.

Gilderbloom, John. "The Impact of Moderate Rent Control in the United States: A Review and Critique of Existing Literature." Sacramento: Department of Housing and Community Development, 1978.

Gillespie, W.I. "Effect of Public Expenditures on Distribution of Income." In *Essays in Fiscal Federalism,* edited by R.A. Musgrave. Washington, D.C.: Brookings Institution, 1965, p. 122-186.

Gleeson, Michael, E. "Effects of an Urban Growth Management System or Land Values." *Land Economics* 55 (August 1979): 350-365.

Goodenough, Richard. "An Approach to Land Use Control: The California Land Conservation Act." *Urban Studies* 15 (1978): 289-297.

Gruen Gruen + Associates. "Proposition 13 and the Future of Construction in California." Photocopy, n.d.

Hager, Philip. "Building Booms in Once Reluctant City." *Los Angeles Times,* February 10, 1980, part 1, p. 1.

Hager, Philip. "Public Employee Pay Freeze Overturned," *Los Angeles Times,* February 16, 1979, part 1, p. 1.

Hamilton Bruce. "Property Taxes and the Tiebout Hypothesis: Some Empirical Evidence." In *Fiscal Zoning and Land Use Controls,* edited by Edwin S. Mills and Wallace E. Oates, pp. 13-30. Lexington, Mass.: Lexington Books, D.C. Heath and Company, 1975a.

——. "Zoning and Property Taxation in a System of Local Governments." *Urban Studies* 12 (1975b): 205-211.

——. "Capitalization of Intrajurisdictional Differences in Local Tax Prices." *American Economic Review* 66 (December 1976a): 743-754.

——. "The Effect of Property Taxes and Local Public Spending on Property Values: A Theoretical Comment" *Journal of Political Economy* 84 (1976b): 647-650.

——. "Local Government the Property Tax and the Quality of Life: Some Findings on Progressivity." In *Public Economics and the Quality of Life,* edited by Lowdon Wingo and Alan Evens, pp. 111-122. Baltimore: Johns Hopkins University Press, 1977.

——. "Capitalization and the Regressitivity of the Property Tax: Empirical Evidence." *National Tax Journal* 32 (June 1979): 169-180.

Hill, G. Christain. "Cut-Rate-Homes Plan Spreads in California, Benefiting Middle Class." *Wall Street Journal,* February 25, 1980, pp. 1, 29.

Hirsch, Werner Z. "The Efficiency of Restrictive Land Use Instruments." *Land Economics* 53 (1977): 145-156.

Institute for Social Science Research. *Rental Housing in the City of Los Angeles.* Los Angeles: University of California, Los Angeles, 1980.

Ishino, Steven A. "Condominium Conversions in the Bay Area." Report to ABAG. University of California, September 1979.

Jamison, Conrad C. *California Tax Study: An Analysis of Revenue and Expenditure of State and Local Government in California.* Security Pacific National Bank, February 1979, March 1980.

King, James R., and Guss, Phyllis A. *Picket Fence Planning in California.* Part 2. *State Financial Planning Requirements and Local Government Planning.* Sacramento: Special Subcommittee on Commuity Development, California Assembly, 1977.

King, Norman R., and Kemp, Roger L. "Proposition 13: The Taxpayers' Revolt." *Management Information Service* (International City Managers Association) 10 (November 1978).

Kirlin, John J. "The Impacts of Proposition 13 Upon California Governments." Photocopy, Los Angeles, 1979.

Kirlin, John J., and Chapman, Jeffrey I. "Research Report: Proposition 13 and the State of California: A Preliminary Analysis of the Impacts of the Jarvis-Gann Initiative." Report to HUD, contract no. AU 91575, December 12, 1978.

——. "California State Finance and Proposition 13." *National Tax Journal* 32 (1979): 269-275.

——. "Active Approaches to Local Government Revenue Generation." *Urban Interest* (in press).

Kirlin, John J., and Frates, Steven B. "Impacts of Rent Control upon the Housing Stock of Selected California Cities." Sacramento: Sacramento Public Affairs Center, 1979.

Kolis, Annette. "Regulation: Where Do We Go From Here?" (part 2). *Urban Land* (February 1979): 4-8.

Ladd, Helen F. "An Economic Evaluation of State Limitations on Local Taxing and Spending Powers." *National Tax Journal* 31 (March 1978): 1-18.

Lafferty, Ronald N., and Frech, H.E., III. "Community Environment and the Market Value of Single-Family Homes: The Effect of the Dispersion of Land Uses." *Journal of Law and Economics* 21 (1978): 381-394.

Lea, Michael J. "Local Public Expenditure Determination: A Simultaneous Equations Approach." *1978 Proceedings of the National Tax Association-Tax Institute of America* (1979): 131-136.

Leftwich, Richard H. *The Price System and Resource Allocation* New York: Holt, Rinehart, and Winston, 1963.

Levy, Frank. "On Understanding Proposition 13." *Public Interest* (Summer 1979): 66-89.

Levy, Frank, and Zamolo, Paul. "The Preconditions of Proposition 13." Urban Institute Working Paper no. 1105-01, October 1978.

Lipson, Albert J. and Lavin, Marvin. "Political and Legal Responses to Proposition 13 in California. RAND Report R-2483-DOJ. Santa Monica: RAND Corporation, 1980.

Longtin, James. *California Land Use Regulations.* Local Government Publications, 1977.

Los Angeles County Economy and Efficiency Committee. "Proposition 13 in Los Angeles County Government." February 1980.

Lovell, Catherine; Kneisel, Robert; Neiman, Max; Rose, Adam Z.; and Tobin, Charles A. *Federal and State Mandating on Local Governments: An Exploration of Issues and Impacts.* Riverside, Calif.: Graduate School of Administration, University of California, NSF Final Report (1979), DAR 77-20482.

McClure, Charles E., Jr. "General Equilibrium Incidence Analysis." *Journal of Public Economics* (January 1975): 125-161.

——. "The New View of the Property Tax: A Caveat." *National Tax Journal* 30 (1977): 69-76.

McDermott, Kelly. "Basic Fiscal Impacts of Development in the Post Proposition 13 Era: Rebuttal to OPR Report." Newport Beach, California: The Planning Center, 1979.

McDougall, Gerald S. "Local Public Goods and Residential Property Values: Some Insights and Extensions." *National Tax Journal,* 39 (1976): 436-447.

McTighe, John J. *Provision and Financing of the Urban Infrastructure in San Diego County.* San Diego, Calif.: Construction Industry Federation, 1979.

McWatters, Ann Robertson. "Financing Capital Formation for Local Governments." Institute of Governmental Studies Research, Report no. 79-3. (Berkeley, Calif.: Institute of Governmental Studies, 1979.

Magaddino, J.P.; Toma, Eugenia Froedge; and Toma, Mark. "Proposition 13: A Public Choice Appraisal." *Public Finance Quarterly* 8 (1980): 223-235.

Meadows, George Richard. "Taxes, Spending, and Property Values: A Comment and Further Results." *Journal of Political Economy* 84 (1976): 869–880.

Merl, Jean. "Eviction—The Price for Her Civic Duty." *Los Angeles Times,* February 14, 1980, part I, pp. 1, 3, 13.

Mieszkowski, Peter. "The Property Tax: An Excise Tax or a Profits Tax?" *Journal of Public Economics* (April 1972): 73–96.

Mills, Edwin S., and Oates, Wallace E. "The Theory of Local Public Services and Finance: Its Relevance to Urban Fiscal and Zoning Behavior." In *Fiscal Zoning and Land Use Controls: The Economic Issues,* edited by Mills and Oates, pp. 1–12. Lexington, Mass.: Lexington Books, D.C. Heath and Company, 1975.

Miscynski, Dean J. "Housing After Proposition 13: Why Housing Construction May Stop." Sacramento: Office of Planning and Research, 1979.

Mitchell, John L. "Condo Conversion Rate is Staggering." *Los Angeles Times,* March 22, 1979, part 7, pp. 1, 6.

Moorehouse, John C. "Optimal Housing Maintenance Under Rent Control." *Southern Economic Journal* (July 1972): 93–106.

Musgrave, Richard A., and Musgrave, Peggy B. *Public Finance.* New York: McGraw Hill, 1976.

Myers, Will. "Proposition 13: Nationwide Implications." *NTA-TIA Proceedings* (1978): 171–175.

Noto, Nonna A. "The Impact of the Local Public Sector on Residential Property Values." *1976 NTA-TIA Proceedings* (1977): 192–200.

Oakland, William H. "Proposition 13: Genesis and Consequences." *Economic Review* (Federal Reserve Bank of San Francisco) (Winter 1979): 1–19.

Oates, Wallace E. "The Effects of Property Taxes and Local Public Spending on Property Values: An Empirical Study of Tax Capitalization and the Tiebout Hypothesis." *Journal of Political Economy* 77 (1969): 956–971.

——. "The Effects of Property Taxes and Local Public Spending on Property Values: A Reply and Yet Further Results." *Journal of Political Economy* 81 (1973): 1004–1008.

Okun, Arthur M. *Equality and Efficiency: The Big Trade Off.* Washington, D.C.: Brookings Institution, 1975.

Olsen, Edgar O. "A Competitive Theory of the Housing Market." *American Economic Review* (September 1969): 612–622.

Orange County Citizens Direction Finding Commission. "The Impacts of Proposition 13 and 4 on Land Planning and New Development." Santa Ana: CDFC, 1980.

Orzechowski, William. "Economic Models of Bureaucracy: Survey, Extensions and Evidence." In *Budgets and Bureaucrats: The Sources of Government Growth,* edited by Thomas A. Borcherding. Durham, N.C.: Duke University Press, 1977.

Polinsky, A. Mitchell, and Rubinfeld, Daniel L. "The Long Run Effects of a Residential Property Tax and Local Public Services." *Journal of Urban Economics* 5 (1978): 241-262.

Pollakowski, Henry O. "Sources of Systematic Error in the Assessment of Urban Residential Property." *1976 NTA-TIA Proceedings* (1977): 89-96.

Pollakowski, Henry O. "The Effects of Property Taxes and Local Spending on Property Values: A Comment and Further Results." *Journal of Political Economy* 81 (July–August 1973): 996-1003.

Pressman, Jeffrey L., and Wildavsky, Aaron B. *Implementation.* Berkeley: University of California Press, 1973.

"Proposition 13 Triggers Varied Land-Use Shifts." *Conservation Foundation Letter* (April 1979): 1-8.

"Proposition 13: Who Really Won?" *Consumer Reports* (September 1979): 546-548.

Quinn, T. Anthony. "In California Government Is Caught with Its Pants Down." *Planning* (September 1978): 11-14.

Reschovsky, Andrew. "Residential Choice and the Local Public Sector: An Alternative Test of the Tiebout Hypothesis." *Journal of Urban Economics* 6 (1979): 501-520.

Rolph, Earl R., and Break, George F. *Public Finance.* New York: The Ronald Press, 1961.

Rood, W.B. "Brown Aide Predicts Near End of Surplus." *Los Angeles Times,* May 30, 1980, part 1, p. 3, 26.

Rose, Louis A. "The Development Value Tax." *Urban Studies* 10 (1973): 271-275.

Rose-Ackerman, Susan. "Market Models of Local Government: Exit, Voting, and the Land Market." *Journal of Urban Economics* 6 (1979): 319-337.

Sansweet, Stephen J. "California's Tax Revolt Slashes Local Spending by Blocking Bond Sales." *Wall Street Journal,* November 27, 1979, p. 1, 35.

Schwartz, Seymour I.; Hansen, David E.; Green, Richard; Moss, William G.; and Belzer, Richard. *The Effect of Growth Management on New Housing Prices: Petaluma, California.* Davis, Calif.: University of California, Davis, Institute of Governmental Affairs, Institute of Ecology, and UC Davis Kellogg Program, Environmental Quality Series no. 32, 1979.

Scott, Claudia DeVita. *Forecasting Local Government Spending.* Washington, D.C.: Urban Institute, 1972.

Security Pacific National Bank, *California Construction Trends.* July 1979, December 1978, July 1978.

Segal, David, *Urban Economics.* Homewood, Ill.: Irwin, 1977.

Shapiro, Perry, and Morgan, W. Douglas. "The General Revenue Effects of the California Property Tax Limitation Amendment." *National Tax Journal* 31 (1978): 119-128.

Shulman, David. "Proposition 13 and the Spatial Allocation of Economic Activities." *University of Southern California Law Review* 53 (1979): 125-137.

Siegan, Bernard H. *Land Use Without Zoning.* Lexington, Mass.: Lexington Books, D.C. Heath and Company, 1972.

Smith, Roger S. "Land Prices and Tax Policy: A Study of Fiscal Impacts." *American Journal of Economics and Sociology* 37 (1978): 51-69.

Sonstelie, Jon. "Maximizing Land Values as the Predominant Goal of Local Government." In *Proceedings of a Conference on Local Governments' Decisions and the Local Tax Base,* edited by George Lefcoe, pp. 125-150. Los Angeles: University Southern California Law Center, 1979.

Sternlieb, George, and Hughes, James W. "Rent Control's Impact on the Community Tax Base." *Land Appraisal Journal* (July 1979): 381-394.

Thomas, Henry B. "Some Estimates of the Distribution of Benefits from Los Angeles City Government Activity." *Bulletin of the Southern California Academy of Science* 77 (1978): 71-81.

Tiebout, Charles M. "A Pure Theory of Local Expenditures." *Journal of Political Economy* 65 (1956): 416-424.

United States Department of Labor. Bureau of Labor Statistics. *CPI Detailed Report, February, 1980.* Washington, D.C.: U.S. Government Printing Office, 1980.

Van Ness, Kathy, and Shoup, Donald. "State and Local Tax Incentives to Attract Business: Will They Work After Proposition 13." In *Proceedings of a Conference on Local Governments' Decisions and the Local Tax Base,* edited by George Lefco, pp. 72-86. Los Angeles, University of Southern California Law Center, 1979.

Vasché, Jon David. "The General Revenue Effects of the California Property Tax Limitation Amendment: A Comment." *National Tax Journal* 31 (1978): 399-400.

Waldhorn, Steven A., and Blakely, Edward J. *Picket Fence Planning in California: A Study of Local Government Planning.* Sacramento: Special Subcommittee on Community Development, California Assembly, November 1976.

Walker, Warren E.; Chaiken, Jan Michael; Jiga, Anthony P.; and Polin, Sandra Segal. "The Impact of Proposition 13 on Local Criminal Justice Agencies." RAND N-1521-DOJ, June 1980.

Wendling, Wayne. *Expenditures and Tax Capitalization: Its Relation to School Finance and Tax Reform.* Denver: Education Commission of the States, 1979.

Williams, Bob. "Renewal Plans Seek New Ideas for Funds." *Los Angeles Times,* October 8, 1978, "Centinela-South Bay," B, part 12, pp. 1, 11.

Wolinsky, Leo C. "Proposition 13 Fouls Up Annexations." *Los Angeles Times,* June 2, 1980, part 1, pp. 1, 14.

Wright, Colin. "Financing Public Goods and Residential Location." *Urban Studies* 14 (1977): 51-58.

Yinger, John. "Capitalization, the Theory of Local Public Finance, and the Design of Intergovernmental Grants." Cambridge, Mass.: Department of City and Regional Planning, Harvard University, September 1979.

Index

Index

About the Author

Jeffrey I. Chapman is an associate professor in the School of Public Administration at the University of Southern California. He received the Ph.D. in economics from the University of California at Berkeley. His articles have appeared in such journals as *Public Choice, National Tax Journal,* and *University of Southern California Law Review.* His current research interests are local public finance, tax reform and limitation, and rent control.